Emily Post's

great
get-togethers

✦ ✦ ✦

casual gatherings &
elegant parties at home

Also from The Emily Post Institute

great get-togethers

✦ ✦ ✦

casual gatherings & elegant parties at home

ANNA POST & LIZZIE POST

Photographs by Sara Remington

WILLIAM MORROW

An Imprint of HarperCollinsPublishers

HarperCollins books may be purchased for educational, business, or sales promotional use. For information please write: Special Markets Department, HarperCollins Publishers, 10 East 53rd Street, New York, NY 10022.

FIRST EDITION

Photographs © by Sara Remington
Styling: Kami Bremeyer

Designed by Alexis Siroc
Produced by SMALLWOOD & STEWART, NEW YORK

Library of Congress Cataloging-in-Publication Data

Post, Anna.
Emily Post's great get-togethers : casual gatherings and elegant parties at home / Anna Post & Lizzie Post.—1st ed.
   p. cm.
   Includes index.
   ISBN 978-0-06-166124-2
1. Entertaining. 2. Cookery. 3. Etiquette—Miscellanea. I. Post, Emily, 1872–1960. II. Title.
III. Title: Great get-togethers.
TX731.P6675 2010
395.3—dc22

                       2009042532

---

10   11   12   13   14   WBC/WCF   10   9   8   7   6   5   4   3   2   1

For our mother, the most lovely and gracious hostess—
your warmth, laughter, and sparkling wit has taught us what a joy entertaining can be.
You not only set a beautiful table but a shining example as well.

contents

acknowledgments

✦ ✦ ✦

Our deepest appreciation goes to our mother, Tricia Post, whose depth of knowledge and eloquence when speaking about entertaining found its way onto every page. We are also extremely grateful for the generous assistance given by Carrie Brown and chef Peter Brown of the Jimtown Store in Healdsburg, California, for sharing delicious recipes and wonderful advice on party style and "how to" catering tips for entertaining at home.

At the Emily Post Institute, Peggy Post, Cindy Post Senning, Peter Post, and Elizabeth Howell provided us with their support and expertise. Katherine Cowles was unstinting in her enthusiasm for this book from start to finish. Royce and Alexis Flippen were wizards at finding the fall line, so to speak, in our sometimes wandering prose, and Smallwood & Stewart has wrapped it all up in a fresh, fun design. Thanks to Sara Remington for the beautiful photographs.

Caroline Sutton, Ann Cole, and Mary Ellen O'Neill, our editors at HarperCollins, gave invaluable advice as to the structure of the book, and Mac Mackie kept us on track through the editing process.

Our Vermont team of experts graciously gave of their time and expertise. They are our number one "go to" sources for professional advice. Our sincerest thanks to Dale Loeffler of Catering by Dale for advice on working with a caterer; to Kris Engstrom and Britta Johnson of In Full Bloom for advice on arrangements and working with a florist; to Deborah, Joe, and Jennifer Jarecki of Scribbles, Vermont, for all things invitations; to Kevin G. Clayton of Village Wine and Coffee for advice on wine and wine pairings; and to Thomas Pierce and Michael Kehoe of Michael Kehoe, Ltd., for the last word on men's attire.

Thanks to "Uncle Mac" Keyser and Louise Roomet for sharing their secret recipes with the world. And most of all, thanks to all the friends who have gathered us to their tables.

introduction

✦ ✦ ✦

We grew up entertaining. Our mother, like her mother before her, is a host both at heart and in every sense of the word. Whether it was our traditional twenty-five-person Thanksgiving dinner, our birthdays, or casual dinners with family friends, we learned at a very young age what it meant to entertain and the wide range the phrase "We're having people over" truly covers.

The word *entertain* has a few definitions: "1. To hold the attention of pleasantly or agreeably; to amuse. 2. To have as a guest; provide food, lodging, etc. for or to show hospitality to." As a verb it simply means "to exercise hospitality." Entertaining is about having a good time, being in good company, enjoying yourself. Our mom showed us through her parties and dinners that to entertain guests is to provide an environment that will raise their spirits, capture their attention, be enjoyable to all, and have just a dash of something special. One thing it doesn't mean is to focus on good manners or etiquette at the expense of having fun. Emily Post didn't blink when a fork was misplaced or a wineglass was the wrong size. To her, what was unforgivable on the part of a host or hostess was neglecting to "do what was comfortable, both for those around you and yourself." That is good manners—nothing more, nothing less—and it applies to hosts of all ages.

The possibility of entertaining brings to mind so many questions. Even just the passing thought *We should have Will and Susan over for dinner* causes one to think further: *Do we invite other couples as well? Whom would we invite? Maybe we'd like to keep it simple? Should I try serving that new dish I've created? When was the last time Will and Susan had us over? What did we do that time? They have kids; do we want to make it a kids night, or just adults? Isn't Will allergic to choco-late . . . should I double-check?* And all this before you've even committed to plans. Not to mention the many questions that arise with having people over in general: *What if something breaks? What if guests don't get the hint that it's time to leave? How do I handle Uncle Randy's politically incorrect sense of humor? Do I have to serve the wine that Ms. Pinot brought over because she says it's her favorite?* Suffice it to say the world of entertaining has options, lots of options, and lots of surprises.

Entertaining can be as simple or complex as you choose to make it, and we think that's what is so wonderful about it! Pizza and beer with a few close friends can be just as enjoyable as a six-course formal dinner. If you're not a master chef there are tons of prepared dish options and catering services to assist you. Decorations can be as simple as wildflowers in a can or as extravagant as all-out themed parties where you transform your home into your fabulous fantasy. Some parties will focus

on an event such as an election, an awards cere-mony, or a competition. Others might focus on an honoree for a special occasion: Jim and Laura's fifth anniversary or Mary Kate's birthday. Simple "girls night" and "Sunday night football" evenings pop up all year round.

Whether you're a beginner or a seasoned host, we hope to inspire you with the menus and ideas in the following pages, as well as encourage you to reach beyond this book and look at Web sites, magazines, and blogs about entertaining to further your creativity. We hope our advice on the nuts and bolts of entertaining will give you confidence, especially if things don't go exactly as planned. We hope you'll be so entertained by the thought of entertaining that you'll experiment and create distinctive parties that will wow your guests—and be fun for you! All the delicious food, the fabulous setting, and the perfect music is just the ribbon and the wrapping for the real gift: the gift of your hospitality to your friends and family, a way to stay connected, to share good times, and to build traditions. It's why we gather, why we celebrate . . . why we entertain.

Cheers!

A Note About the Recipes

Our good friend Carrie Brown—caterer and stylist par excellence, inventive cook, and owner of the famous Jimtown Store in Healdsburg, California—has graciously worked with us on the menus and recipes for this book. Our goal is to provide a core collection of recipes and menu suggestions that are not only yummy but also easy to prepare, seasonal, and interchangeable. They could become the base of a host's party repertoire. Except where noted, the recipes are from *The Jimtown Store Cookbook*, by Carrie Brown, John Werner, and Michael McLaughlin, and from the Jimtown Store's current offerings, created by Carrie Brown and Chef Peter Brown. With Carrie and Peter's kind permission, we offer you menus and dishes that are exciting and delicious. Menu suggestions without accompanying recipes, such as tomato bruschetta, for example, are easily found in cookbooks, food magazines, or cooking and recipe Web sites.

✳

create
your party
style

✳

CHAPTER ONE

how to be party ready anytime

Let's face it: The secret to successful entertaining is hardly classified information. In fact, anyone can throw a great party—even raw beginners—as long as you follow some basic advice: Stick with what you know, then build on your knowledge base. Even if your only party-giving experience is inviting friends over for pizza and beer, you can take it up a notch by throwing a make-your-own-pizza evening, using store-bought dough, sauce, and toppings. Add a bottle of wine, toss a salad with your own vinaigrette, light some candles, and you're in business (see the Basic Vinaigrette recipe, page 12). The quickest way to trip yourself up? Making the leap from take-out pizza and beer to a full-blown multicourse dinner requiring dazzling culinary skills, exotic ingredients, pricey equipment, and all the pots and pans you own—especially if you're not really much of a cook. At least not yet!

✦ ✦ ✦

This, then, should be your mantra: Start simple and grow with experience. Every time you throw a party, give yourself a couple of new challenges: a more complicated dish from your repertoire perhaps, or a serious centerpiece.

Over time you'll gain the confidence and know-how to pull off that twelve-person five-course extravaganza. And most important, you'll be having fun doing it.

the impromptu party

✦ ✦ ✦

Not every party is a planned event. In fact, some of the best, most memorable parties are those that happen on the spur of the moment, like the time we picked too many mussels and Mom and Dad called all the neighbors over for mussel spaghetti. Soon, eighteen people were crammed in the living room eating one of the best spaghetti dinners ever—laughing, joking, having a wonderful time. People still talk about what a great party it was.

what to have on hand

You can be party ready anytime simply by having some basic items on hand. While this may seem like a lot, you don't have to run out and buy everything all at once. Over time, here are some items to collect:

+ **IN THE PANTRY:** prepared tapenades; nuts; a variety of chips and crackers; salsa or your favorite bottled dip; various pastas and a good sauce; imported tuna and anchovies; olive oil and good vinegar; Dijon mustard; great pickles; onions and garlic; dates, apricots, or other dried fruit; simple cookies.

+ **IN THE FRIDGE:** olives; cheese (including real Parmesan for grating or shaving); bacon, or cured meats like salami or sopressata; pesto; lemons and limes.

+ **IN THE FREEZER:** homemade or organic chicken stock; ice cream or sorbet; frozen pasta sauces.

+ **IN THE BAR:** seltzer and tonic water; sparkling or mineral water; fruit and tomato juices; wine, beer, and a bottle of Champagne or sparkling wine.

The Chef Is Out

Too busy to cook or just not that into cooking? Don't worry: You can still throw a great party.
Many a celebrated hostess has served delicious food someone else has prepared.
Here are a few ways to go:

✳ **FORAGE CREATIVELY** at farmers' markets for gorgeous fruit and crudités (raw veggies for
dipping); at specialty stores for cheese and salumi; at a favorite pastry shop for desserts and breads.

✳ **BUY PREPARED FOOD,** like lasagne, that you just heat in the oven. Many specialty markets
prepare casseroles, entrées, side dishes, and salads.

✳ **GET TAKEOUT** from a local restaurant or specialty food store and just heat and serve.
This can range from the simple—picking up ribs, for example—to something more elaborate,
such as arranging for a restaurant to cook a salmon or roast beef. (Lots of Thanksgiving
turkeys get to the feast this way.)

✳ **HIRE A CATERER.** Caterers' services aren't limited to big events like weddings; they do
small parties as well.

+ BY THE PHONE: a stash of take-out menus.
+ EXTRAS: cocktail or dinner napkins, candles, coasters, cocktail picks.

Now turn on the music and it's a party!

Certainly if you're just having one or two friends over for dinner, the prep and planning is fairly simple. But for something a little grander you'll need to take stock of what you have and what you can do: for example, how many people your party space can accommodate; what "party stuff" you already have, such as dishes and glassware; how much you can spend; and where to find party help and supplies. The good thing is that once you've completed your inventory, you'll know just what you have or need for any party in the future. You only have to do this once!

the party space

✦ ✦ ✦

While visions from the Food Network dance in your head, it's time to get down to the nitty-gritty of planning your party. First, size up your entertaining space. How many people can fit comfortably in your living room, dining room, kitchen, or outdoor space? Is your outdoor space available at this time of year? If you have a small apartment with no dining room, can you rearrange your space and your furniture to accommodate your guests? Your answers will determine where and even when you hold your party, and how many guests you can have. If you're having trouble visualizing how many people will fit—and there's no easy way to figure this out—start by inviting only a few guests. That will give you an idea if you can accommodate more—or fewer—people at your next party.

Your goal is to make sure your guests can move about comfortably and everyone has a place to sit. Expandable tables, folding tables, tabletops (placed on top of smaller tables and covered with a tablecloth), and folding chairs can turn dinner for four into dinner for six or eight. Plus there's no rule that says dinner needs to be at a dining room table. Smaller tables placed around a room are a cozy and relaxed way to entertain. If you don't have a formal dining room, you can set up folding tables in the living room. No tables? At the most casual parties, guests can eat on their laps.

your party stuff

✦ ✦ ✦

Take stock of your stuff—and by that we mean dishes, glasses, cutlery, serving dishes, linens, vases, the works. Determine exactly what you need for the party, and then buy, borrow, or rent to fill the holes. If you're hosting a dinner party, do you have enough place settings? If you're having a cocktail party with hors d'oeuvres, do you have plenty of serving dishes, glassware, and small plates? If you're going the disposable route, will you be using paper or plastic—or going green (see "Green Entertaining," opposite)? If you're on a budget, this is a good time to get creative with the stuff you have. Borrow a giant metal tub and fill it with ice, beer, and wine or use wooden bread boards as serving platters.

It's a good idea to invest in at least one **tablecloth** or a set of **place mats** along with a set of eight to twelve **cloth napkins**. White is very formal; colors or patterns may be more versatile: A colorful tablecloth can work overtime as both a table covering *and* instant décor. Over time, you can add **runners** and **additional sets of napkins** (eight to twelve) in colors that complement your other dining accessories. Think of it as building a wardrobe for your table.

If you plan on doing a lot of entertaining, consider investing in inexpensive **glassware, extra flatware**, and **dinner and dessert plates**—even **platters** and **serving bowls**. Enamelware (aka tin) and melamine are attractive and well-priced alternatives to china. You can buy stylish and quite inexpensive wine and beverage glasses at national home-goods chains like Bed, Bath & Beyond and Target. If you have the room to store them, it could save not only on rentals but on your everyday or formal dinnerware as well. Our parents purchased four dozen Champagne glasses just so they'll have enough for their annual New Year's Eve party. The forty-dollar investment has more than paid off over the years—and they don't worry if a glass gets broken.

Finally, think about any kitchen equipment you might need to prepare your party food: **pots and pans** or specialized equipment such as **mixers or food processors**. Appliances are a convenience

---

Green Entertaining

These days, you can find great alternatives to plastic dinnerware. Enamelware or melamine is an investment, but are unbreakable and reusable. We love plates and utensils made of bamboo— a renewable resource and a reusable product. Look for bamboo plates and, if you really want your tools to multitask, "sporks"— a cross between a spoon and a fork, perfect for outdoor parties. Bamboo products can be washed and reused several times, making them economical as well.

If your neighborhood, homeowners', or condo association has occasional potluck suppers, do as one California group does and have members bring a dish and their own dishes—plate, knife, and fork! It saves on the landfill and on cleanup, as everyone takes their own dishes home to wash.

---

and a time-saver, but before you shell out the big bucks for one, think about how often you're really going to use it. Think, too, about your available space—is there room in your kitchen for a big appliance? And of course, consider your budget: Is this something you simply can't live without, or can you improvise with what you have? For instance, instead of investing in a big, bulky, expensive stand mixer, you can get a small hand blender or use a whisk to beat egg whites into stiff, frothy meringues—and get a great arm workout at the same time! Instead of a large food processor, consider going with a mini version (ours is a real workhorse).

One thing we don't recommend skimping on is a **good knife**. Trust us, a sharp, well-made knife will cut your prep time in half. Lizzie particularly favors her Wüsthoff 10-inch chef's knife, and Anna can't live without her L'économe paring knives. Also, a nice-size, good-quality **skillet** will go a long way in any kitchen. Beyond the basics, we think the following items make party prep much easier:

+ **An instant-read thermometer:** Critical for grilling or roasting meat.
+ **A juicer:** The old-fashioned manual kind is handy.
+ **A microplane or multipurpose grater:** For fruit zest and cheese.
+ **Tongs:** We can't cook without them.
+ **A salad spinner:** It really does save time.
+ **A blender:** If you're really into margaritas.
+ **A thermal carafe:** Make coffee *before* the party and keep it hot without burning it.
+ **A hot tray:** For warming plates or keeping food hot; whoever invented this was a genius.

your budget

✦ ✦ ✦

Decide up front what you can spend on your party. For most party givers, food and beverages are the main attraction, so first and foremost, budget whatever you need for that. A gorgeous floral centerpiece can be a beautiful mood setter, but not if it means skimping on the food and drinks to pay for it. If you're planning a big party, your budget will also determine if you can afford to hire help or rent supplies.

If your budget is limited, don't feel you have to pull the plug on your plans. Instead, consider the following cost-cutting tips:

+ **BUY IN BULK AT WAREHOUSE STORES.**
Purchasing food and supplies in party-size
quantities is one way to save. You'll not only
find great deals on paper goods, but you can
also get good prices on party foods sold in
bulk (nuts, crackers, chips, and salsas).

+ **FIND A HOUSE WINE.** Look for a reliable,
drinkable red and white in your price range
that you can serve for most occasions. Discount
warehouses usually have a good bottle price, but
you may be able to save more at wine or grocery
stores that offer a case discount. (See Chapter
8, Delicious Drinks, page 95, for more
information on choosing wines.)

+ **BUILD YOUR MENU AROUND LOCAL AND
SEASONAL PRODUCTS.** Not only will you
be doing your part for the environment
and supporting local farmers but you'll also
be buying the freshest foodstuffs available.
By cutting out the middleman (grocery
stores) and buying when a crop is flooding
the market, you'll often be paying less. In
the summer, for example, delicious fresh
tomatoes, corn, lettuce, and beans are in
abundance at farmers' markets; in the fall, the
stalls are overflowing with just-picked apples,
pears, squashes, kale, and brussels sprouts.

your party helpers

✦ ✦ ✦

Determine whether you need to enlist help
to throw your party. If you're planning a
big event, research options for caterers, bartenders,
and servers (see Chapter 5, When You Need a
Supporting Cast, page 49). Know that for liability
reasons, it's always a good idea to hire a professional
bartender. Check with a local caterer or a favorite
restaurant to see if they can recommend one. If
you can't afford professional waitstaff, enlist the
help of your neighbors' high school–age children
or local college students to pass hors d'oeuvres,
serve food, clear, and clean up the kitchen. (We've
waitressed many parties for our mom and her
friends.) Pay them by the hour, and be sure to
include a 10 to 15 percent tip.

Having your resources at your fingertips makes your planning easier. Keep a sourcebook
(or file on your computer) with business cards, contact information, prices, and notes
for florists, caterers, wine and specialty food sources, take-out menus, and rental
companies. Added bonus—your friends will start looking to you as the ultimate resource.

your sources

✦ ✦ ✦

Whatever your budget or the size of your party, you'll want to offer the best you can for your guests. Base your choices on quality, not just price. Learn to forage and gather great components for entertaining. Think about:

✦ **FARMERS' MARKETS:** The best for fresh and local foodstuffs, farmers' markets offer an amazing variety of produce, baked goods, flowers, cheeses, and more.

✦ **SPECIALTY STORES:** Shop for great guest-worthy products: cheeses, cured meats and fish, olives and tapenades, artisanal breads and crackers, freshly prepared sides and salads, and main dishes, such as soups and chilis. *Always* ask for a taste. Wine, cheese, and gourmet food shops can offer more than just

great products. Owners and staff are usually enthusiasts, willing to answer questions and give advice.

✦ **SPECIALTY WINE STORES:** You don't have to be an expert to know good wine, but an expert at a wine shop can help you pick out the right wine at the right price for your party. If you're looking for a good wine pairing in your price range, bring along your menu. Look for a shop where the staff really know their stock and aren't saying things like, "Oh, pinot goes with everything."

✦ **GROCERY STORES:** You may need to check around at more than one store to get the best-quality foods. Find out who has the best meat, fish, produce, cheeses, breads, and selection of staples, like olive oils, vinegar, quality pastas, grains, and odd ingredients. If you're lucky to have a good all-around market in your neighborhood—especially one that also carries flowers and a decent beverage selection—it can be a big time-saver.

+ **WAREHOUSE STORES:** You can save by buying your food, beverages, and party goods at one of the big chains (Sam's Club, Walmart, Costco, Trader Joe's), most of which also offer a solid array of frozen foods—pizza, desserts (tiramisù, cheesecakes, mini éclairs), and appetizers (mini quiches, bacon-wrapped scallops, crab cakes)—as well as large jars of salsa and pesto, dips and sauces, meat, vegetables, fruit, wine, and beer. *Be sure to read the ingredients and check out their source. Never serve guests something you haven't first sampled yourself.* If it passes the

quality and taste tests, consider adding extra spices or garnishes to make it your own.

+ **TAKEOUT—THE ULTIMATE DIY CATERER:** You'd be amazed at the number of restaurants that offer takeout. Think beyond Thai, Chinese, and pizza—although they're great, too. Your favorite barbecue restaurant might supply ribs or pulled pork, and a local bistro may be a good source for main courses. Prepare your own fresh salad to serve with the main course and learn to make a good, reliable vinaigrette.

+ **A STATIONER OR PARTY STORE:** When the party calls for more than a phone or e-mail invite, you'll want a fun source for invitations. While you're at it, you can also buy cocktail napkins and other paper goods, as well as decorations for theme parties.

our favorite vinaigrettes

A few good vinaigrettes will greatly expand your salad repertoire.

basic vinaigrette

Makes just over ¼ cup, enough to dress a salad for 6 or 8. Make more if people will be dressing their own.

1 teaspoon Dijon mustard
1 tablespoon red or white wine vinegar
¼ teaspoon kosher or ground sea salt
Ground pepper, to taste
Optional: ½ teaspoon minced garlic or shallots
3 tablespoons extra virgin olive oil
Herbs of choice: 1 teaspoon chopped fresh parsley, chervil, thyme, or tarragon

In a small bowl, whisk together the mustard, vinegar, salt and pepper, and optional garlic or shallots. Continue whisking and slowly add the olive oil. Dress the salad and sprinkle with the fresh herbs and additional salt, if needed.

champagne vinaigrette

Makes 1¼ cups

¼ cup Champagne vinegar
1 teaspoon Dijon mustard
1 teaspoon minced shallot
½ teaspoon salt
¼ teaspoon sugar

¼ teaspoon ground pepper
1 cup neutral oil such as extra virgin olive oil
   or canola oil

Whisk together all the ingredients except the oil. Continue whisking and slowly drizzle in the oil until all of it is incorporated. Taste the dressing—if it seems too tart, drizzle in a little more oil. For more bite, add a little more vinegar. Keeps tightly covered in the refrigerator for up to 1 week.

balsamic vinaigrette

Makes 1¼ cups

¼ cup balsamic vinegar
1 teaspoon Dijon mustard
1 teaspoon minced shallot
½ teaspoon minced garlic
1 teaspoon honey
½ teaspoon salt
¼ teaspoon ground pepper
1 cup extra virgin olive oil

Whisk together all the ingredients except the oil. Continue whisking and slowly drizzle in the olive oil until all of it is incorporated. Taste the dressing—if it seems too tart, drizzle in a little more oil. For more bite, add a little more vinegar.

caesar dressing

This eggless Caesar dressing really flatters beans, especially something as simple as a big
platter of cool, crisp-cooked garden green beans. Upon the good base of two, three,
or four types of beans and the dressing, other summery salads can also be built:
Consider adding halved red or yellow cherry tomatoes, tender hearts of romaine, boiled
new potatoes, or sweet corn cut off the cob. For a picnic salad, omit the lettuce.
Makes about 1 1/2 cups

1 tablespoon red wine vinegar
1 tablespoon chopped anchovies
2 tablespoons Dijon mustard
1 tablespoon chopped garlic

1 teaspoon freshly ground black pepper
2 tablespoons fresh lemon juice
1 cup extra virgin olive oil
Several dashes of Worcestershire sauce

1. Combine the vinegar, anchovies, mustard, garlic, pepper, and lemon juice in the bowl of a food processor. Pulse to combine. With the motor running, add the olive oil in a steady stream until incorporated. Season to taste with the Worcestershire sauce.

2. Use immediately or store, tightly covered, in the refrigerator for a week.

✳

CHAPTER TWO

producer, director, and star

there's an art to being a good host. It's like being the producer, director, and star of your own show. As producer, you're responsible for all the details of party prep, from invitations to last-minute errands. Just before the doorbell rings, you take off your producer's hat and step into the roles of director and star. As the director, you guide the action, letting guests know when it's time to come to the table and when it's time to say goodbye. As the star, you add the sparkle and set the tone of the party. Successful hosts make this transformation seem easy; guests have no sense of the planning and work that's gone on behind the scenes. Their time is spent wrapped in your kind attention, stimulated by conversation, and cheered by a meal created for their enjoyment—all of which leaves them feeling, well, entertained.

✦ ✦ ✦

Being a good host isn't all that difficult, but it does take forethought, practice, and a little talent for multitasking. Above all, you want to make sure your friends feel comfortable and welcome. The following suggestions will help you hit all the right notes:

+ **INVITE CLEARLY.** Make sure your invitation lets your guests know what to expect. Whether you invite by phone, e-mail, or written invitation, let your guests know:

  Who: Host(s)

  What: Cocktails

  When: 6 P.M., Saturday, May 6

  Where: Burlington Country Club

  Why: Jane and Ben's Engagement

  Add how and when to respond, and any special info your guests should know, such as what they should wear or what they should bring. (See Chapter 4, The Invitation Tells All, page 35.)

+ **PLAN WELL.** Prepare as much as you can *before* everyone arrives. Have your meal ready and your table set and be dressed at least fifteen minutes before party hour. (See Chapter 3, Planning to Have Fun, page 25.)

+ **DRESS FOR YOUR EVENT—OR ONE NOTCH UP.** After all, this is your party and you're the star! Just don't tell guests "casual" and then open the door draped in an evening dress and dripping with bling.

+ **REMAIN CALM.** Your mood sets the tone. Take five minutes simply to enjoy the beauty of the stage you've set before the guests arrive. And no matter what happens, never let your guests think you're stressed out—it will make them feel anxious and uncomfortable, too.

+ **BE WELCOMING.** Making your guests feel at home and seeing to their comfort are what being a host is all about. Greet them enthusiastically as they arrive, even if it means excusing yourself from a conversation with another guest. (Note: If you're hosting with a partner, only one of you needs to greet guests at the door.)

+ **BE THE SPARK.** Circulate among all your guests. Be sure to introduce newcomers and stay with them long enough to get a conversation going. If one of your guests doesn't know any of the others, enlist a friend to make introductions and make sure he isn't left on his own.

+ **BE MINDFUL.** Keep an eye on guests' drinks and offer refills before they have to ask. (At the same time, keep an eye on the guest who's had one too many!) Rescue others from being trapped in overly long conversations, and make an effort to gently draw out the shy ones. Above all, be sure to spend time with each guest.

+ **BE THE LEADER/DIRECTOR.** It's your job to call guests in to dinner and to raise your fork so they can begin eating. If you plan to serve yourself last, say, "Please begin" once three or four guests have been served so their meal doesn't get cold. It's also up to you to signal when it's time for the next course, and to get up from the table to indicate when the meal is over.

+ **MAKE A TOAST.** To many people, making a toast seems like a daunting prospect. But it's really as simple as welcoming your guests, thanking the chef (if it wasn't you), or wishing health and happiness to the guest of honor or to your friends around your table. A thoughtful toast transforms any gathering into an occasion, and is a wonderfully special way to extend a warm welcome to all. (See Chapter 12, Traditions and Special Occasions, page 173.)

+ **BE APPRECIATIVE.** Let your friends know how much you enjoy spending time with them. Thank them not just for coming, but also for any gifts or contributions to the meal. Guests who've experienced your enthusiasm and appreciation for their company are sure to want to return.

greetings and introductions

+ + +

As the host, it's your job to greet your guests and introduce new and old friends. Before the party, take a little time to think about each guest. Does everyone know each other? Is there someone new who needs to meet everyone? Do you have some shy guests who may not be comfortable introducing themselves to people they don't know? Think about your guests' interests and general background information—who likes music, films, wine, sports, trekking, finance. Offering a point of common reference between two people is an easy way to get a conversation going when strangers meet. At a large party, be on the lookout for guests who are sitting quietly on the sidelines, and make it a point to draw them into a conversational group.

"i'd like you to meet..."

Making an introduction is easy: Simply speak to the person you wish to honor first—the guest of honor, your grandmother or other elderly person, your client, your boss. "Samantha [your guest of honor], I'd like you to meet John Parker. John, this is Samantha Evans. Samantha's just moved here from Seattle."

lively conversation

In the same way that you keep an eye on your guests' glasses, keep an ear tuned to the conversation. As the host, you'll need to fill in the gaps or redirect a discussion that's gone astray. Small talk is a characteristic of the cocktail party, where conversations tend to be short exchanges of information or light give-and-takes about what's going on.

Dinner parties lend themselves to more in-depth discussions. Even though the classic advice is to steer clear of the four unmentionables (politics, religion, sex, and money), our present society loves to talk about politics, religion, sex, and money! As the host, it's your job to make sure the discussion remains friendly and respectful, no matter what the topic. In some circles, a really heated debate is a sign of a great evening. That's

fine, if everyone's in on it and understands the (often unspoken) ground rules. If that's not the case, then you'll need to change the subject if the sparks start flying. Stepping in with "How 'bout those Red Sox?" (or some other completely off-topic comment) is a clear way of saying to guests, "We've hit the uncomfortable zone." At the same time, it injects some humor and lets another discussion begin. Then, again, if you're in Yankees territory, that quip might set off an explosion, so be aware of your context.

avoid the awkward moment

Whether you're enjoying the company of new friends or old, it's never a good idea to bring up deeply personal issues at a party. It's one thing if your dinner partner chooses to divulge a bit of personal info, but you shouldn't be the one to go down that road ("So, Karen, how was rehab?"). The top ten one-liners to avoid are:

1. "When are you getting married?"
2. "Why aren't you married?" (or its corollary, "Why don't you have kids?" or "So, are you going to have kids?")
3. "When are you due?"
4. "You look great—have you lost weight /had an eye lift/been getting Botox?"

5. "You look awful—are you okay?"

6. "How much does someone in your line of work make?"

7. "How much did that cost?" or "Wow, is that real?"

8. "That can't be right."

9. "Should you be eating that?"

10. "As my good friend _____ was telling me the other day..."(fill in name of celebrity).

making small talk

To engage in small talk with your guests, you'll need to have something to talk about besides the weather. Here are some tips to help you jump-start the conversation:

+ **KNOW YOUR CURRENT EVENTS.** Make an effort to know what's going on in your community, your state, the world, and current sports and entertainment. Take a little time to think about the topics you've come across in newspapers and magazines and on television and you'll be surprised at how naturally you can get a conversation going.

+ **KNOW YOUR GUESTS.** Consider their interests, hobbies, jobs, and accomplishments. This gives you lots to talk about—plus your guests will be flattered by the attention.

+ **ASK PEOPLE'S OPINIONS.** Asking questions is the easiest way to start a conversation and/or to keep one going. People *love* to be asked for their opinion—so instead of simply giving your own take on the latest sports or celebrity gossip or that weird new diet you just read about, bring the topic up and ask your guest for *her* thoughts on the subject.

+ **BE A GOOD LISTENER.** Focus on the person you're talking to and maintain that focus. Wandering eyes make the other person feel as if you're just killing time. As you talk, respond with comments and questions to show you're engaged.

accidents will happen

✦ ✦ ✦

Sometimes being the host means coping with accidents, mishaps, or even bad behavior. It's inevitable that at some point red wine will be spilled or something will break. For starters, if you're worried about having your heart broken over an accidental mishap, *don't* use glasses or dishes that are beloved heirlooms, or vases so valuable that a guest couldn't possibly afford to replace one if he breaks it.

The truly good host is gracious and unflappable, no matter *what* happens. This is where a sense of humor and an awareness that "stuff happens" come in handy. So does a supply of OxiClean and paper towels. Stay relaxed and look for creative solutions if an accident occurs. The more you take things in stride and handle them gracefully, the better your guests will feel.

staying flexible

It's not easy to keep calm when you've been thrown for a loop, but by maintaining your cool you can turn even the most socially awkward situation into a success. Let's look at a common scenario: You've invited three couples for dinner. The table's perfect: flowers, place cards, candles—the whole nine yards. You open the door to find that Katherine and Rob have unilaterally taken the liberty of bringing along their friend Jane, who's visiting. You could say,

(A) "What were you thinking, bringing an extra person to my dinner party?! I don't know how I'm going to cope. My menu, my seating plan—everything is ruined!"

And you'll be absolutely right—because while it's true that Katherine and Rob never should have brought Jane without asking you first, your reaction has now ruined the evening for everybody.

Or you could say,

(B) "Jane, it's a pleasure to meet you. I'm so glad Katherine and Rob brought you along! Let me get you something to drink while they introduce you."

Make sure your facial expression, tone, and body language match your gracious words or the whole effect will be lost.

Sure, you'll have to rearrange a few place settings and fiddle with portions, but your gracious welcome has smoothed over what could have been a very uncomfortable moment. In fact, the other guests may not even notice that Jane wasn't on the original guest list! (By the way, it's okay to call Katherine and Rob the next day and let them know how much you enjoyed having Jane at the party, but that if this kind of situation comes up again, you'd really appreciate a call ahead of time.)

friends don't let friends...

The one thing you can't ignore is a guest who's over the limit. First, stop serving him alcohol, and second, take away his car keys. Offer a bed or a couch for the night or take on the responsibility of seeing Mr. Not-So-Sober safely home—but whatever you do, *never* let him drive. And remember, calling a cab or asking a friend to take the drunk person home only makes him someone else's responsibility.

FHB:
Three Magic Letters

Sometimes, for whatever reason—extra guests, a dish that didn't make as much as anticipated, a potluck that's long on salad and short on entrées—a host realizes there isn't quite enough food. FHB stands for "Family Hold Back." Whispered to your immediate family, it's a secret signal that they should either take a mini portion of whatever's in short supply or wait until all the guests have been served.

CONTINGENCY PLANS

Some guests are late	Wait 15–20 minutes, then start without them.
A guest breaks or spills something	Smooth over the incident and clean the mess up quickly. The guest should apologize and offer to do what he can to resolve the situation—but if he doesn't, chalk it up to the cost of entertaining a less-than-considerate guest.
A guest makes an ethnic slur or an offensive joke	Interrupt and change the subject, or ask for his help in another room, where you can tell him that his off-color jokes or remarks are making others uncomfortable. Be sure to apologize privately to anyone who might have been offended.
Unexpected guests show up at your door	Greet them graciously and do your best to include them. Set extra places at the table if possible (even if your place settings aren't an exact match). If all else fails, eat on laps in the living room.
A guest has had too much to drink	Cut off the alcohol and take away the car keys. Offer him a place to sleep for the night or drive him home yourself.
There's not enough food	Plate the food, using smaller portions of what's short and larger ones of what's in good supply. Augment the salad and add bread if possible. Signal "FHB" (Family Hold Back) to family members.
Dinner is overcooked, undercooked, or an otherwise complete disaster	Laugh and order pizza!

wrap it up

✦ ✦ ✦

Since even the most awesome parties have to end sometime, it's a good idea to have a few exit lines prepared for die-hard guests who show no sign of leaving. Of course, if you're game to party till dawn, there's no worry here. But if you really need to call it a night you can, in the following order:

✦ Close the bar.

✦ Turn off the music.

✦ Start cleaning up.

✦ Yawn—repeatedly.

✦ Be direct: Stand up and say, "Wow—look at the time! I've got yoga [a meeting, a class] first thing tomorrow. Let's call it a night."

✦ Start turning out the lights.

✦ Go to bed.

sharing the joy:
tips on cohosting a party

✦ ✦ ✦

Cohosting with friends is a great way to throw a big party or dinner that may be too expensive or too much work for an individual or a couple, or for events honoring others, such as birthdays, anniversaries, graduations, engagements, weddings, promotions, or retirements. It's a fun way to bond with friends and can be a great way to expand your entertaining skills.

Communication is the key to successful cohosting. As soon as possible after you say, "Let's do it!" sit down together to discuss dates, guest list, budget, and who's doing what. Divide the duties as evenly as possible, taking advantage of each person's skills and interests: Put the decorator in charge of the table, and the cook in charge of the meal. Decide who greets, who's in charge of drinks and hors d'oeuvres, who preps, and who serves. All the hosts share in the usual hosting responsibilities throughout the party—welcoming guests, making introductions, and seeing to the guests' comfort. Be aware that the "home host" will bear the brunt of the event, so visiting hosts should offer to help with the pre- and post-party cleaning and supplement any tableware or kitchen equipment.

Your Partner Is Your Cohost

When you entertain as a couple, it doesn't mean that one of you does all the prep and acts
as host while the other acts like a guest. Consider yourselves cohosts. Communicate clearly
with each other and divvy up the hosting duties ahead of time. Also agree on what
those duties are and don't assume that being the bartender means the same thing to both of you.
Your idea might be to actually pour and serve drinks; her idea may be, "Help yourself."
At the end of the party, thank each other and compliment each other on a job well done.

planning to have fun

believe it or not, having fun at your own party is largely about careful preparation. The more planning you put into your party, the easier and more enjoyable the experience will be because you won't be eaten up with worries. We recommend breaking down the process into four parts:

Anna and Lizzie's four-step party plan

1. Work out your **overall party plan**—including the type of party you're going to throw, the number of guests, and your budget.

2. Make a **planning timeline** so that you'll know when to send the invitations, hire help, purchase or rent supplies, order flowers, shop for food, clean the house, decorate, set the table, and prepare the food and drinks.

3. Draw up **to do lists** for all these tasks, along with **detailed shopping lists** that cover your entire menu and beverage needs.

4. Most parties or small gatherings won't need this step, but if you're having a serious party—sit-down dinner, lots of courses, mailed invitations—map out a **party timeline** to ensure that your party flows smoothly from beginning to end. (For a sample party timeline, see page 30.)

working out your overall plan

✦ ✦ ✦

Let's pretend that you're planning to host a thirtieth birthday party for your close friend Carolyn. You've discussed it with her husband, John, and he's on board. Now what? Work out your initial plans on paper, jotting down all your ideas and amending as you go. Lizzie likes to use a kitchen whiteboard so the plan can be easily updated. Use your own favorite planning method, or a simple grid like the one below can help pull your ideas together.

Next, begin to expand and refine your plan—adding a new column for your to do and shopping lists and other notes—and start filling in the details to create a general timeline:

	GENERAL PLANS	DETAILS, NOTES, TO DOS
Event	Carolyn's 30th Birthday— Cocktails & Cupcakes Saturday, June 18; 6–8 p.m.	Check date and time with John
# Guests	24	Consult with John on guest list
Time to event	4 weeks	This week, 5/20: Make guest list and run it by John Buy invitations and paper goods Hire bartender/helper Plan menu and drinks
		5/27: Mail invites
		6/4: Check on RSVPs Call florist

GENERAL PLANS		DETAILS, NOTES, TO DOS
		Party week, 6/11–18: Shopping Cleaning Cooking Set up
I can handle	Invitations, flowers, drinks, hors d'oeuvres, birthday cupcakes, paper goods	Scribbles Stationery: Invitations, napkins, birthday candles In Full Bloom: Flowers—peonies? Hors d'oeuvres: Marsha—shellfish allergy Cupcakes: Carolyn loves chocolate with coconut Drinks: Full bar? OR Champagne cocktails or margaritas? White & red wine, beer, iced tea, sparkling/mineral water
I need help	Bartender, server/cleanup	2 people @ 4.5 hours (4:30–9:00) @ $25/hour = $225 plus $50 tips = $275—too much???
Budget	$350—split with John	Hmm…maybe skip the bartender and full bar, keep a server/busser

As you look at each item on your list, you'll be able to see whether it's realistic and if it accomplishes your goals. For example, if more than half of your budget is going to a bartender and a helper, will you have enough left for food, flowers, and drinks? One solution could be to skip the bartender and stick to serving wine, beer, sparkling water, fruit juice, and a premade cocktail that your cohost, John, can serve. On the other hand, hiring someone to take coats, pass hors d'oeuvres, pick up plates and glasses, and do basic cleanup will let you spend all your time with your guests—so you may not want to give that up.

fun and games

✦ ✦ ✦

Entertaining isn't just about serving a meal. There are lots of ways to add fun to a party. If you're planning an activity as part of your party, you'll need to figure out where it fits into your party timeline and how long it will take to complete. A How to Host a Murder dinner can take all evening. Depending on the players' enthusiasm, charades could last twenty minutes to an hour, cards or Scrabble an hour or all night, and sports as long as the daylight and the players' stamina lasts! Keep the focus on the fun, and be flexible enough to call a halt to the game if your guests start to lose interest.

INDOORS	OUTDOORS
Charades	Bocce or boules
Cards: Hearts, poker, bridge	Croquet
Fictionary	Volleyball
Scrabble	Badminton
How to Host a Murder	Touch football

managing your schedule

✦ ✦ ✦

Our advice in a nutshell: *You can never, ever be too prepared.* A successful party looks effortless, but that's only because of the careful prep work that went into it. And one of the most vitally important parts of party preparation is *managing your schedule.* Prep is truly personal, so this means knowing how much time *you* need to set aside to prepare: to shop, clean or straighten up your house, set the table, set up the bar, prep and cook your meal, and shower and dress for the party (really!).

We strongly recommend sitting down and creating an actual timeline. That way you'll have what you need when you need it, and you'll also be sure to leave plenty of time for your cooking and setup. You can follow the same approach whether you're hosting a formal dinner party or a simple get-together: The idea is to walk through all the steps involved in preparing for the party, working backward from the party date, and try to estimate how long each step will take. As you become more experienced entertaining, this step will become automatic and simpler. For a serious party, we like to print out a blank calendar that begins a month ahead of our party date, and then we fill in all our various party tasks on the calendar. Spread the work out, filling in a few items at a time. That way you'll keep it fun and won't feel overwhelmed.

Shopping Tips

✳ Preorder meat or fish. Have the butcher or fishmonger do the prep for you: butterfly a leg of lamb, trim a tenderloin, fillet a salmon.

✳ Check on pantry and cooking staples as you're making your master list. Don't forget to stock up on butter, cooking oil, spices, herbs, and condiments.

✳ Shop as early as you can before the party: a week ahead for staples; one or two days ahead for fresh ingredients.

✳ Wash and store produce right away so it's ready for prepping.

SAMPLE TIMELINE

Although the actual time frame may vary somewhat according to the particular party,
this timeline covers the elements involved in planning most parties.

4–5 weeks ahead	Establish date, purpose, budget, guest list
	Purchase invitations, if mailing
	Hire help
3–4 weeks ahead	Mail, e-mail, or phone invitations; as guests respond, inquire about food allergies
	Choose and reserve any rental items; arrange for pickup or delivery
2 weeks ahead	Finalize menu—food and beverages
	Gather all recipes; photocopy and keep in a folder
	Begin making shopping lists: food, beverages, flowers, decorations, equipment rental
	Check party linens; send to dry cleaner or wash and iron if necessary
1 week ahead	Call any non-RSVPers
	Purchase wine, liquor, and other beverages—either take with you or arrange for delivery
	Order meat or fish and arrange pickup time
	Purchase decorations, candles
	Prepare music: make playlist or choose CDs
	Order flowers; arrange for pickup or delivery
3 days ahead	Take care of any major housecleaning
	Replace missing lightbulbs
	Check and tidy walks, entryways
	Order ice for delivery or pickup, or start making and bagging your own
2 days ahead	Shop for all remaining ingredients
	Pick up beverages, flowers, rental items
	Make seating plan; write place cards
	Begin food prep, if necessary

Day before	Choose serving dishes for meal and/or hors d'oeuvres
	Set dining table
	Lay out buffet table, label serving dishes, wrap silverware in napkins
	Set up bar area
	Check and restock guest bathroom
	Set up coat area
	Tidy party spaces, if needed
	Arrange decorations
	Do as much food prep and precooking as your recipes allow
Morning of	Chill wine, water, juices, and mixers
	Arrange flowers if doing it yourself
	Make any sauces; fill condiment dishes and refrigerate; fill saltcellars, pepper grinders
	Prepare salad and dressing and refrigerate (separately)
	Assemble crudités, cheese platters, or antipasto platters; wrap and refrigerate
	Retidy party areas, if needed
	Make a mental "What can I do?" list in case guests offer to help (See Chapter 5, When You Need a Supporting Cast, page 49)
4 hours – 1½ hours before	Pick up ice if it's not being delivered
	Finish any food prep—you want to have as little as possible to do when guests arrive
	Slice bread—wrap until ready to put on the table
1½ hours before	Get yourself ready!
45 – 15 minutes before	Set out any platters/hors d'oeuvres that need to be at room temperature
	Set out butter to soften—wrap until ready to put on the table
	Fill ice buckets; place cold beverages, wine, beer at the bar
	Open wine

continued on next page

15 minutes before	Dim the lights
	Turn on the music
	Do a mental run-through of the evening and any other meal-related tasks you need to attend to
	Take a few minutes to enjoy your creation
	Take a deep breath and *smile*
Party time	Greet your guests

Day-Before Prepping Tips

 ✳ Marinate meat or chicken.

 ✳ Make baked desserts, fillings or dips for hors d'oeuvres, sauces, and salad dressing.

 ✳ Chop vegetables; bag and store.

 ✳ Wash, spin, and store lettuces and salad greens.

write it down, make it happen

✦ ✦ ✦

While you can throw a party without making lists, you'll only drive yourself crazy. The beauty of making lists is that they relieve you from having to remember so many things at once. Believe us, you'll be much more relaxed. So repeat after us: "Lists are my friends."

The easiest thing to do is to keep separate lists for specific reasons: a **to do list** that you can check off and add to as needed plus several **shopping lists** for groceries, beverages, and supplies. For a big party or important event it helps to **organize lists by supplier** once you have a **master list**.

After you've recalculated your recipes for the number of guests you'll be serving, make a **master list of ingredients and amounts**. Do a careful inventory of what you already have on hand and what you'll need to purchase. Our parents regularly host this incredible clambake, sometimes for upwards of seventy people. They developed a master list and timetable that covers everything, right down to the sticks for the s'mores and how far in advance to collect seaweed. My mom keeps it on her computer so that it's ready for the next time—a huge time-saver.

the essential checklist

This is a general list of party-prep essentials. You may not need each item, but use it as a guide when preparing your own party checklist.

- ☐ Make a party outline or budget
- ☐ Create a timeline
- ☐ Start a master to do list
- ☐ Start a master supply list
- ☐ Purchase and send invitations
- ☐ Hire help: bartender, servers, caterer
- ☐ Rent or purchase equipment and supplies; arrange pickup or delivery
- ☐ Purchase liquor, wine, beer, mixers, ice, water (sparkling and still), other beverages; arrange pickup or delivery
- ☐ Purchase paper goods
- ☐ Purchase or make decorations
- ☐ Send linens to dry cleaner, if necessary
- ☐ Prepare party music
- ☐ Prepare menu
- ☐ Gather recipes and recalculate all amounts for the number of servings
- ☐ Make a detailed grocery shopping list
- ☐ Shop for all ingredients
- ☐ Check /clean entryways
- ☐ Clean house/party area
- ☐ Set up party area and decorate
- ☐ Pick up any orders: rental items, liquor, flowers, meat or fish
- ☐ Set up bar
- ☐ Set table/buffet
- ☐ Set up coat area
- ☐ Cook/prepare dishes
- ☐ Make a seating plan
- ☐ Choose a party outfit and accessories

the party notebook

✦ ✦ ✦

Our grandmother has these beautiful red leather notebooks in which she records the details of every party she gives. It's fun to look through them and read about our mom and dad's engagement party or her famous New Year's Day parties. For our grandmother, it's also an invaluable resource in terms of remembering what was successful and what wasn't. Here's what she includes:

✦ The occasion, the date, and the time
✦ Who was invited, and whether they could come or not. Sometimes, for special occasions, she kept a copy of the invitation, too.

✦ The menu
✦ Wines, liquor, and other beverages—what she served and how much of it was used. (This is especially useful information for cocktail parties.)
✦ Flowers—which flowers and if she arranged them herself or used a florist
✦ Table linens and other decorations
✦ The seating plan
✦ Help: bartender, servers, caterer
✦ Notes on what worked and what didn't
✦ Jottings about costs

fifteen minutes fashionably early

✦ ✦ ✦

With all the hustle and bustle of party preparation, there's one more important thing to factor in: No matter what it says on the invitation, start your party a little early, just for you. Plan to be dressed and refreshed about fifteen minutes before your party begins. That leaves some wiggle room for you to look over the scene one last time and take care of any remaining details. Do a quick mental run-through of your overall plan and spend a couple of minutes thinking about your guests. Then take a deep breath, turn on the music, and smile!

✴

CHAPTER FOUR

the invitation tells all

What's your occasion? Are you celebrating a birthday or an anniversary? Throwing a holiday affair or welcoming new neighbors with a potluck party? Or have you simply decided to host your favorite crowd with a cocktail or dinner party? Determining the type of party you want to give makes the main elements of your celebration—guest list, time of day, formality, and even menu—fall into place naturally.

Let the circumstances of your celebration guide you in choosing the type of party to throw. If, for example, you want to introduce your new friends Carrie and Sean to a group of your old friends, a dinner or cocktail party is a good bet. A surprise birthday party for your best friend means that the guest list will be comprised largely of her relatives and friends.

Once you've chosen the type of party you want to give, turn your thoughts to your guest list and invitations.

◆ ◆ ◆

who's coming?

✦ ✦ ✦

No matter the occasion, the right group of people will go a long way toward making your party a hit. The key? Invite people you like and people you think *they'll* like, whether they know one another or not. Your mix of guests can actually determine the personality of your party—whether the vibe is laid-back and relaxed or vibrant and exciting.

Often it's the occasion that drives your guest list, such as a business dinner for work associates or a lunch for members of a club. If the event is in someone's honor—a birthday, an anniversary, a shower, or a graduation—then the honoree usually helps prepare the guest list.

the invite

✦ ✦ ✦

Back in Emily Post's time, mail was delivered twice daily, and local mail was often delivered the same day, so mailed invitations were fast, convenient, inexpensive, and reliable. The telephone was considered too informal; besides, it was expensive, and you never knew if operators or people sharing party lines were listening in. With a mailed invitation, it was hard to go wrong.

Mailed invitations are still the preferred mode for formal celebrations like weddings or black-tie affairs (an invitation received in the mail comes with an invisible IMPORTANT stamped on the envelope), but for expediency's sake, phone and e-mail invitations are now an accepted part of the invitation establishment. No matter how you issue your invitation, the main thing to remember is that all your guests should receive their invite the *same way*. If you mail out invitations to every other guest but invite your best friend by phone, she may think that she's an afterthought.

Whichever way you choose to deliver it, don't forget to include your Ws: **Who**, **What**, **When**, **Where**, and **Why**, a **Way to Respond**, and any info, if necessary, on **What to Wear**.

by phone

The phone is perfect for those occasions when you want to invite close friends to an informal gathering such as brunch; a small, casual dinner; or a birthday party, barbecue, cocktails, or dessert. You'll know right away who can come and who can't, plus you'll be able to settle any "What can I bring?" or "What should I wear?" issues on the spot.

Start with the facts: "Hi, Chloe, it's Trish. We're having a few people over for dinner next Saturday night. We'd love it if you and Sam could join us." This is a much better way of inviting someone than ambushing Chloe with "What are you doing Saturday night?"

What if no one's at home? It's fine to leave a voice-mail message, but do try to call again and issue the invitation "in person" in case the message doesn't get delivered.

e-vitations

Using e-mail or online services like Evite® or Socializr.com (which organize and customize the invitation process for you) can save time and money and build some excitement at the same time. The key is knowing when the situation is right to use an e-mail invite—and when it's not. The bottom line is that your guests get the message.

pros

+ You don't have to go to the store.
+ It's free.
+ You have lots of design choices.
+ You can send your e-vitations 24/7.
+ Sites like Evite and Socializr.com are well organized.
+ It's easy and fun.

cons

+ It's not as personal as a phoned or written invitation.
+ It might not provide enough fanfare for a formal event or be special enough for an intimate gathering.
+ It may end up in a spam folder or undelivered as a result of a computer glitch.
+ E-vitation RSVP messages are seen by all—so guests may angst over sending a clever response.
+ You still may have to follow up with people who don't respond.

tips for e-vitation success:

+ Make sure the e-mail addresses you use are correct and all your invited guests check their e-mail regularly.
+ Make yourself familiar with all the options.

For example, you may want to turn off the feature that lets guests see who else is invited. This is especially important to people who don't know each other well. (Between privacy issues and abuse of the "Reply All" button, this can save the party before it starts!)

+ Be sure you've included all the important info: who's hosting, what kind of party it is, why the party is being thrown (if there's a reason), when and where it is (including links to maps if necessary), and RSVP details.

+ If using a service like Evite® or Socializr.com, fill in all the details the site asks for and remember to include a personal message.

+ Proofread before you hit "Send." Invitations are the first hint of what a party will be like, so make a good impression.

+ Be prepared to follow up by phone if you don't receive an RSVP in a timely fashion, just in case your message has not been delivered or is lingering unopened in an inbox. (Note: One of the advantages of Evite®, compared with using your own e-mail account, is that it lets you know if the recipient has viewed the invitation.)

+ Follow up with a reminder to the group a day or two in advance.

by mail

If you're hosting a more formal event—honoring a special guest or celebrating a milestone, for example—a mailed invitation is the way to go. Of course, you can mail invitations for informal dinners and parties, too—even the simplest get-together is elevated to party status by an invitation in the mail.

Be sure to pick invites that match the event or the style of the party. More formal events call for more formal invitations (see The Pleasure of Your Company, opposite). For less formal parties, choose a fill-in invitation from a stationery shop that suits the occasion. Many stationers carry computer-friendly invitations: Supply the wording, select a font, and either have the invites printed out for you at the shop or do it yourself on your home computer.

The most personal invitation? A note handwritten on your own stationery. Handwritten invitations are few and far between these days, but wow, what an honor it is to receive one! Your guests will know they're cherished friends.

the pleasure of your company

✦ ✦ ✦

When your party's formal and the occasion fancy, it calls for third-person formal invitations. These invitations are printed, engraved, or handwritten. The most formal invitations are engraved in black ink on white or cream cards. But for slightly less lofty occasions, colored papers and inks, thermography, and letterpress can add personality and style.

A formal invitation can be handwritten, too. Use the same wording and spacing as the engraved model on plain white or cream notepaper or stationery printed with your monogram or house address. To make it as easy as possible for your guests to respond, include a phone number or e-mail address below RSVP. And make sure your voice mail is active and that you check your e-mail! Another option is to enclose a reply card with a stamped, preaddressed envelope or postcard.

Tina and Thomas Giordano
request the pleasure of your company
for dinner and dancing
on Saturday, the tenth of April
at half after seven o'clock
The Coach Barn at Shelburne Farms
Shelburne, Vermont

RSVP   *Black tie*
802-555-1234

when do the invitations go out?

✦ ✦ ✦

Whether you mail, e-mail, or phone your invitations, timing is key. Nowadays, sooner rather than later is the rule, to best accommodate guests' busy work and social schedules. How soon? Give your invitees enough time to respond—and give yourself enough time to organize the party. If you're hosting a holiday party or if guests have to travel to get there, invitations might go out as early as six weeks ahead. Here are some general guidelines on timing your invitations, but feel free to adapt them to fit your particular circumstances:

Formal dinner	3–6 weeks
Informal dinner	A few days to 3 weeks
Cocktail party	1–4 weeks
Lunch or tea	A few days to 2 weeks
Casual get-together	Same day to 2 weeks
Birthday or anniversary	3–6 weeks
Graduation	4 weeks

Christening, Bar/Bat Mitzvah	4 weeks
Housewarming	A few days to 3 weeks
Holiday party	4–6 weeks
Thanksgiving or other holiday dinner	2 weeks to 2 months

invite clearly

Make sure your invitation lets your guests know what to expect. Whether you invite by phone, e-mail, or written invitation, let your guest know:

+ WHO'S hosting, include the names of any cohosts.
+ WHAT type of event it is (lunch, brunch, dinner, tea, cocktails, barbecue, picnic).
+ WHERE it's taking place (your house, a park, the beach).
+ WHEN: State the date and the time you'd like guests to arrive or, for an open house or cocktail party, the beginning and the end time (6:30 P.M. to 8:00 P.M.).

+ **WHY:** Let guests know the reason for the celebration, such as a birthday or an anniversary, and the name of the honoree.

+ **HOW TO RESPOND:** Provide a phone number, an e-mail address, or a postal address. It's also okay to include a "reply by" date if this is critical to your planning.

+ **ANY SPECIAL INFO:** Put any information into the invite that guests should know ahead of time, such as what to wear or what to bring or not bring: "It's a surprise!"; "No gifts, please"; "Bring a bathing suit"; "Casual."

rsvp

+ + +

RSVP is the abbreviation of the French phrase *Répondez, s'il vous plaît*, which means "Please respond." Of course, you can always just say in plain English, "Please respond by [date]." Most invitations include some sort of RSVP; it lets the host or hostess know how many guests will be attending the party—crucial if you're having a sit-down dinner, for example, or a catered party that demands specific headcounts. Add a physical address, a phone number, or an e-mail address on written or e-mailed invitations, and if calling, include your number if you leave a voice-mail message. A guest is obligated to reply to an RSVP, so if you haven't heard back from someone within a reasonable amount of time, it's perfectly okay to call and ask (politely of course!) for a yes or a no. (Include a "Could you let me know by Thursday?" for any wafflers.) Remember, the hope is to have that person there!

For a big party, you might be tempted to add "Regrets Only" to save yourself from being inundated by phone calls. We really don't recommend this. It's confusing, and guests often call anyway or simply forget to call and fail to show up. It's best to include a "Reply By" date, usually a week or more before the event—especially if you need to provide a headcount for a caterer. For weddings, large events such as balls or benefits, and business events, reply cards make it easy for guests to make a menu choice or send payments or donations. If you just need a yes or no answer, go green and ask for an e-mail reply.

invitation extras

✦ ✦ ✦

Some invitations aren't so cut-and-dried. Here are a few more tips for those party invites that require a little extra:

✦ **If more than one person is hosting,** be sure to list all the hosts on the invitation: "Please join Marcia and Bob Heiddecker and Linda and Ian Williams for..."

✦ **If your party is in someone's honor,** list the honoree on the invitation as well: "Please join us for cocktails to celebrate Antoine's thirtieth birthday."

✦ **End times** aren't generally included on an invitation, with a few exceptions. Children's parties list an end time so parents know when to pick up their kids. Invitations to cocktail parties or parties that precede another scheduled event (theater, sporting event) have a start and end time so that guests can go on to dinner or the next event. End times are also given for open houses and other events where guests are free to come and go during the specified time.

✦ You may need to include other information for your guests with, but not on, the invitation. This is done using enclosures. Simply place enclosures in front of the invitation, which is inserted with the written side facing the flap side of the envelope. This way, the recipient sees the writing on the invitation and the enclosures as the invitation is removed from the envelope. Some typical enclosures are:

✦ **MAPS AND DIRECTIONS:** Be sure to add a contact number—just in case!

✦ **SCHEDULE OF EVENTS:** Useful for weddings or reunion weekends.

✦ **TICKETS:** For graduations, say, or if you're inviting friends to a concert or game.

✦ **RAFFLE TICKETS:** For charity events, for example.

✦ **REGISTRY INFORMATION:** For bridal or baby showers.

✦ **RESPONSE CARD:** Make sure the envelope or postcard is addressed and stamped.

decoding dress codes:
what (or what not) to wear?

✦ ✦ ✦

Parties are a great time to dress up a bit. The question is "How much?" That's why it's helpful to include any information about attire on the invitation. Not only does it help ensure the comfort level of your guests, but it lets them enjoy all the party has to offer—*especially* if they need to bring a change of clothes: BRING YOUR SWIMSUIT AND TOWEL; WEAR YOUR WHITES AND BRING YOUR RACQUET; COSTUMES.

On what occasions, then, do you need to specify a dress code on the invitation? On formal invitations, BLACK TIE or WHITE TIE is printed or written in the lower right corner. On informal invitations, it's not necessary to mention a dress code, but for those in-between occasions, guests appreciate any guidance you can give, such as CASUAL DRESS, BUSINESS CASUAL, NO JEANS, PLEASE, or JACKETS REQUIRED. The idea is to be helpful, which means being clear. Not everyone will understand SAFARI CHIC. If there's nothing on the invitation about dress and a guest is unsure, it's perfectly fine to call the host or another invitee and ask. (See Chapter 16, Be Invited Back, page 233.)

potlucks, byob, and byof

✦ ✦ ✦

Potluck suppers, in which guests contribute food and/or beverages, are a fun and easy way for family and friends to share time together without one person bearing the brunt of the work. While these group events don't have an official "host," often one person or couple provides the party venue and organizes the party. When you're inviting people to the party, it's important to be clear that the event is a potluck—so spell it out on the invitation or simply tell people if you're inviting them in person. As the organizer, you can assign food categories (appetizer, main course, salad, dessert) to keep the menu balanced. If you do, be sure to note it on your invitation: "Please bring a salad to share." To be sure that everyone gets their containers back, have masking tape and markers on hand to label the bottom of the dishes.

BYOB means "Bring your own beverage." The host generally supplies the glasses, ice, and appetizers or a meal. Although BYOB commonly refers to alcohol, a guest can bring any beverage he or she chooses. BYOF means "Bring your own food." Guests come with food for themselves, not necessarily dishes to share. In this case, the host may be providing the venue, such as access to a private beach.

what not to put on an invitation

- **No Smoking:** The absence of ashtrays in your house should let smokers know they need to take it outside.
- **No Children:** If your invitation doesn't include the kids, then they aren't invited. Period. If you're concerned that a certain someone will try to bring her children, it's best handled with a phone call.
- **No Pets:** Most people know better than to show up with Fido in their purse—they should always call and ask first. That's the time to let them know if it's okay or not.
- **Gift Information:** A request for gifts or any mention of gifts or where someone is registered is *never* put on the invitation itself. This is an inviolable rule for wedding invitations, but it also applies to birthday, anniversary, graduation,

shower, or other invitations when the occasion calls for a gift for the honoree. Remember—the choice of a gift is *always* up to the giver. That said, people do like to give gifts that please the recipients, and suggestions are helpful. So, for bridal or baby showers, it's okay to add a separate enclosure with registry information or a list of items on the mother-to-be's or bride's wish list.

If a group gift is planned, this information also goes on a separate enclosure: *"Some of us are getting together to give Anne Marie and Matt a tent for their 10th anniversary. The total cost is $425. If you'd like to join in, please call Tara at 987-555-1234 by June 10."* This way a guest is free to contribute or give a gift of his or her choosing. Note, too, that no amount was suggested, but that the contribution was left up to the individual.

No Gifts, Please

There is one exception to the "no gift information on the invite" rule. Though once considered a faux pas (and still the case for wedding invitations), putting NO GIFTS, PLEASE at the bottom of an invitation is fine for birthday and anniversary parties and for any occasion when a gift would otherwise be expected. You may also tell invitees in person or by phone.

what's in a name?

✦ ✦ ✦

To some people, everything. When addressing invitations, be careful to spell names correctly. Although it's fine to omit titles when addressing casual invitations, titles are a must for more formal ones. This can be an etiquette minefield: Jane and John are married, but she doesn't want to be addressed as "... and Mrs. John Kelly"; Shana's married but uses her maiden name; Colleen's a doctor and so is her husband. (Women have so many options these days!) It's always nice if you can find out how people prefer to be addressed, but if you aren't sure, use this chart to guide you:

How Do I Address?

SITUATION	OPTIONS/NOTES
ADDRESSING A WOMAN	
Maiden name	Ms. Jane Johnson Miss Jane Johnson* *Usually Miss is for girls under 18.
Married, keeping her maiden name	Ms. Jane Johnson
Married, uses her husband's name socially	Mrs. John Kelly Mrs. Jane Kelly* *Nowadays this is acceptable. Ms. Jane Kelly
Separated, not divorced	Mrs. John Kelly Mrs. Jane Kelly Ms. Jane Kelly
Divorced	Mrs. Jane Kelly Ms. Jane Kelly Ms. Jane Johnson (maiden name)
Widowed	Mrs. John Kelly* *If you don't know the widow's preference, this is the traditional and preferred form. Mrs. Jane Kelly Ms. Jane Kelly

ADDRESSING A COUPLE

Married, she uses her husband's name socially	Mr. and Mrs. John Kelly

NOTE: Traditionally, a man's name preceded a woman's on an envelope address, and his first name and surname were not separated (Jane and John Kelly). Nowadays, the order of the names—whether his name or hers comes first—does not matter and either way is acceptable. The exception is when one member of the couple "outranks" the other—the one with the higher rank is always listed first.

Married, she prefers Ms.	Mr. John Kelly and Ms. Jane Kelly Ms. Jane Kelly and Mr. John Kelly *Do not link Ms. to the husband's name: Mr. and Ms. John Kelly is incorrect.
Married, informal address	Jane and John Kelly John and Jane Kelly
Married, she uses her maiden name	Mr. John Kelly and Ms. Jane Johnson Ms. Jane Johnson and Mr. John Kelly If you can't fit the names on one line: Mr. John Kelly and Ms. Jane Johnson Note the indent; either name may be used first.
Unmarried, living together	Mr. John Kelly and Ms. Jane Johnson Note: Either name may be used first.
A woman who outranks her husband: elected office, military rank	The Honorable Jane Kelly and Mr. John Kelly If you can't fit both names on one line (note indent): The Honorable Jane Kelly and Mr. John Kelly

continued on next page

How Do I Address?

A woman who outranks her husband: professional or educational degree	Dr. Jane Kelly and Mr. John Kelly
Both are doctors (PhD or medical) and use the same last name	The Doctors Kelly (omit first names) Drs. Jane and John Kelly / Drs. John and Jane Kelly Dr. John Kelly and Dr. Jane Kelly Dr. Jane Kelly and Dr. John Kelly
Both are doctors (PhD or medical); she uses her maiden name	Dr. Jane Johnson and Dr. John Kelly Dr. John Kelly and Dr. Jane Johnson

BUSINESS

Woman	Ms. is the default form of address, unless you know positively that a woman wishes to be addressed as Mrs.
Professional designations—use only for business	Jane Kelly, CPA Note: Do not use Ms. or Mr. if using a professional designation. Socially, drop the professional designation and use Mr., Ms., or Mrs.: Ms. Jane Kelly.
Esquire: Attorneys and some court officials	Jane Kelly, Esquire Note: If using Esquire, do not use Ms. or Mr. In conversation or socially, Esquire is not used; use Mr. or Ms.: Ms. Jane Kelly.
Attorney at Law	Ms. Jane Kelly Attorney at Law This is an alternative to *Esquire* for attorneys. Use Mr. or Ms. and use two lines with no indent.

when you need a supporting cast

parties are as much about coordinating as they are about planning—and when all the main elements of the party are in full swing, what host hasn't wished for more than two hands? Even the most determined do-it-yourselfer throwing the most casual of parties can benefit from a little help, if only to tidy up the mess afterward. (Wouldn't it be nice to say good night to your last guest and *not* have to do the cleanup?)

Depending on your entertaining experience and the type of party you're throwing, you may want to consider enlisting some help: asking a friend to serve at an informal dinner, hiring nonprofessional help to clean up, or bringing in the big guns—professional caterers, bartenders, and servers. In determining just how much help you need, consider your time, your comfort level, and your budget—and then go and create your team.

◆ ◆ ◆

No matter who's assisting you, it's up to you to give clear instructions about what you want done as well as when and how to do it. Here are your four main options for getting party help:

+ **TAKE GUESTS UP ON THEIR OFFERS OF HELP.** Have a list of tasks in mind before guests arrive. (See Can I Help?, opposite, for specifics.)

+ **ENLIST THE DEDICATED HELP OF A CLOSE FRIEND OR FAMILY MEMBER.** This is a good option when you just need an extra pair of hands. Ask early—when the party is in its planning stages, if possible. Have a few specific jobs in mind: Taking coats, passing hors d'oeuvres, filling glasses and lighting candles, delivering plated entrées to the table or helping with clearing or cleaning up. These are all things you can ask a good friend to do— as long as you don't ask her to do too much! You still want her to feel like a guest and have plenty of time to socialize and enjoy the

receiving end of your hospitality. A small gift accompanied by a note of thanks is a wonderful way to show your appreciation for her graciousness and generosity.

+ **HIRE A FRIEND OR NEIGHBOR'S TEEN OR A COLLEGE STUDENT TO HELP.** This option is easy on the pocketbook, but do factor in the time you might need to show your help what you'd like them to do and how to do it. Of course, if it works out, you know you have reliable help for future parties. (See Working with Nonprofessional Help, opposite.)

+ **HIRE PROFESSIONALS.** Professionals can save you time, stress, and even money. For time-stressed hosts, it may be a better value than you think—it means no shopping, no running around, no cooking, no serving, no cleaning up. Caterers come with all the equipment they need so you don't need to rent it, clean it, or return it. Plus, you can be a guest at your own party!

"can i help?"

✦ ✦ ✦

In these casual times, most guests (especially close friends) will make a genuine offer to pitch in. If you aren't using professional help and are feeling slightly overwhelmed, by all means take your friends up on their generous offers. Here's a list of possible light chores a guest can do without being made to feel that he's suddenly "on staff":

✦ Passing hors d'oeuvres
✦ Lighting candles
✦ Filling water glasses
✦ Opening and pouring wine
✦ Delivering plated courses to the table
✦ Bringing bread or salad to the table
✦ Helping to clear between courses (one person per six guests)
✦ Helping to serve dessert and/or coffee

working with nonprofessional help

✦ ✦ ✦

In high school, we were often the designated help at our mom's and aunt's dinner parties, passing hors d'oeuvres, serving and clearing the table, and doing the cleanup. It was a great way to earn extra money, and a fun way to learn about entertaining. At first we were tapped because we were family members, but word got out, and soon other people around town were asking us to help serve at their parties.

Using high school or college-age kids for basic serving and cleanup help at your party is a great resource. It's a good idea to hire two kids (it's more fun for them to work in tandem, and you'll have plenty of help), and if you're planning a large holiday party, consider hiring one or two teens and providing them with large flashlights to direct guests to parking. Here are some things to discuss with your help in advance:

✦ SET AN HOURLY RATE.
✦ BE CLEAR ABOUT ARRIVAL TIME. Have the kids come over a day or two before the party to familiarize themselves with your house and to

All Together Now

A much-loved, creative winery owner who lives in California's Alexander Valley recently gave a memorable informal dinner party for twelve neighbors. Here, guest Carrie Brown (owner of The Jimtown Store in California's Alexander Valley and author of *The Jimtown Store Cookbook*) describes the hostess's novel approach to service:

"When we arrived, our hostess offered us a glass of wine and asked each of us to find our name on a handwritten dinner menu with a schedule for the evening that she had posted in her open kitchen. Each course had two names listed to help plate and serve, and two other names were listed to clear that course. All the plates and extra utensils had been organized for each course and a place had been set aside for the dirty dishes. A rubber spatula was handy for scraping scraps into the garbage, and a soapy water bucket for utensils was ready in the sink—with explicit instructions to simply stack, not wash, the dishes and return to the table.

"By the end of the three-course meal we had all contributed to the service and had a great, lively time doing so. We lingered at the table swirling our reserve vintage wine and then were sent on our way home—a final cleanup was not allowed. Our hostess's kitchen was left neat and tidy and I'm sure it didn't take long to finish up."

---

get instructions. On the day of the party, ask them to arrive an hour or two in advance to help out with the final preparations.

✦ **DETERMINE WHICH JOBS THEY'LL PERFORM.** Among their possible duties: taking coats, passing hors d'oeuvres, picking up glasses and napkins, emptying bowls for pits or toothpicks, refreshing platters and bar items, and, for a dinner party, serving and clearing the table.

✦ **SET EXPECTATIONS FOR ATTIRE.** This is especially important for high schoolers. Typically, servers wear black pants or skirts with a white or black shirt, and clean, appropriate shoes. (Clean black sneakers are fine.) Otherwise, ask for conservative, clean and ironed clothing.

+ **ESTABLISH THE GROUND RULES.** Discuss when it's appropriate for the helpers to take a break, whether smoking is permitted, and if food will be provided. Also, let them know that they shouldn't accept any tips from guests for services such as valet-style parking.

It's important to set the tone and standards for service beforehand with professionals and nonprofessionals alike. Show them explicitly how you want things done. For example, use a tray to clear dirty napkins and empty glasses; pick glasses up by the stems or bottoms, not by sticking your fingers *in* the glasses; when serving and clearing the table leave, on the left, remove from the right (LL/RR). Show them how you want platters plated and refreshed. Depending on their experience, nonprofessionals may also need your direction during the party. You might need to remind them to refresh platters, pick up glasses, check on the status of the guest bathroom, and keep the kitchen tidy.

How Much Help Do I Need?

Depending on your particular party, your professionals will recommend the number and type of help you need. If you want things to run flawlessly, so that you can be a guest at your own party, count on:

Cocktail party for 20	2–3 servers who can share passing, bussing, and kitchen duties (a bartender is optional)
Cocktail party for 50	2 servers, 1 bartender, 1 kitchen duty, plus 1 to "back the bar" and buss
Dinner party	1 cook, 2 kitchen duty with at least 1 who can assist the cook, 1 server per 8 people, 2 servers if the dinner involves changes of silverware and pouring wine, water, coffee

You can hire fewer people, but if you do, it's likely you'll still need to keep a vigilant eye on everything as the party proceeds.

what can I expect from:

+ **BARTENDERS:** Bartenders mix and serve drinks and keep the bar neat and refreshed. They should arrive before the party starts to set up the bar and learn the layout of your home. For a larger party, professional bartenders will require around two hours to properly set up the bar and polish all the glasses, hide the flats, boxes, and cooler for extra ice, and make it all look neat and clean. Bartenders ordinarily don't leave until the last guest has been ushered out and the last glass washed and put away. This may take an hour to an hour and a half, depending on how long guests linger and the scale of the party.

+ **SERVERS:** Servers arrive ahead of time to prepare platters or assist in the kitchen, and they leave after all the dishes have been washed and the kitchen and party areas are immaculate. During the party, they take coats, pass hors d'oeuvres, pick up glasses and napkins, empty ashtrays or bowls for pits or toothpicks, refill platters, refresh bar items if there's no bartender, and serve and clear the table at a dinner party. Professionals will know exactly what to do once you show them how you want things presented and explain your timeline for the event. Beware that servers, whether professional or amateur, are not necessarily skilled at food presentation, so take the time to show them how you want trays and platters arranged, garnished, and replenished. For example, ask servers to either switch almost empty trays with fresh trays or take the almost empty trays into the kitchen to be rebuilt.

Kid and Animal Wranglers

Kids and pets are adorable, but their unpredictability can disrupt a party (unless your celebration is casual or family style to begin with). Your focus should be on your grown-up guests, not wayward kids or unruly pets. Solution: Hire a babysitter to take care of little tykes in an area separate from the party. Preferably, have the sitter come an hour or two ahead so you have enough time to get yourself ready and finish last-minute preparations or give instructions. If your party is during dinnertime, be sure to arrange for food for the kids. And if your favorite furball can't behave with guests or if someone is allergic, confine him to a yard or a room away from guests.

what can a caterer do for you?

✦ ✦ ✦

A full-service caterer can work with you in several ways. She can do it all—cook, serve, and clean up for the entire event—or she can simply deliver meals or hors d'oeuvres at a specified time (which you then serve yourself). A caterer can even help you plan and manage your entire party, creating a menu that fits your budget while taking into account food allergies and preferences. In addition, she can provide professional waitstaff and make reliable recommendations for bartenders (some catering companies offer bartending service) and other vendors such as wine retailers, rental companies, or florists.

when is a caterer a must?

✦ ✦ ✦

In truth, there's no set rule. Some people hire caterers to prepare elegant dinners for four; others wouldn't think of hiring a caterer for fewer than fifty guests. If you feel you don't have the time or the skill to pull off *any* size party—and the party has to be perfect—catering is the way to go.

finding and hiring a caterer

✦ ✦ ✦

The best way may be firsthand experience: If you go to a party where the catering is outstanding, get the caterer's card for future reference and keep it in your resource file. Another good way to find a caterer is through word-of-mouth recommendations. A catchy ad with a great photo is no substitute for a rave review from a friend. Was the food delicious? Did everything go as planned? Was everything attractively presented and appealing? Was the staff helpful, pleasant, and efficient? Were they on budget?

You'll want to hire your caterer *at least* four weeks before your event. Count on an even greater lead time during the holidays or busy times of year like wedding season. In fact, don't even send out invitations until you're sure you have the help you need.

meeting with the caterer: be prepared

✦ ✦ ✦

Start off on the right foot by being organized and clear. Before the meeting, do some homework. Don't worry if some of the details are sketchy—the caterer will help you round out your plan or suggest alternatives to meet your budget. Go to your first meeting with:

✦ A clear idea of your budget

✦ The number of guests you wish to invite

✦ A preliminary plan for your event:

  ✦ the purpose or theme

  ✦ the time of day

  ✦ the style: casual or formal

  ✦ brunch, lunch, tea, cocktails, dinner

  ✦ stations or passed hors d'oeuvres

  ✦ buffet or sit-down meal

✦ A list of food allergies or special dietary needs and any special food requests

At the meeting, discuss the type of help, equipment, or supplies you'll need at your party, the menu, and the contract.

Staff and supplies. Depending on the type and size of your party, your caterer may recommend cooks, servers, bartenders, and possibly a captain (the head server or a "director" for the evening who oversees the staff). Be sure to mention if you have other staff needs, such as valet parkers, too. Discuss what equipment and supplies you might require, like extra dishes, glasses, utensils, serving dishes and utensils, trays, and linens. Do you need a grill, a tent, an outdoor heater, or a portable oven? As you develop your party plans and your menu, the caterer will be doing a cross-check of what you have and what she needs to supply.

Choosing your menu. Now for the fun part! It's easy to go overboard with all the tempting choices of hors d'oeuvres, entrées, sides, and desserts, but a good caterer will be able to gauge just how much food you'll need and help you build an interesting and balanced menu—one that also meets your budget. Always ask to set up a food tasting to narrow your selections.

The contract. Once you're satisfied with your menu choices and have established staff and supply needs, it's time to sign the catering contract. Get all the details in writing: an itemized list of the food, supplies, and the staff, including duties, and arrival and departure times, each matched with a price. The contract should list separate amounts for food, labor, tax, and gratuity—otherwise, ask if it's included. Ask if you'll be charged extra for things like garbage disposal, ice delivery, or linens. Once you've signed the contract, you do have some leeway for making changes, but be sure to get a new price each time so there are no surprises. Expect to pay a deposit on signing the contract, and establish

when and how the balance will be paid. Be sure cancellation policies are clearly spelled out.

Two weeks before your event, all the details of your party should be finalized. Remember, you've hired a caterer so that you don't have to micromanage your party. One week before the event, you have carte blanche to call any absent-minded guests who haven't RSVP'd and give your caterer a final head count.

before help arrives

+ Designate parking areas.
+ Have as much cleared, clean counter space as possible in the kitchen. Consider providing an extra table for a prep area.
+ Empty the dishwasher.
+ Have emptied bins for trash and recycling and a good supply of trash bags.

who's the boss?

✦ ✦ ✦

You are! Whether you use a caterer or hire help on your own, you're still the one in charge, and it's up to you to give the staff instructions. They'll need to know how the party will flow: when hors d'oeuvres should be passed and which hors d'oeuvres should be placed on tables; when to stop serving drinks; when dinner or dessert will be served. A caterer's staff should be able to take it from there, leaving you free to relax and have fun.

Tipping Your Help

If you're working with a caterer, check the contract to see if the gratuity is included.
It should be listed separately and based on a percentage of the food and beverage bill, not
the tax or labor, just as it is in a restaurant. An 18 percent gratuity is average.
If it's not included, calculate it as you would a restaurant tip, and deliver it to the staff directly
or to the captain, or add it when you make your final payment with a note to the caterer
expressing how pleased you were with the staff.

When you hire your own help, you should tip a percentage of the hourly rate.
Be prepared to pay and tip the staff before they leave—but don't pony up until the cleanup
is done to your satisfaction.

a word about insurance

✦ ✦ ✦

Any time you serve alcohol to a guest, you are considered responsible for his sobriety when he leaves your premises. If you hire a bartender, check to see if he comes with a liquor license. If so, he (or his company) is required to carry liability insurance, and thus assumes the responsibility of serving alcohol, not you. If you hire a local college student with no liquor license, you, the homeowner, are liable—which makes hiring a professional a very good idea. Remember, no one under twenty-one is allowed to serve liquor. Depending on the nature of your party, consider adding a rider to your homeowner's policy to cover your event. Whatever the scenario, *never* let a guest drive under the influence.

✳

setting
the stage

it's safe to say that most of us don't live in a party-ready house—
most of us, in fact, inhabit homes: comfortable, lived-in spaces
surrounded by the clutter of everyday life. But whether you're inviting
two people to dinner or throwing a cocktail party for fifty, you'll need
to think about fashioning a party space out of your cozy nest. Your goal
is to create a party with its own unique atmosphere and personality.
Whether that means sweeping away the clutter for a minimalist look or
artfully arranging your space so that it glows with shabby-chic ambience
is entirely up to you. Keep your creative vision in mind as you tackle
some of the more practical aspects of setting the stage.

◆ ◆ ◆

transforming your space

✦ ✦ ✦

Transforming your space for a small group may involve little more than adding a chair or two from another room, or making your existing living room seating more intimate to encourage conversation. A large group poses different challenges: You're looking to maximize your space and seating. Pretend you're a guest, and imagine moving through the space. Are there places to set down food and drinks? Is there enough seating? Does the space have room for flow or are there cramped areas with potential for human gridlock? You may have to move or remove some furniture or add seating or small tables. *Think out of the box:* Ottomans, low stools, and trunks can do double duty as seating and tray tables. Floor pillows work well for casual gatherings. If you find you still don't have enough chairs, borrow or rent a few more. If you plan to entertain a lot in the future, consider investing in some folding chairs. Here are a few more tips for working with your space:

✦ Cocktail parties are mostly stand-up affairs, but you should provide several seating clusters for small group chats (and to provide relief for those wearing high heels!).

✦ Place tables strategically so that guests have somewhere to put glasses or plates.

✦ A buffet dinner requires that everyone has a seat—whether eating at a table or on laps—and a surface for drinks.

✦ Make sure bars and buffet tables don't inhibit traffic flow or cause congestion. Avoid placing them near the front door or the entrance to the kitchen. (Do a walk-through to see where you end up.)

✦ Establish a designated spot for coats—a rack, a closet, or a bed. In inclement weather, set aside a space for wet coats, boots, and umbrellas.

✦ Check that your entry space flows directly into your party space.

you can rent almost anything!

✦ ✦ ✦

Sometimes renting party equipment and party supplies is the smart way to go. Shop around for a company with an assortment of quality goods and a range of price points. Ask about delivery prices and whether you have the option to pick up a small order yourself. Among the party stuff rental companies can provide:

+ Coatracks for large parties

+ Tables and chairs (look for attractive painted or natural wood ones instead of plastic or metal)

+ Everything for the table setting, from enamelware plates to white ironstone dishes to crystal Riedel wineglasses—including tablecloths and linens, glassware, dishes, utensils, platters, votives, and even little dishes for nuts or olives

+ Just about anything you can think of for a party—grills (charcoal or gas), outdoor heaters, strands of lights (à la Italian street parties) or Japanese lanterns, plants, warming trays, chocolate fountains—everything, pretty much, but the kitchen sink

seasonal space: the great outdoors

✦ ✦ ✦

We love summer in Vermont! That's when we get to throw big parties outside. Having a party in the great outdoors means less strain on your house (guests only need access to the bathroom and maybe the kitchen) and less need to decorate—after all, who can top Mother Nature on a sunny Vermont afternoon? Lawns, patios, and screened-in porches make ideal party spaces. Don't forget to consider rain insurance—can your guests fit inside or will you need to rent a tent?

decorating with flowers

✦ ✦ ✦

In our book, it's not a party without flowers. You don't need to invest a fortune in masses of roses and lilies to make an impact, though. Small, simple arrangements can be just as effective as big sprays of flowers.

Fresh flowers are available year-round from a variety of sources, including your local grocery store. But where flowers are concerned, you get what you pay for. Flowers from a reputable florist generally cost more but should last up to a week, while bargain-priced blooms may not be as fresh and generally fade after a day or two. Buying fresh, seasonal flowers from the farmers' market or direct from a grower is a wonderful and reasonable way to go. Bottom line: Always buy the freshest flowers you can afford.

flower arranging 101

✦ ✦ ✦

When it comes to flower arranging, the only "rule" is to make sure your arrangement is low enough so it's not blocking guests' views of other guests. If you're clueless about flower arranging, a florist can give you suggestions or even prepare a sample arrangement you can copy. Don't be afraid to ask for a lesson.

A few well-placed arrangements can enhance your space and add personality and life—think entryway, coffee table, mantelpiece, bar, buffet, or sideboard. Don't forget your guest bathroom— even a small vase containing a bud or two will add elegance and charm. Here are some tips on using flowers to set the stage for your party:

+ Just like produce, pick what looks freshest and best to you.
+ A centerpiece is just that—an arrangement for the center of your dining table. It doesn't have to be just one arrangement, however; you can easily fill small vases and place them along the length of the table, or group them in clusters or at each guest's place. Single large blooms floating in shallow bowls make a stunning centerpiece.

- Keep it simple—choose one to three colors and one to three shapes or textures.
- Odd numbers work best: one, three, or five of each color, shape, or texture.
- When you're feeling more confident, choose multiple colors that harmonize.
- Colors that are analogous (next to each other on the color wheel) are often more sophisticated when paired than you might expect. Try combinations of red/orange or red/pink. Hold the flowers together in your hands to see if you like the combinations.
- Let the seasons inspire you: soft shades of pinks to magenta and pale greens for spring; bright orange, yellows, and blue for summer; fiery reds, burnt orange, deep purple, and gold with chocolate brown for accents in the fall; all white for winter with greens or tiny red berries.
- Take your color scheme from something you love that speaks to you: your kilim carpet, a favorite fabric with unusual colors, or a bird print. It's a great way to train your eye for pleasing color combinations.
- Flowers with strong scents are better for the powder room or entryway than on the dining or buffet table, where they can overwhelm the aroma of the food.
- Let the vase show off the flowers. Choose a vase or container and hold the image in your mind (or bring a digital photo) when you choose the flowers. Or let the vase dictate what will flatter it. It's kind of like putting an outfit together—imagine a chocolate brown bottom with a deep pink top, for example.
- Subtly echo the color of food you're serving in the floral arrangements—using pinks and greens if you're serving salmon and asparagus, for example, or yellows and reds if you're having polenta and heirloom tomato sauce. We're not suggesting that everything should match by any means, but it's lovely to see colors reverberate on the table.
- Borrow a trick from food magazine stylists: Go one step further and dress to match your color scheme. The overall effect can be playful or subtle—and chances are people will notice and comment favorably. Check out the next dinner party article you come across and see how the hosts are styled.

Spring in Winter

Make an arrangement of tightly budded flowering branches in late winter and "force" them open. You do this by keeping the vase full of clean, fresh water until the buds bloom and reward you with an indoor spring in approximately ten days to two weeks.

the simplest arrangements

✦ ✦ ✦

Make a tight bouquet using one type of flower: baby roses, small calla lilies, alstromeria, hydrangea, gerbera daisies, daffodils, lilacs, or tulips. Wrap stems with twine, raffia, or ribbon to hold tight. Cut stems evenly so flowers sit above the lip of the vase. Or choose something spectacular like peonies and add them one at a time to a vase with a small mouth (the blossoms are top-heavy; you don't want them flopping around). Offset the height of each flower by cutting stems at different lengths so each one has its own space. Anna loves to do this with carnations, that often-dismissed flower. She also likes to repurpose the glass holders from stylish scented candles or votives, using them as vases. (Remove any leftover wax with hot water.)

allergic to flowers?

✦ ✦ ✦

Silk flowers are always an option, but only use those that are so well made they truly fool the eye. You can also create centerpieces or arrangements using edible combinations of fruit, nuts, and seasonal vegetables such as miniature eggplant and long green sautéing peppers. Search out exotic fruit such as Buddha's Hand lemons and fragrant citrus like clementines, Kaffir limes, and Meyer lemons. Play with scale: Use tiny crabapples and seckel pears; richly colored pomegranates or persimmons; purple Concord grapes mixed with fresh pecans, almonds, or walnuts in their shells. Think still life paintings. For the minimalist, a pottery bowl of farmers' market brown-speckled eggs could be all that's needed. Forage from the roadside—but watch the poison oak and ivy! Scout out vacant lots or take a drive in the country with clippers and buckets ready for boughs of greenery. Wear your gloves and harvest teasel thistles, dock, or cattails for drama. Do be respectful and make sure you're not clipping from a public park or someone's private property.

let there be light

✦ ✦ ✦

Lighting really sets the mood for your party. It's true: Everyone looks better by candle-light, but be sure there's enough light to see your plate! Even for daytime events you might turn on table lamps or overhead lighting if sunlight is lacking. Events that start in the early evening and go late into the night call for different lighting at different times, so be prepared to flip the switch. In the evening, a lighted house always says "welcome," so open curtains or blinds before your guests arrive—you can always close them once the party begins. Here are some tips on using lighting to your best advantage:

+ **OUTDOOR LIGHTING:** Before the party, check the outdoor lighting. Pretend you're a guest and walk up to your front door at night. From the curb, be sure that your pathway lighting is adequate, and that lights by the front door are in good working order. Also, check that your house number is well lit and not blocked by a car, a hanging plant, or a flag. If you live in an apartment, is the lighting in the hall and stair-way in good order? If not, call maintenance.

+ **DAYTIME LIGHTING:** Use table lamps or overhead or wall lighting in a dark room or on a cloudy day. Candles aren't usually lit during the day. They don't really stand up to natural sunlight, and in the old days it seemed wasteful to burn candles when there was adequate light. That said, candles can certainly provide cheery warmth at a formal luncheon on a gloomy day.

+ **EVENING LIGHTING:** You need lighting in the evening, and what you choose is determined by the kind of party you're having and the kind of atmosphere you wish to create. At a large party—a holiday cocktail buffet, say—bright and festive is the key to keeping the party cheery and upbeat. So you'll want more lighting, perhaps not glaring overheads but plenty of table lamps and wall sconces. A more intimate cocktail or dinner party calls for softer lighting. Dimming overheads and using a few table lamps and candles sets the mood for conversation and even romance. For a dinner party, dim the overheads, use wall lights, and light the candles—again, just be sure it's not too dark, or your guests won't be able to see their food!

+ **CANDLES:** Candles are the all-time mood setter. From pillars to votives to the classic taper, they're available everywhere (and make a great hostess gift, too). Candles lend drama and elegance to the space and can be the feature of your table—using candlesticks of varying heights, for example, or votives at each place setting or down the center of the table interspersed with tiny arrangements. Candles are not just for the dining room table; think sideboards, mantelpieces, coffee tables, and the guest bathroom. In general, choose unscented candles. Scented candles can overpower the food, irritate some people, and create soot, which clings to surfaces. Keep safety in mind at all times. Never leave candles unattended and don't place them near fabric

Baby, It's Cold Outside

Don't forget to think about temperature! A large group of people will warm up a room quickly, as will a fire in a fireplace, so adjust your thermostat before the party begins, lowering the heat setting or raising the setting for air-conditioned spaces. Adjust as needed during the party. Outdoors, you can still enjoy cool evenings if you rent large propane heaters or use a firepit. (See also Chapter 11, A Breath of Fresh Air, page 151.)

or flammable decorations or in drafty areas. And be sure to extinguish any candle before it burns down to nothing.

+ **STRING LIGHTS:** Strings of lights aren't just for Christmas anymore. We've seen lights in the shapes of dragonflies, mini Chinese lanterns, flowers, chilies, spiders, pirate skulls, even lobsters. Practically every party theme is covered, and they're all you might need for decoration. White string lights can be added to garlands and hung over windows and doorways or wrapped around a banister to add holiday sparkle. Outside, drape porches or trees with string lights to add romance to evening parties.

+ **LANTERNS AND TORCHES:** Lanterns hung from porches or trees are another charming way to light an evening party. Luminaria—paper bags cut with a lacy pattern and filled with sand and a lit votive—light pathways or outdoor tables. Tiki torches illuminate yards or pathways and have the added benefit of keeping away insects if you burn citronella oil. Again, always keep safety in mind when fire is involved.

start the music

+ + +

Computers, iPods, and MP3 players make it easier than ever to create the perfect playlist for your party. The sky's the limit, subject to your CD collection or iTunes account. Matching the music to your party should be fun, not stressful. Give a thought to the party's flow—when you want your music quiet and when you want it more lively. If you don't feel like mixing your own playlist, let a store-bought collection do the work for you.

A word on volume: Unless the focus is on dancing and you want to crank it up, lower the volume so the music subtly sets the mood and isn't overbearing. Conversation should flow easily—no one should have to shout to be heard.

the preparty cleanup

✦ ✦ ✦

It goes without saying: Your house needs to be clean and tidy if you want it to be fit for company. If you have cleaning help, see if schedules can be rearranged for the day of or the day before the party. If you're on your own, start several days ahead, so that when it's time to decorate or prep food, your space is ready. Dust, vacuum, polish; you'll want any spaces your guests will use to look their best—including the bathroom. Your kitchen needs to be shipshape, too: dishes put away, dishwasher emptied, counters cleared and wiped, floor swept or vacuumed. Be kind to yourself, however—if you run out of time, sweep the table and countertops clean, hide the mess of unedited mail, magazines, and odd bits in a bag, and stuff it in a closet. (Just remember to unearth it after the party!)

pov—what your guests see

✦ ✦ ✦

Take a big step back and give your house the once-over. Look at it the way your guests will see it. Watch for:

✦ **The Outside:** Even if your party isn't at night, your driveway, walkway, and entryway should be swept and any ice, snow, or slush removed. If you live in an apartment, remove any clutter from the hallway.

✦ **Pet Hair:** You may not even notice it, but guests will—and it's a real annoyance. A thorough vacuuming of floors and furniture will also lower the chance of a reaction from guests with pet allergies.

✦ **Clutter:** Books, magazines, CDs and DVDs, papers and projects should all be put away or stowed in a box out of sight for the duration of the party.

✦ **Cushions, Pillows, and Throws:** Plump cushions, fluff pillows, and fold throws—an instant neatening trick.

✦ **Windows:** For a daytime event, wash the windows in your party room. It will make the entire room sparkle!

✦ **A Shared Bathroom:** If your guests must share your bathroom, turn it into a guest bath.

Put all of your personal items—toothbrushes, razors, brushes, hair dryer, toiletries, and medications (yes, people snoop!)—into a temporary storage box or crate that you can store in a closet during the party. Give the room a thorough cleaning and empty the wastebasket. Fold bath towels neatly and leave clean hand towels and a fresh bar of soap for guests.

Remember the Loo

Make sure your bathroom is well stocked: Have guest towels available, either hanging or a stack of cloth towels or decorative paper towels. If you stack cloth towels, have a bin for used towels. Put out a fresh bar of soap, a fresh roll of toilet paper plus a spare roll stored in an obvious place, and a neutral-scented spray air freshener. It's also thoughtful to have some feminine supplies available, either in a drawer or in a discreet container. For a nice extra touch, add a few fresh flowers, some good hand cream, or a pretty candle.

the blitz

✦ ✦ ✦

This is what you do when you get the fifteen-minute warning ("AHHH, my parents are stopping by in fifteen minutes!"), or when you've decided to invite friends over on the spur of the moment. There's no time for the big cleaning—but a tidy house *looks* cleaner. So grab the disposable wipes, put on some high-energy music, and set the timer for fifteen minutes. Next, as fast as you can:

✦ ENTRY OR FOYER: Hang up coats and hats. *(1 minute)*

✦ LIVING ROOM: Straighten the coffee table, books, and magazines; throw out newspapers; put away CDs and DVDs; plump pillows and cushions and fold throws; quickly wipe tabletops. *(4 minutes)*

✦ KITCHEN: Put dishes in the dishwasher and close the door (then run it if the machine's not too noisy); pile mail and papers; wipe counters, fold and hang dish towels. *(5 minutes)*

✦ BATHROOM: Put dirty clothes in the hamper and toiletries in a drawer; fold and hang towels neatly; give a quick wipe of the sink and toilet. *(4 minutes)*

✦ CLOSE DOORS TO BEDROOMS. *(30 seconds)*

✦ TURN OFF THE MUSIC and breathe deeply. *(30 seconds)*

You'll be amazed at how much you can accomplish in 15 minutes!

A Word About Coasters

Even if you serve guests drinks with a napkin, condensation can leak through the paper and damage tabletops. Have plenty of coasters and stash them all around the rooms where you entertain—not just in the bar. Then, before the party starts, scatter them around anywhere a drink is likely to land.

setting up the dining room

✦ ✦ ✦

Learning to set an attractive table isn't difficult—just let balance and symmetry be your guides. Of course, you'll also need to know how many people will be at your table and what your menu is. Finally, everything you use should be crisp and sparkling—linens ironed, glasses and flatware spotless, and dishes shining. Let's look at a basic setting for eight at a rectangular or oval table.

table setting, part 1

If necessary, expand your table to accommodate eight people. Place **chairs** evenly around the table, one at each end and three on each side.

Choose your **linens**. Place mats are less formal than a tablecloth and work well for a luncheon or a less formal dinner; tablecloths of any color are great for most dinner parties or a very formal luncheon. A white tablecloth and white cloth napkins are considered the most formal of all. Your napkins can match or complement your tablecloth or place mats. If you really want to dress up your table, table runners are another great option. On a rustic table, try

some roughly woven material or a beautiful shawl folded in thirds (just make sure it's something that can be cleaned). Once the runner is down you can place votives, flowers, trivets for wine, a bread basket, and saltcellars on it. Create place settings by putting the utensils directly on the table.

Place mats are centered in front of each chair, about one to two inches from the edge of the table. If you use a **tablecloth**, spread it to hang evenly on each end and on the sides. Twelve to eighteen inches is the average drop, but don't worry if it's a little long or a little short—you just don't want it hanging too low, or it'll end up in the diners' laps. **Runners** can fit exactly on the tabletop or hang off each end.

Place the **dinner plate** in the center of each place mat or on the tablecloth, centered in front of each chair. (If you're serving buffet style, you can remove the plates later. Meanwhile, they'll help you judge where to put silverware, napkins, and glasses.)

Next, place the **silverware**: The dinner fork goes to the left of the plate, dinner knife to the right of the plate, and dinner or soup spoon to the right of the knife. This is the basic setting. Utensils for other courses are placed in the order they'll be used, from the outside in. For example, if you're serving salad as a separate course before the main course, the salad fork is placed to the left of (outside) the dinner fork. If salad is going to be served *after* the main course, the salad fork is placed to the right of (inside) the dinner fork. The dessert fork or spoon may be placed above the plate, parallel to the edge of the table, with the handle of the fork facing left and the handle of the spoon facing right; or they may be brought in on the dessert plate. Never put out silverware that won't be used at some point during the meal. Don't put out a spoon, for example, if your meal doesn't call for one.

Another option is to set your table restaurant or Euro style. If you feel that having all the utensils on the table at the beginning of the meal looks too formal or cluttered, you can set the appropriate utensils for each course right before you serve it. Start out the meal with just the utensils for the first course being served. When that course is completed, clear the plate and utensils and then reset each place with the utensils for the next course. Even if you don't use this style for all of your courses, it's especially handy for the dessert course: Before serving dessert, clear away anything that pertained to dinner—including any unused utensils, bread, butter, salt, and pepper—then set the dessert fork and spoon. This is more of a restaurant style of service, and it's guaranteed to make your guests feel that you're paying special attention to them.

Napkins are folded and placed on the dinner plate, to the left of the fork(s), or under the fork(s), depending on your style.

Now, where to put all the glasses? Water glasses are set above and slightly to the right of the knife (think 45-degree angle). Wineglasses are grouped to the right of the water glass. If you're serving more than one wine, follow the "outside in" rule, with the wine that's being served first placed farthest to the right.

Put salts and peppers (at least one set for every four people) either at each end or each side of the table. If you want to up the quality of what you're serving your guests, small, attractive bowls of kosher or sea salt are a great alternative to salt-shakers, as are pepper grinders for pepper shakers. (See She Sells Sea Salt, page 94, in Chapter 7, Fabulous Food.)

Take a moment to study the effect. Then take another moment to straighten any crooked silver-ware and check to see that the bottoms of the handles are evenly aligned with the edge of the table. Perfect!

table setting, part 2

Now for the creative part—the decorating! It's time to add flowers, candles, place cards, or any other decorations that come to mind. The space not taken up by place settings is your available real estate. Arrange your decorations so diners sitting opposite can see each other, and choose flowers, centerpieces, and candles that complement your tablecloth, place mats, or dishes.

If you have a single centerpiece, place it in the exact center of the table. For a formal and traditional look group a series of smaller arrangements or decorations either symmetrically or in a single line down the center. You can also step outside the box and create an asymmetrical arrangement for a less formal and predictable effect. Whatever approach you take, the key is to make a balanced arrangement.

Scatter votives in clusters of twos, threes, and fives, or zigzag the candles and alternate with little flower arrangements in small, unmatched containers, like a collection of white pottery in different shapes. Candles can also be placed symmetrically, in pairs, or grouped asymmetrically. It's fine if they're of differing heights—again, the idea is to create a balanced, pleasing tablescape.

If you're using place cards, center them above each plate.

Quiet, Please

A silence cloth is a pad placed underneath a tablecloth to protect a table from spills and to muffle the sound of silverware, plates, and glasses on the table. The pad can either be cut to the size of the table or overhang the edges. Years ago, silence cloths were made of felt; today thick felt is hard to find, so most silence cloths are made from padded vinyl or plastic. These can be stiff, though, and while they protect the table they can make candles and glasses a little wobbly. We both like to use a thin ivory or white microfleece blanket. Besides keeping the tablecloth nice and smo oth, it has the added benefit of letting it drape beautifully.

the buffet

✦ ✦ ✦

Another important consideration is how the meal will be served. Plating the meal in the kitchen may take a few extra minutes, but it has certain advantages: It lets you compose and garnish each plate to your liking, and it also gives you portion control. If you're planning to serve the food buffet style, you'll need to set up your buffet table ahead of time. Think about traffic flow when deciding on location—you want your guests to move easily through the line and to the table. Protect surfaces such as wood with a tablecloth or runner, or use trivets or hot trays under hot dishes. Stack the dinner plates at the beginning of the line and lay out platters and serving utensils for each item being served. **Hint:** Use a Post-it to label each serving bowl or platter with the dish that will be going in it. That way, when it comes time to fill them, you or your helpers will know exactly what goes where.

setting a beautiful table

✦ ✦ ✦

Part of the fun of hosting a dinner party is setting the table: creating a centerpiece and choosing the linens, dishware and glasses, serving pieces and candles. Cooking and style magazines are full of ideas for simple ways to dress your table. Let the occasion, theme, or season inspire you. A beautiful table only enhances the dinner party ambience. Here are some ideas:

Summer. Fill a glass bowl with lemons or peaches; put bright zinnias or garden flowers in canning jars; place heirloom tomatoes of different colors in a wooden bowl. Straw or raffia place mats or runners give a summery feel, and outside, colorful oilcloth is cheery and practical.

Lobster dinner. Sprinkle beach glass and shells down the center of the table; use new dish towels for "lapkins." Butcher paper on the table is fun for lobster, crab, and crawdad dinners, and makes for easy cleanup.

Easter. For the centerpiece, surround a tray

of green grass with a scattering of dyed or colored eggs in varying sizes; use tiny pots of tête-à-tête (mini) daffodils as place cards.

Let the cuisine determine the decor. For example, a Chinese menu could be enhanced by a black tablecloth, white plates, and red napkins wrapped with white bands printed with fortunes; hang Chinese lanterns and arrange a centerpiece of red chrysanthemums.

Winter white. Simplicity can be stunning. Set the entire table in different textures and shades of white and off-white, with one, two, or three coral red camellias for color.

Fall harvest dinner. Lay clipped bay branches or other local greenery directly on a bare wood table, radiating out from the center on a round table or down the center on a rectangular table. Nestle tiny apples, quinces, pomegranates, the last of the season's small peaches, and purple grapes with lots of bloom (that delicate mistiness) among the greenery. Scatter votives around the table.

setting the buffet table

Traditionally, the meat is first, then side dishes, with any gravies, sauces, or condiments at the end. We actually like to do the reverse: green salad first, then side vegetables or starch, and then the protein, which can nestle on top of the other elements if need be. Condiments go near their intended accompaniments—chutney or salsa verde alongside meat, herb butter next to biscuits—so it's clear what they're intended to be used for. Why do we prefer to do it this way? Aesthetically, guests tend to compose a more balanced looking plate when they serve themselves in this order. And psychologically, filling the plate with salad and sides first avoids the my-eyes-are-bigger-than-my-stomach syndrome, in which people load their plates with more of the meat or fish course than they can actually eat, helping to ensure that the salmon or steak won't go to waste.

beverages and napkins

If you're eating at the table, guests who have filled their plates at the buffet table now head to their places, which have already been set with wine and water poured ahead of time.

When eating lap style, wrap utensils in cloth napkins by making a pocket so they don't fall out, and place them at the end of the buffet table. That way, guests' hands are free for filling their plates. Similarly, drinks—poured glasses of wine or water—can be set up on a separate table for pickup when hands are free.

fabulous food

Sometimes food is the main reason to have a party—like the summer day we collected so many mussels that our parents called the neighbors over for an impromptu spaghetti with mussels party or the make-your-own pizza parties we have to celebrate just about anything. Sometimes all it takes to spark our party imagination is an enticing recipe in a food magazine, seeing fresh peas at the farmers' market, or watching lobstermen bring in a fresh catch. It makes us want to share the wealth and celebrate with friends. Whatever the spark, let it inspire your menu, whether it's a simple luncheon or an elaborate buffet. As you do, you'll want to keep the following basics in mind:

✦ ✦ ✦

✦ **CELEBRATE THE SEASONS.** Let your menu celebrate the here and now: Plan your menu around the seasonal foods in your local markets. Soft-shell crabs, peas, and asparagus are a sure sign of spring. Fresh sweet corn, tomatoes, and berries abound in summer. Mushrooms and squashes herald the fall. Even winter has bay scallops to offer. By using fresh, seasonal food, you'll get the best results with your recipes and you'll save money, too. You can also plan a menu that plays off the seasons: Salads and cold soups are refreshing foils for summer's heat; stews and braises warm us from the inside out in winter.

✦ **ALWAYS LOOK FOR BALANCE.** Your menu doesn't have to be an item-for-item mirror of the USDA food pyramid, but you don't want to serve your guests too much of one food group either. A balanced meal includes **protein**, usually in the form of meat, fowl, or fish, (though it can also be beans and rice, dairy, cheese, eggs, yogurt, or other vegetable protein like tofu), **fresh vegetables**, and a **starch**, such as rice, grains, potatoes, beans, or bread.

✦ **COMPLEMENT AND CONTRAST.** Choose dishes that complement each other: Pair roast pork and garlic mashed potatoes, for example, or wild salmon and sautéed corn with cherry tomatoes. Think about contrasting elements as well, such as tart and sweet, sweet and savory, spicy and cooling. Serving your guests one spicy dish after another may only overwhelm their palates. Avoid repeating the same ingredient over and over—unless the theme of your party is celebrating one food. Anna was once served a meal whose every dish used Mexican chocolate.

✦ **CONSIDER TEXTURE AND TEMPERATURE.** Contrast raw with cooked, for example, or pair a crisp or crunchy element with something soft or sticky (pulled pork on a soft roll with buttermilk coleslaw) or hot and cold (warm apple pie à la mode or hot lentil soup with a dollop of cold crème fraîche).

✦ **CONSIDER COLOR AND APPEARANCE.** Have fun with color. Pair lightly sautéed spinach with butternut squash; sprinkle steamed snap peas with black sesame seeds; serve swordfish with red pepper coulis. Garnish an all-brown dish like a winter stew with a sprinkling of chopped fresh herbs.

✦ **BE KIND TO YOURSELF.** Be realistic about what you can handle. You don't have to cook the entire meal; don't be afraid to use prepared foods. Remember, as important as good food is, entertaining is really about getting people together—not about being a gourmet cook.

menus IOI

✦ ✦ ✦

Creating a menu for your party can be delicious fun, whether you cook the party food yourself or have it prepared for you. For inspiration, look to cookbooks, food magazines, TV cooking shows, or food Web sites, like epicurious.com. Make a note of restaurant meals you particularly enjoyed. Look to your own repertoire as well. We like to take our favorite ingredients and mix and match, creating variations on a theme and seeing just how many menus we can create from these building blocks.

Take, for example, a classic fall combination—butternut squash, mushrooms, and fall vegetables; pork; tomato, arugula, and goat cheese salad; pears and walnuts. Let's see how many menus we can build using these and similar elements.

Menu 1: For a simple supper or lunch, substitute bacon for the pork and make a sophisticated BLT:

Roasted Butternut Squash and
Apple Soup with Sage
(page 81)

Grilled Bacon, Tomato, and Goat Cheese
Sandwiches with Arugula

Menu 2: Now let's create a three-course fall supper out of our main ingredients, substituting a hearty salad for the sandwich and adding a dessert:

FIRST COURSE

Roasted Butternut Squash and
Apple Soup with Sage
(page 81)

SECOND COURSE

Arugula Salad with Crumbled Goat Cheese,
Cherry Tomatoes, Red Onion, and Bacon
with Red Wine Vinaigrette

Artisanal Whole Grain Toasts

DESSERT

Roasted Pears with Ginger and
Crème Fraîche

Walnuts in their shells for cracking

Fresh Mint Tea

Menu 3: For a more substantial dinner party, soup can be passed in little cups or glasses as an appetizer. A smaller, plated version of the arugula salad makes a pretty first course, but try a variation, using pomegranate seeds and toasted walnuts instead of the cherry tomatoes and bacon. Substitute baguette toasts brushed with extra virgin olive oil for whole grain toasts. Feature pork tenderloin for the main event, and pears for the dessert.

APPETIZER

Roasted Butternut Squash and
Apple Soup with Sage
(*opposite*)

FIRST COURSE

Arugula Salad with Goat Cheese,
Pomegranate, and Walnuts

SECOND COURSE

Herb-Crusted Pork Tenderloin
with Mushroom Pan Gravy
(*page 82*)

Roasted Fall Vegetables
(*page 83*)

Garlic Mashed Potatoes
(*page 84*)

DESSERT

Buttermilk Feather Cake with Nutmeg
(*page 85*)

Roasted Pears with Ginger and
Crème Fraîche

We created three menus from our theme ingredients. By using a little imagination and substituting similar ingredients—bacon for pork, pomegranate seeds for cherry tomatoes—and mixing and matching different types of bread, we built a fall repertoire that covers many occasions, from a simple lunch to a four-course dinner. As you add new recipes to your repertoire, think about how many ways you can put them to use.

roasted butternut squash and apple soup with sage

This soup has fall colors, fall flavors, and even "fallen leaves" by way of garnish.
Its apple-sage and squash-allspice flavor combinations may well have thoughts of
Thanksgiving dancing in your head. Full-flavored and silky—but without cream—it's elegant
enough to be served as the first course of a dinner party, but hearty enough for a soup
and salad supper on a busy weekday night. Serves 6 to 8

2½ pounds (2 medium) butternut squash,
  halved, seeds and strings scooped out
2 tablespoons vegetable oil
2 tablespoons unsalted butter
1 cup finely chopped yellow onion
1 small tart apple, such as Granny Smith, cored
  and chopped
4½ cups chicken stock or reduced-sodium
  canned chicken broth, preferably organic

1 tablespoon finely chopped fresh sage
Kosher salt
Freshly ground black pepper
1/8 teaspoon ground allspice
20 Crisp Fried Sage Leaves (page 84) as garnish,
  optional

1. Position a rack in the middle of the oven and preheat the oven to 400°F.

2. For easier cleanup, line a half-sheet pan with parchment paper or foil. Brush the squash halves all over with the oil and lay them cut side down on the prepared pan. Bake until tender when pierced with a knife, about 50 minutes. Remove from the oven. When cool enough to handle, scoop the flesh out of the peels and roughly chop it.

3. In a medium pot over moderate heat, melt the butter. Add the onion and apple, partially cover, and cook, stirring once or twice, for 10 minutes. Add the stock, chopped sage, ½ teaspoon of salt,

½ teaspoon of pepper, and the allspice and bring to a simmer. Partially cover and cook, stirring occasionally, for 30 minutes. Add the squash and simmer uncovered, stirring once or twice, until the squash is very tender, about 10 minutes.

4. Cool slightly, then in a food processor or blender, puree the soup until smooth. The soup can be prepared up to 3 days in advance. Cool, cover, and refrigerate.

5. To serve, rewarm the soup over low heat, stirring often, until steaming. Adjust the seasoning. Ladle into bowls, garnish with fried sage leaves if you are using them, and serve immediately.

herb-crusted pork tenderloin
with mushroom pan gravy

Serves 4 to 6

2 tablespoons finely chopped rosemary

3 tablespoons chopped parsley

2 tablespoons chopped thyme

1 tablespoon Dijon or whole grain mustard

4 teaspoons salt

1 teaspoon freshly ground pepper

3 tablespoons extra virgin olive oil

2 pork tenderloins, about 4 pounds total

3 tablespoons butter, at room temperature

1 small onion, finely diced

3 garlic cloves, minced

1 pound any type of fresh mushrooms, or a
variety such as cremini and chanterelles,
brushed clean and roughly chopped

1 cup dry white wine

1 cup chicken stock

1 tablespoon flour

1. Preheat the oven to 350°F.

2. In a small mixing bowl, mix together the herbs, mustard, salt, pepper, and 1 tablespoon of the olive oil. Mix into a paste and rub all over the tenderloins. Heat the remaining 2 tablespoons of olive oil in a large sauté pan (not a nonstick pan) over medium heat. When the pan is good and hot, add the tenderloins and brown slowly on all sides, being careful not to scorch anything in the pan. This may take about 8 minutes.

3. When the pork is golden on all sides, transfer to a roasting rack and bake to an internal temperature of 145°F. This may take 15 to 18 minutes. Cover loosely with foil and rest for 5 to 10 minutes. Slice crosswise into ½-inch medallions and serve.

for the gravy

1. While the tenderloins are roasting and resting, pour out any excess oil in the pan and place over high heat. Add 2 tablespoons of the butter and the onion and cook until the onion is soft and lightly browned, about 5 minutes. Then add the garlic, cook for 2 minutes, and add the mushrooms. Cook for an additional 5 minutes, stirring constantly, until the mushrooms have cooked down and browned a bit. By now a nice layer of browned bits called fond should have formed on the bottom of the pan. Be careful not to let this burn.

2. Remove the vegetables, set aside, and add the wine. Cook for 5 minutes, scraping up the fond with a metal spatula or wooden spoon. Add the chicken stock and continue to cook over high heat, reducing the wine and stock until only about a cup of liquid remains.

3. In a small dish, mix the flour and remaining tablespoon of butter into a smooth paste. Whisk this paste into the wine and stock, and boil for 3 more minutes, stirring constantly, to thicken the gravy. Add the mushroom and onion mixture to the pan, return to a boil, then hold over very low heat until ready to serve.

roasted fall vegetables

Serves 4 to 6

1 pound parsnips, peeled and cut into 1-inch dice

1 pound carrots, peeled and cut into 1-inch dice

2 red onions, cut into large 1-inch dice

4 tablespoons extra virgin olive oil

4 teaspoons balsamic vinegar

4 teaspoons salt

1¼ teaspoons pepper

2 tablespoons chopped flat-leaf parsley

1 pound zucchini, cut into 1-inch dice

1. Preheat the oven to 350°F.

2. In a large mixing bowl, combine the parsnips, carrots, and onions. In a separate bowl, whisk together the olive oil, balsamic vinegar, salt, pepper, and parsley. Pour about three quarters of this mixture over the vegetables and toss until they are evenly combined. Spread in a single layer on a baking sheet pan (parchment-lined for easy cleanup), using more than one if necessary.

Roast in the oven for 30 to 45 minutes, until soft and lightly browned, stirring the vegetables three times during cooking.

3. Combine the remaining seasoning mixture with the zucchini and roast in the same manner as the other vegetables, but for only 10 to 15 minutes, until soft but not mushy. Combine the zucchini with the rest of the vegetables, toss lightly, and keep warm until ready to serve.

garlic mashed potatoes

Serves 4 to 6

3 pounds (5 or 6) russet potatoes, peeled and cut into 1-inch dice

4 ounces (1 stick) unsalted butter

10 garlic cloves, minced (or more to taste!)

1 tablespoon salt

1 teaspoon freshly ground pepper

½ cup heavy cream

1. In a large heavy saucepan, cover the potatoes with lightly salted cold water and gently boil over medium-high heat until tender but not falling apart.

2. Meanwhile, heat the butter in a saucepan over medium heat. When all the butter has melted, add the garlic and continue to cook until the garlic is soft and golden in color, 4 to 5 minutes. Add the salt, pepper, and cream, and bring to a boil. Turn the heat down to very low and keep warm until the potatoes are done cooking.

3. Strain the potatoes. Press them through a sieve, food mill, or ricer into a large mixing bowl. Fold in the warm cream mixture using a rubber spatula, working quickly and gently so as to keep the potatoes as light in texture as possible. Taste and adjust the seasoning with salt and pepper if needed. Serve immediately.

crisp fried sage leaves

These make a nice garnish for the Roasted Butternut Squash and Apple Soup with Sage (page 81) and are a great little appetizer, too. Makes approximately 20

1 bunch fresh sage leaves (about 20 medium leaves)

Vegetable oil like canola or safflower for frying

1. Rinse and pat dry the sage leaves. Pour an inch of oil into a medium skillet and heat until very hot (the surface should appear wavy but should not smoke). Test one sage leaf to see if it fries crisp quickly, without absorbing too much oil.

2. Carefully lower the sage leaves in small batches into the hot oil and cook until crisp, about 15 seconds. With a slotted spoon, transfer to paper towels to drain. Use immediately or hold at room temperature for up to 3 hours.

buttermilk feather cake with nutmeg

This cake may be plain, but it's not lacking in finesse. It's featherlight, moist from the buttermilk, and nutmeg scented—simply scrumptious. Because it's so restrained, it's versatile, good with pear compote and crème fraîche or whipped cream, or in season with juicy ripe fruit (like peeled, lightly sugared peaches, pitted sliced plums, or berries), or just pristinely on its own. P.S. Don't skimp on the multiple siftings—it ensures the featherlight texture.
Makes one 9-inch, 2-layer cake. Serves 8

About 2 cups unbleached all-purpose flour

2 teaspoons freshly grated nutmeg

1 teaspoon baking powder

1 teaspoon baking soda

¼ teaspoon salt

1 stick (¼ pound) unsalted butter, softened

1½ cups granulated sugar

3 large eggs, at room temperature

1 teaspoon vanilla extract

1 cup buttermilk

Buttercream Filling (recipe follows)

Confectioners' sugar (optional)

1. Position a rack in the middle of the oven and preheat the oven to 350°F. Butter two 9-inch round cake tins. Line the bottoms with parchment or wax paper cut to fit. Butter the paper, then flour the tins and tap out the excess.

2. Onto a piece of wax paper, sift the flour. Spoon the sifted flour into dry measure cups and sweep level; return the rest of the flour to the canister. Onto a piece of wax paper, sift together three times the 2 cups sifted flour, the nutmeg, baking powder, baking soda, and salt.

3. In a large bowl, with an electric mixer on medium, cream the butter. Gradually beat in the granulated sugar and beat until light and fluffy. One at a time, beat in the eggs just until incorporated. Beat in the vanilla. Add the dry ingredients to the butter mixture in 3 batches, alternating with the buttermilk in 2 batches, beginning and ending with the dry ingredients. Divide the batter evenly between the prepared pans.

4. Bake until golden and the center, when pressed gently with a finger, springs back (20 to 25 minutes). A tester inserted into a layer should come out clean. Let the layers cool in the pans on a rack for 10 minutes. Turn the layers out onto the rack, turn right side up, and cool completely.

5. Invert one layer onto a cake plate. Spread the buttercream over the layer almost to the edges, using it all. Top with the second layer, right side up. Dust the top of the cake with confectioners' sugar if desired.

buttercream filling

Too much buttercream is sometimes too much of a good thing. That's why we like this formula, which produces a restrained amount of buttercream that neatly fills but does not overwhelm the delicate feather cake. Makes enough to fill a 9-inch cake

6 tablespoons (¾ stick) unsalted butter, softened
1 cup confectioners' sugar
2 tablespoons whipping cream

1 tablespoon brandy
Pinch of salt

1. In a bowl, with an electric mixer on medium speed, cream together the butter and sugar until smooth. Beat in the whipping cream and brandy. Taste. Beat in a pinch of salt, if needed.

2. Use immediately or cover and refrigerate for up to 1 day. Return to room temperature before using.

too much vs. too little:
getting the portions just right

✦ ✦ ✦

Regardless of what menu you're thinking of serving, it's always better to have *too much than too little.* When you're shopping for meat or fish, ask the butcher or fishmonger for their suggested raw weight to buy per person. Or check the recipes in cookbooks to get a feel for how much to purchase per person. Here are some other points to consider:

+ Lunch portions are generally smaller than dinner portions.
+ When you're serving fewer courses, the portions can be larger.
+ When you're serving multiple courses, the portions are smaller. (For example, you might serve a bowl of soup with a sandwich at lunch, a cup of soup before a main course at dinner.)
+ Take the weather into account as well:
  ✦ When it's very hot, people tend to eat less. This is the season for food that is light, cool, and refreshing, dishes like ceviche and tuna Niçoise, chilled soups, or anything grilled with a big salad. Or take a cue from culinary India and stimulate the appetite with a spicy curry and cooling raita (yogurt dip)—but keep portions small to avoid overwhelming guests' taste buds.
  ✦ Freezing cold temperatures call for generous portions of richer, heartier food: pâtés, risottos, pasta with meat or creamy sauces, stews, braised meats in wine sauce, wild game, roasts with potatoes and gravy, casseroles and cassoulets.
+ Consider the length and timing of the meal—you wouldn't serve as much food for supper on a work night as you would if you were hosting a long, leisurely multicourse Saturday night dinner with wine.
+ Men tend to eat more than women.
+ When you're serving family style—placing platters and bowls of food directly on the table—you'll need enough of each dish to encourage seconds. The same holds true when you're serving a buffet where people help themselves.

- If you're serving a plated meal, you control the portions, so you probably don't need to prepare as much extra food as you would for a buffet or serving family style—but you should still have enough food so you can offer seconds to those who request it.

the bread box

It's become a puzzle whether or not to serve bread with a meal. For some people it's a critical meal element; for others it's a low-carb-diet no-no. The split tends to run along gender lines, with men saying "yes" and women "no thanks." Many restaurants no longer serve bread as a matter of course, not wanting customers to fill up before the main event. So, when is bread a good thing?

- **When it's artisanal, freshly made, and warm.** Who can resist fresh bread in all its varieties from a farmers' market, bakery, or specialty food store? Breads that can hold their own and earn a place at any table include baguettes (long and thin), boules (round), focaccia (a flat, chewy sheet), rolls, biscuits, challah and brioche (eggy) and croissants (flaky), semolina, white, rye, whole wheat, apple-raisin, seeded-crust, and herbed.

- **When there's a sauce worth savoring.** Definitely offer bread when serving stews, bouillabaisse or mussels, hearty soups, sauced pastas, braises, and anything in garlic butter. Pick a good, crusty white bread that stands up to but won't overwhelm the sauce.

Sop It All Up!

Who can resist the last bit of sauce or gravy? In a restaurant or at someone else's house, put a bite-sized piece of bread into the gravy or sauce, spear it with your fork, sop well, and eat. At home, go ahead and hold the bread in your fingers while you mop the plate. The same goes for hearty soup: At home, dip away. At a restaurant, tear off a piece, drop it in the soup, and eat with a spoon.

+ With the salad or cheese course. Having already eaten their main course, guests are more likely to enjoy bread guilt-free—and you don't even need to serve butter or olive oil.

how to serve bread

At most meals, put sliced bread, rolls, or biscuits in a napkin- or cloth-lined container such as a basket. Bread can be served buffet style or passed at the table and is put on the dinner plate or bread plate. At a more formal dinner, place the bread on bread plates before the meal begins. If you'd like guests to slice their own bread, provide a cutting board and knife, and wrap the bread so that guests don't hold it with bare hands while cutting.

Butter is served several ways: Place a stick of room-temperature butter on a small serving dish with a butter knife, or slice a stick of butter and serve the pats on a small plate with a small fork. At a formal meal, pats of butter can be put on bread plates ahead of time along with the bread.

Bread is also served with **olive oil.** Its rich flavor is an ideal and healthy alternative to butter. Use only high-quality extra virgin olive oil, and enhance the flavor with garlic, hot peppers, or herbs for variation. Serve the olive oil in a cruet or small dish with a spoon on a saucer, and plan on using bread plates. Guests spoon or pour the olive oil onto their plates, then dip their bread into it.

DIFFERENT PARTIES, DIFFERENT MENUS

What to serve when? Here are some basic guidelines:

Brunch	2 courses, served buffet or family style or plated: a mixture of hot and cold breakfast and lunch dishes Beverages: juices, hot coffee, and tea; Bloody Marys, mimosas
Luncheon	2 to 3 courses: First course: soup, salad, or appetizer Main course: soup, composed salad, sandwiches, quiches, poached fish or a small-portion balanced plate of protein, vegetable, and starch Dessert: fruit, cookies, sorbet, fruit tart Beverages: water, juices, iced or hot tea or coffee, a light wine or Champagne

continued on next page

Tea	Elegant tea sandwiches: miniature sandwiches of a thin filling on thin bread Small cookies, scones, pastries, cupcakes, or slices of cake Beverages: tea and coffee, hot or iced (optional: sherry or Champagne)
Cocktails	An assortment of appetizers (hot or cold), crudités, cheese and fruit, breads, crackers, dips and chips, olives, nuts
Dinner—simple	2 courses: Main course and dessert Or 3 courses: Salad, main course, and dessert or first course, main course, and dessert Beverages: water, wine, milk, beer, coffee, tea
Dinner—all out!	Up to 6 courses: (hors d'oeuvres, served before the meal) First course: soup, fruit, shellfish, or small composed plate Second course: fish (omitted if shellfish is served as a first course) Third course: main course, usually meat or fowl, vegetables, and starch Fourth course: salad (may be combined with a cheese course) Fifth course: cheese and or fruit* Sixth course: dessert, followed by coffee and cordials Beverages: water, wine, coffee, cordials

*Traditionally the cheese course came after dessert; now it's up to you.

food bling

✦ ✦ ✦

We're talking luxury food here—caviar, truffles, and fancy chocolates. Sure they're expensive, but a little goes a long way—and in these instances, less can be more.

caviar

Caviar is the salted roe (eggs) of sturgeon. Caviar has a wonderful briny, nutty, mineral flavor; each little grain literally pops in your mouth.

The most celebrated caviars—sevruga, osetra, and beluga (from least to most expensive)—come from the Caspian Sea and are black, grey, or golden in color. Because of overharvesting, however, the fish have become endangered, resulting in periodic bans on the import of Caspian Sea caviar and limits on production. American-produced caviars provide a more ecologically responsible—and much less expensive—alternative. Red caviar is actually salmon roe, and each grain, or berry, is quite large. It's usually used as a garnish.

Store caviar on ice in the coldest part of your fridge, but don't freeze it. It's best used as soon as possible after opening. Serve it icy cold so the grains don't collapse. When serving it straight, put it in a glass dish on top of crushed ice or snow. Never put caviar in contact with metal—it will develop a horrible metallic taste. Little spoons made of horn or mother of pearl are made for serving caviar, but a wooden spoon will do in a pinch. Don't mush up the caviar—it's very delicate. Lift and spoon it gently.

How much caviar should you buy? It depends on how you're going to use it.

One ounce of caviar =

+ Four 1-teaspoon servings
+ Eight to ten ½-teaspoon servings
+ Twenty scant ¼-teaspoon servings

Straight up—for real enthusiasts:
½ to 1 ounce per person

On toast points or in an appetizer where you want to feature the caviar:
½-teaspoon servings

As a garnish:
Scant ¼-teaspoon servings

A 2-ounce jar will do nicely for four people if it's served with crackers or toast points.

how to eat caviar

When caviar is served in a bowl with a little spoon, gently scoop a spoonful onto a toast point, cracker, or your plate. Then, if they're offered, top off the caviar with sour cream, crème fraîche, chopped egg, or onion, using the little spoons provided. When caviar is presented already prepared or as an appetizer, just pop it into your mouth. Most important: If you have to share caviar, don't be piggy.

best ways to serve caviar

+ On toast points—little triangles of thin, crustless, lightly toasted white bread. (Pepperidge Farm thin white bread is perfect.

Place small triangles on a baking sheet and bake at 200°F until just browned.)

- On toasted, great-quality, thinly sliced whole grain or rye bread.
- On top-quality home-style potato chips (fun!).
- Accompanied by sour cream or crème fraîche, chopped onion, chopped hard-cooked egg, or thin lemon wedges.
- To garnish omelets, with a dollop of crème fraîche.
- With blinis (tiny yeast-leavened buckwheat pancakes) and sour cream.
- Scoop tiny, steamed red potatoes, slice off the bottom, fill with sour cream mixed with minced red onion, and top with caviar.
- Any of the above with Champagne or chilled vodka.

truffles

The very name makes our mouths water and our noses quiver. A truffle is the edible fruiting part of underground fungi of the genus *Tuber*. The fungi have a symbiotic relationship with certain trees, like oaks, and are harvested in the late fall to early winter, "sniffed out" by pigs or trained dogs. The most famous are the white truffle (*Tuber magnatum pico*) from the Piedmont region of northwestern Italy, and the black truffle (*Tuber melanosporum*) from the Périgord region of southwestern France. Each has a fabulous, distinct aroma and a flavor that brings sauces and egg, potato, risotto, and pasta dishes to sublime heights. Speaking of sublime heights, truffles may be the ugliest and most expensive food items on the planet. White truffles can, in a good year, average $4,000 a pound (a record $330,000 was paid in 2007 at auction for a 3.3-lb. white truffle). Black truffles are less pricey, averaging $300 to $800 per pound, depending on the season. If you find fresh truffles featured on a restaurant menu, be sure you're clear about the price before you order or you'll be in for severe sticker shock.

Don't despair of never experiencing this delicacy—a little truffle goes a long, long way, and you don't have to purchase fresh ones to enjoy the experience. Truffle salt is a delicious way to add the aroma to foods—it's incredible sprinkled on French fries. Truffle honey pairs beautifully with a nice ripe Taleggio cheese. Truffles also come packed in water or oil or as a paste. Be sure to add them to your dish at the last minute. If you're lucky enough to meet a fresh truffle, shave it over pasta with olive oil or on scrambled eggs with butter. Fresh truffles don't last long—just a few days—so if you have enough for more than one or two servings, by all means celebrate your good fortune with a party! Store truffles in dry uncooked rice in a sealed jar in the refrigerator.

chocolate

Who can say no to chocolate? Truffles (the chocolate kind, so named because they look like the fungal ones) and specialty chocolates make a great dessert or a little après dessert with coffee. As in the movie *Chocolat*, today's chocolatiers are pairing dark and milk chocolate with the exotic and the unusual: Think curry, chiles, green tea, lavender, pink peppercorns, chipotle roasted pecans, rosemary with juniper berry, or cardamom with rose hips. You can also find chocolates that are gorgeous to look at, covered with "foils" of gold and copper or patterns of greens, blues, reds, and lavenders. And for a twist, seek out handmade chocolate-covered toffees and caramels with sea salts. Unlike inexpensive milk chocolate candy bars, dark chocolate is very satisfying—just a little does the trick—and is even reported to have heart-healthy properties. Whatever you choose, chocolate is an elegant finish to any meal.

more of the good stuff

Remember, a little of these delicacies goes a long way. Some, like artisanal oils and vinegars, may be a tad hard to find but are worth the effort. Look for specialty foods at gourmet markets, farmers' markets, and specialty stores. You can also find some interesting food products online or through mail-order ads in the back of gourmet food magazines.

+ Domestic or European imported artisanal cheeses

+ Foraged (by professionals, not by you!) mushrooms: morels, chanterelles, porcini

+ Smoked fish, such as salmon

+ Pâtés: meat, fish, or vegetable

+ Rillettes: slowly cooked meat (usually pork) or game, mixed into a paste with rendered fat

+ Confit: slowly cooked duck legs, preserved in their own rendered fat

+ Artisanal honeys: chestnut, lavender, acacia, or linden to serve with cheese

+ Single-producer olive oils: for dipping or a finishing drizzle

+ Specialty vinegars: balsamic, raspberry, Champagne, sherry, herb

a tip from Anna
SHE SELLS SEA SALT

A world of beautiful sea salts is available—from U.S. varieties like red and black salts from Hawaii to Maldon salt from Britain, grey fleur de sel from France, and pink Murray River salt from Australia. Sea salts are pretty, and they taste better, too. Plus, they're full of essential trace minerals. Almost every country with a coastline produces sea salt. Some salts are chunky and some flaky, but because sea salts are coarser than fine table salt, they provide more of a flavor wallop, so you'll need less salt—a plus for anyone watching salt intake. A pinch or a sprinkle ought to do it. Find a tiny spoon to place alongside. But be careful of ones made of silver—they tarnish if left in the saltcellar beyond dinner. (We use tiny mussel shells as scoops.)

Delicious Reading: Our Favorite Cookbooks

Or maybe we should say our favorite cooks! These tried-and-true food tomes offer inspiration for recipes and presentation:

Irma S. Rombauer, Marion Rombauer Becker, and Ethan Becker: *The Joy of Cooking*

Ina Garten, aka The Barefoot Contessa: *Back to Basics; Barefoot in Paris*

Martha Stewart: *What to Have for Dinner; Entertaining*

The Silver Palate: *The New Basics Cookbook*

Julia Child: *Mastering the Art of French Cooking*

Carrie Brown, John Werner, and Michael McLaughlin: *The Jimtown Store Cookbook*

Molly Stevens: *All About Braising*

Editors, *Cook's Illustrated: The New Best Recipe*

Nancy Silverton: *A Twist from the Wrist*
(crafting good, attractive food from quality pantry staples)

※

delicious
drinks

if food provides the sustenance to a celebration, drinks—alcoholic or non—add the fun. You'll want to pay just as much attention to choosing drinks as you do to planning your menu. A luncheon or afternoon event might skip anything alcoholic and feature lemonade, iced teas, or fruit juice spritzers. At cocktail hour, offer a seasonal cocktail, like a Lemon Drop martini in the spring or a manhattan in the winter—easier on you and your pocketbook than having an open bar. Most likely, you'll serve wine, or even a specialty beer, with your dinner menu. Coffee or a mint tea, perhaps with a liqueur or vintage port, could bring the evening to a perfect close.

✦ ✦ ✦

choosing wine

✦ ✦ ✦

While some foods pair naturally with certain drinks, such as chili or beef carbonnade with beer or a hearty pasta bolognese with a Zinfandel, there are no longer any carved-in-stone "rules" about serving white wines with white meat and fish or reds with red meat. Nowadays, it's simply a matter of creating a pleasing pairing, choosing a wine (or other beverage) that complements—and doesn't overwhelm—the food. On the other hand, if you have a really spectacular wine to share, you might plan your entire menu around it.

Sound complicated? It's not, really. Expert help is on hand at your local wine merchant. Bring him your menu, and he'll help you choose complementary wines within your budget. You can also find good advice on Web sites that feature food and wine, or by reading up on wines in magazines, reference guides, and consumer publications (see To Learn More About Wine, page 99).

WHAT TO SERVE WHEN

Aperitif	Sherry, Lillet, Dubonnet, Campari, Cinzano, vermouth, Champagne, white wine, rosé
Soup or appetizer course	White, light red, rosé, or sparkling wine
Fish course	White or red wine
Main course	White or red wine
Dessert	Ice wine, moscato, vin santo, sparkling wine
After dinner / digestif	Cognac, brandy, single malt Scotch, Port, liqueurs (Grand Marnier, crème de menthe, Frangelico, Baileys, Amaretto), eaux de vie (Pear William, Calvados, schnapps, slivovitz), grappa, Limoncello, a Post favorite! Digestifs (Averna, Fernet Branca)

Wine and Food Pairings

WINE	DESCRIPTION	COMPLEMENTS
RED		
Barbera	Fruity. Cherry and plum. Mild with medium tannins.	Red meat, pork, poultry, sausages, tomato sauces, barbecue
Cabernet Sauvignon	Full-bodied and complex. Deep fruit, chocolate, and spice. Dry and rich in tannins.	Red meats, game, pork, rabbit, stews, hearty sauces
Merlot	A smoother, softer version of Cabernet Sauvignon. Berry and herb.	Red meat, pork, poultry, stews, hearty sauces, pastas, fish such as tuna or swordfish
Pinot Noir	Lighter than Merlot and Cabernet Sauvignon. Cherry, spice, and herb.	Red meat, game, pork, rabbit, salmon, seafood, poultry, rich risottos, vegetable dishes
Sangiovese	Light when young, complex as it ages. Versatile.	Red meat, sausage, grilled meats, poultry, seafood, tomato-based sauces, pasta, risotto, vegetable dishes
Syrah (Shiraz in Australia)	Well-rounded. Fruit and berry. Pairs well with many foods.	Red meat, game, rabbit, poultry, stews, hearty sauces, sausages
Zinfandel	Rich and spicy. Berry, vanilla, chocolate, and herb.	Red meat, barbecue, duck, burgers, lasagne and other tomato-based pasta dishes, sausages, spicy foods

continued on next page

Wine and Food Pairings

WINE	DESCRIPTION	COMPLEMENTS
WHITES		
Chardonnay	Rich and buttery or light and citrusy. Apple, pear, and vanilla plus oakiness, if aged in oak barrels.	Pork, poultry, seafood, fish, pâtés, risottos, vegetable dishes, triple cream cheeses like Brie, nutty cheese like Gruyère. It's also a nice aperitif wine.
Pinot Gris/ Pinot Grigio	Light and mineral tasting. Apple and citrus.	Pork, poultry, seafood, rabbit, fish, sausages, vegetable dishes
Riesling	Very fruity. Sweet or dry styles. Peach, apricot, and spice flavors.	Appetizers, pork, duck, seafood, Asian dishes
Sauvignon Blanc	Crisp and dry. Melon, fig, grapefruit, herb, or grassy.	Appetizers, pork, poultry, seafood, Asian dishes, pasta, vegetable dishes
Viognier	Spicy. Apple, peach, melon, and herbs.	Appetizers, pork, poultry, seafood, Asian dishes
OTHER WINES		
Rosé	Fruity, dry, and light. Versatile, it pairs with many foods. Serve chilled.	Appetizers, pork, poultry, seafood, steak, Asian dishes. An excellent choice for spring or summer dining.

WINE	DESCRIPTION	COMPLEMENTS
Sparkling Wines: Champagne, Prosecco, Cava	Fairly dry, sometimes "toasty." Apple, pear, citrus, or peach. "Crisp" or "soft," depending on the bubbles.	Appetizers, oysters, caviar, duck, seafood, salad, desserts, cheeses like Parmesan, Camembert, Gorgonzola Dolce
Dessert wines, white: Sauternes, late harvest Sauvignon Blanc, Vin Santo	Highly intense sugar. Floral or fruity.	Blue cheeses, fruit, cake or pastry desserts, biscotti, but not chocolate
Dessert wines, red: Madeira, or made from varietals like Zinfandel	Full-bodied, intense, sweet. Port-like.	Anything chocolate! Cake, biscotti, Stilton, Gorgonzola, aged Cheddar, nuts, cigars or other grapes

To Learn More About Wine

The *Wine Spectator*, a consumer wine magazine and Web site (www.winespectator.com), provides ratings and discussion about wines, especially those being currently released. To learn more about wine and the great wine regions around the world, browse your bookstore for works by Hugh Johnson, best-selling wine author who has been writing about wines for almost fifty years, and Robert Parker, influential wine expert, author, and the man behind the 100-point wine ratings system.

pouring wine, demystified

✦ ✦ ✦

There's really no big secret to pouring wine. The trick is to make sure it doesn't drip: Hold the bottle around its widest part, pour, and just before you finish, twist the bottle toward you while raising the neck. This prevents drips. It's also not a bad idea to wrap the bottle in a napkin—especially for red wine (easier to clean the napkin than a tablecloth or a guest's dress).

Glasses should be filled to the widest point of the bowl, both to allow the wine the most surface area to "breathe" and so that the wine can be swirled in the glass. And no, this isn't some affected wine-tasting thing: The swirling releases the wine's aromas. Using a wine coaster under the bottle can help prevent stains on a tablecloth.

cheers! a champagne primer

✦ ✦ ✦

The very mention of the word evokes celebration, glamour, and sophistication. It's the star of every happy occasion and makes even the most humdrum of days special. Serve it at your next party and watch what happens.

The term "Champagne" actually refers only to the sparkling wine made in the Champagne region of France. All other bubblies are called sparkling wines or noted as being produced by the *méthode champenoise*. True Champagne is made from a blend of Chardonnay, Pinot Noir, and Pinot Meunier grapes. Here's what the label is telling you:

+ **BRUT:** dry
+ **EXTRA DRY:** sweet
+ **BLANC DE BLANCS:** made entirely with Chardonnay grapes
+ **BLANC DE NOIR:** made from 100-percent Pinot Noir, Pinot Meunier, or a blend of the two
+ **VINTAGE:** made from at least 85 percent of the grapes from the year it was harvested. A producer usually makes a vintage wine only in a great year. Because they're rarer, vintage wines are quite pricey.

✦ **Nonvintage:** The base is made mostly from grapes grown in a particular year but may contain a percentage of grapes from previous years. This blending produces a very consistent style, replicable year to year. Nonvintage Champagne is generally less expensive than vintage, and worth it for the occasional splurge.

In most of the rest of the world, by treaty or agreement, bubbly wine is called sparkling wine, and there's lots of it at a great price. Look for Italian Spumante or Prosecco and Spanish Cava, to name a few. Many U.S. producers have French parents and produce excellent, affordable sparklers as well.

When serving Champagne, it should be well chilled—ideally to between 43 and 47°F. Prechill the bottles in the fridge, then transfer to a bucket filled with water and ice. The chilling helps the cork contract a little, making it easier to open the bottle. Once open, the Champagne can be left out of the ice bucket to let its aromas continue to develop. Ideally, Champagne is served in flutes—slender, narrow glasses with long, thin stems—which best preserve both aroma and effervescence. Fill the flute two-thirds of the way and hold it by the stem so that the wine doesn't warm too fast. You can count on six flutes per 750ml bottle. Cheers!

pop! goes the cork: how to open champagne or sparkling wine

✦ ✦ ✦

Sure, it's fun to let the cork fly and see the bubbly spray, but save that for when your team wins the big championship. (Frankly, it's a waste of good wine!) But the biggest reason for restraint is safety. The thick Champagne bottle and heavy cork are designed to withstand pressure between seventy and ninety pounds per square inch. If you think about it, that's about double the pressure in your car's tires. That cork can be a dangerous missile. Take the following precautions to safely open a bottle of Champagne:

1. Hold the bottle at a 45-degree angle and point it away from yourself and anybody else.
2. Remove the foil.

3. Place a napkin over the bailed cork while you untwist the "pigtail" to loosen the bail. (The napkin will lesson the impact of a cork that accidentally pops.)

4. Remove the bail and replace the napkin.

5. Hold the cork with one hand and twist the bottle with the other. You get more torque this way. Slowly loosen the cork, letting it uncork with a soft sigh instead of a pop.

Opening the bottle this way may be less dramatic, but it's safe—both for people and for your breakables—and you'll be sure to get every drop.

big, bigger, biggest: a party in a bottle

Not all Champagne comes in a standard 750ml bottle. In fact, some are the size of a small child! So, let's do the math: If one bottle contains 750ml, then . . .

EQUIVALENT OF STANDARD BOTTLES (LITERS)	IS CALLED A . . .	NUMBER OF GLASSES
Two (1.5L)	Magnum	12
Four (3.0L)	Jeroboam	24
Six (4.5L)	Rehoboam	36
Eight (6.0L)	Methuselah	48
Twelve (9.0L)	Salmanazar	72
Sixteen (12.0L)	Balthazar	96
Twenty (15.0L)	Nebuchadnezzar	120

beer—it's not just for keggers anymore

Man has been producing beer since biblical times and, like wine, beer is made in all parts of the globe. Microbreweries abound, and more and more people are making their own homemade beer as well. As a serious food companion, beer is growing in popularity, and you'll often see both beer and wine recommendations given in food magazine menus and recipes. The styles and flavors are endless, from sweet to dry, fruity, yeasty, even chocolaty, so there's lots to choose from.

In general, beer is made from malted grain—usually barley, but also wheat, rice, oats, rye, and in some parts of South America, corn. It's often flavored with hops, the flower of the hops vine, which gives it a slightly bitter taste and acts as a preservative. Water is the other main ingredient crucial to a beer's flavor and style. There are two main brewing styles: lager and ale. Lager is fermented at a cooler temperature over a longer period of time, resulting in a mild-tasting beer; it's a popular style in Germany and central Europe. Ale is fermented quickly and at a higher temper-ature. Ales have a sweeter, fruitier taste and a fuller body than lagers. From here, the variables and varieties are endless. Wherever you travel, be sure to sample the local brews or visit a micro-brewery for a tour and a tasting. Beer festivals are held all over the world, the largest and most famous being Oktoberfest in Munich, Germany.

The following books and Web sites provide great references, both for rating and discussing beer:

Michael Jackson's Great Beer Guide or *Ultimate Beer:* Two top-ranked books about beers around the world by the late British beer critic.

The Beer Guide, by Josh Oakes: complete guide to beers in the United States.

BeerAdvocate: a magazine and Web site for "global, grassroots network" of beer aficionados (www.beeradvocate.com).

Single Malt Scotch and Single Barrel Bourbon

Increasingly popular as an after-dinner drink, these whiskeys are to a distiller as a vintage reserve is to a vintner. So what's the buzz? A single malt Scotch is whiskey that must be made in Scotland from a single grain (barley) malted at a single distillery and aged for at least three years in old oak barrels, although many are aged much longer. The only ingredients used are barley, yeast, and water. The barley is malted—mixed with water and left to germinate for several days—then the mixture is air dried, with the introduction of peat smoke to varying degrees to help impart the whiskey's unique flavor.

Bourbon, by law, is an American whiskey, made from at least 51 percent corn (usually it's 70 percent) with the addition of wheat and/or rye or malted barley. It's aged in new charred oak barrels, imparting a vanilla flavor. Single barrel bourbon is whiskey that literally is bottled from a single barrel. A promising barrel is chosen and bottled, so each bottling is unique. Small batch production takes whiskey from a number of selected barrels and combines them to give a more consistent bottling. Then there's small-scale production, as done at Maker's Mark, which is simply dedicated to producing a consistent, high-quality whiskey in all their barrels.

Purists serve it neat—adding no ice or water.

when it's cocktails

✦ ✦ ✦

While the trend at smaller cocktail parties is to offer a seasonal cocktail along with beer, wine, sparkling water, juices, and other nonalcoholic options, a large cocktail party usually offers a full bar. To know how much you'll need, start by doing a little math.

✦ Generally, count on 3 drinks per person for a two-hour party.

✦ A one-quart bottle will provide twenty-one 1½-ounce drinks, or serve approximately seven people.

✦ A 750ml bottle of wine yields 4 to 5 glasses.

✦ A 12-ounce bottle is a standard serving of beer.

✦ It's better to buy liquor in quart or liter bottles—they're much easier to pour from—and be sure to ask the store if you can return bottles that haven't been opened or chilled.

✦ Don't forget mixers, garnishes, and non-alcoholic options, including sparkling and mineral waters, tomato juice, and fresh fruit juices.

For a large party, have plenty of glasses on hand. Guests tend to put glasses down and lose track and end up getting a refill in a new glass. Consider renting or investing in an extra set of inexpensive barware. Plastic glasses are perfect for an informal pool party (where broken glass is a danger); otherwise real glasses are more in keeping with a party atmosphere.

The most critical ingredient is ice. Crushed ice will keep wine and beer cool, or you can fill tubs with cubes and water. For mixed drinks, have a bucket full of ice cubes at the bar and refill as needed. If your freezer can't produce what you need, cubed ice is available at most grocery and convenience stores. Just buy it close to party time so it doesn't melt. Commercial ice, which holds up best, can be ordered through a liquor store. If you live in an urban area, save time by having your liquor and ice order delivered.

the well-stocked bar

✦ ✦ ✦

This is a soup-to-nuts list of what you might need for a large cocktail party. In general, stock what you like to drink and have on hand what close friends usually like. Pimm's isn't stocked at every bar, but Anna would never throw a party without it. Add equipment and garnishes—like a martini shaker and cocktail onions—as the occasion arises.

Liquor: Vodka, vermouth (sweet and dry), rum, Scotch, bourbon, tequila, gin, triple sec, Champagne or sparkling wine, rosé, red and/or white wine, a variety of beers.

Mixers: Tomato, Clamato, cranberry, fresh orange and grapefruit juices, tonic water, seltzer or club soda.

Additional ingredients: Bitters, Worcestershire sauce, seasoned salt, Tabasco, Rose's lime juice, Rose's grenadine syrup. See Simple Syrup (page 112).

Garnishes: Lemons, limes, lemon twists, green cocktail olives, cocktail onions, orange slices, maraschino cherries, rimming salt for margaritas. Get creative with unexpected fruits and berries.

What's an Aperitif?

From the Latin *aperire*, to open, an aperitif is an alcoholic drink served before a meal or as a cocktail, accompanied by salty little nibbles—olives, pistachios, chips, Parmesan shavings, or salted nuts. A number of aperitifs are sweetened and infused with fruits, flowers, herbs, or seeds and pack a wallop of flavor—sometimes sweet, sometimes bitter. Lillet, Dubonnet, Cinzano, sherries, vermouths sweet and dry are fruity or floral in nature (served chilled over ice), while Campari and Cynar (made from artichokes) are bittersweet and prepare your palate for what's to come. They are cocktails pared to their essence. Cocktails, too, can be made with aperitifs, such as Campari and soda served over ice with a twist, or a Negroni—Campari with vodka or gin, sweet vermouth, and a twist of orange or lemon.

Glasses and paper goods: Napkins (3 to 4 per person; 6 to 8 if serving hors d'oeuvres), glasses (3 per person), toothpicks, coasters (place plenty of these around *before* the party to protect furniture).

Equipment: Jigger, corkscrew, bottle opener, ice bucket, tongs or ice scoop, shaker, long-handled cocktail spoon or stirrer, paring knife and small cutting board, bar towel or paper towels, pitchers for water and mixed bases such as Bloody Marys or margaritas, cocktail picks, bowls for garnishes, blender.

a primer on glassware

✦ ✦ ✦

It's a sure bet that your favorite bar has a special glass for almost every drink. At home, having a different glass for every drink you serve isn't really practical. But you can build a collection of basics, including the following:

Wine: White wine is served in a glass with a tulip-shaped bowl. The bowl of a red wineglass is rounder and wider than that of a white wineglass. If you're on a budget, an 11-ounce, all-purpose glass will work for red and white wine, spritzers, wine punches, even sparkling water. Choose a shape in between the narrow white wineglass and the balloon-shaped red.

Champagne: If you're a real fan, flutes are the way to go. But if you have your grandmother's old-fashioned Champagne coupes and want to use them, why not?

Rocks or Old-Fashioned: This is a short tumbler, usually holding 5 to 10 ounces.

Highball: A tall tumbler, this 8- to 14-ounce glass will accommodate mixed drinks, beer, soda, water, or iced tea.

Pint or Pilsner: These are classics for serving beer. The pint is a tall tapered tumbler, wider at the top than the bottom, holding a pint of liquid. A Pilsner, named for the beer, is a tall, narrow, tapered, and footed glass that usually holds less than a pint.

Martini: A classic Y shape, the modern-day glass is available in sizes ranging from a demure

6 ounces to a whopping 16 ounces. Remember: A martini is to a martini glass as Champagne is to a Champagne flute. Serving one in anything else doesn't quite cut it!

Nice, but not critical:

Margarita: A shallow, widemouthed glass on a sturdy stem, typically holding 10 to 12 ounces. True aficionados feel about the margarita glass

the way martini and Champagne drinkers feel about their special glasses.

Sherry: A 4- to 6-ounce small wineglass, it's also great for aperitifs like Campari or Lillet, or liqueur-based drinks.

Shot: Not really appropriate for the cocktail party (savor, savor, savor) except to serve single malt whiskey neat.

To Stem or Not to Stem— That Is the Question...

Until recently, all serious wineglasses came with stems—the idea being that a wineglass is held by the stem rather than by cupping the bowl, so the temperature of the wine isn't affected by the warmth of your hand and icky-smeary fingerprints aren't transferred to the glass. Then along came the stemless wineglass, popularized by a line introduced by Reidel in 2003. This is really a case of "everything old is new again": In France and Italy, regular everyday wine is just as likely to be served in a tumbler as in a wineglass—and what is a stemless wineglass but an upmarket, crystal version of its glass cousin? On the plus side, stemless glasses are less likely to tip over, and they can go—and fit—in the dishwasher.

On the negative side, you *have* to cup them in your hand, which may put them out of the running for white wines and makes smeary fingerprints a given. And then there's the whole issue of how they look on your table. Some people just love the drama and height created by stemmed glasses. There's no right or wrong here; your taste and preference is what counts.

top five cocktails
everyone should know how to make

mimosa

Makes 1 drink

2 ounces juice of your choice: fresh orange or blood
    orange, pomegranate, or passion fruit
4 ounces Champagne or sparkling wine

Pour the juice into a flute and top with the
Champagne or sparkling wine.

Note: If you use white peach juice, it's called a
Bellini, made famous by Harry's Bar in Venice.
Regular peach juice also works just fine. Anna
loves mimosas of all kinds, but one of her favorites
uses elderflower liqueur, such as St-Germain.

martini

Makes 1 drink

3 ounces dry gin (the classic!) or top-quality vodka
1 teaspoon dry vermouth
Ice, for shaking
Lemon twist or olive, for garnish

Pour the gin or vodka and vermouth into a shaker.
Add ice and shake. Strain into a chilled martini
glass and garnish.

"top-shelf" margarita

Makes 1 drink

1½ ounces 100% agave reposado tequila or high-
    quality mescal
Juice of ½ lime
1 ounce Grand Marnier
1½ ounces Simple Syrup (page 112)

Shake all ingredients together and pour over ice
into a salt-rimmed glass. Or serve up by shaking
with ice and straining into a salt-rimmed margarita or martini glass.

Frosting Rims

1. Rub a citrus wedge along the rim of the
   glass or dip the rim in water.
2. Now dip the rim into a shallow bowl of
   salt or sugar.

Note: Colored sugars can be a fun way to
dress up cocktails.

uncle mac's cosmo

Divine! Makes 1 drink

Lime wedge
2 ounces Ketel One Citron Vodka
1 ounce triple sec
1 ounce Rose's lime juice
1½ ounces cranberry juice
Ice, for shaking

Squeeze the lime into a martini glass. Leave the squeezed lime in the glass. Pour the vodka, triple sec, lime juice, and cranberry juice into a shaker. Add the ice and shake. Strain and pour into the glass over the lime.

bloody mary

Makes 1 pitcher or 8 drinks

16 ounces vodka
32 ounces tomato juice or Clamato juice
8 tablespoons Worcestershire sauce
8 dashes Tabasco
Ice
Lemon or lime slice or leafy celery stalk, for garnish

Combine the vodka, tomato juice, Worcestershire sauce, and Tabasco in a pitcher. Stir and pour into tall glasses filled with ice and garnish.

For a Bloody Maria, substitute tequila for vodka and definitely garnish with a lime slice.

Note: For a party, especially for a brunch, make a pitcher of Bloody Marys without the vodka—called a Bloody Shame—so friends who want to skip the alcohol can enjoy them, too. Just add the vodka as you pour each drink.

and a few extras . . .

the lemon drop

A variation on the martini. Makes 1 drink

1½ ounces vodka
¾ ounce freshly squeezed lemon juice
1 teaspoon Simple Syrup **(page 112)**
Ice, for shaking
Lemon twist, for garnish

Pour the vodka, lemon juice, and syrup into a shaker. Add ice and shake. Strain into chilled martini glasses and garnish with the lemon twist.

Note: You can also rim the glass with sugar (see Frosting Rims, page 109).

manhattan

Makes 1 drink

2½ ounces rye or bourbon
1 ounce sweet vermouth
Ice, for shaking
Lemon twist or maraschino cherry, for garnish

Pour the rye or bourbon and sweet vermouth into a shaker. Add ice and shake. Pour into a martini glass and garnish with a lemon twist or a cherry.

Note: These can also be made by the pitcher.

gin and tonic

Makes 1 drink

2 ounces top-quality dry gin
4 ounces tonic water
Ice
Lime wedge, for garnish

Pour the gin and tonic into a tall, ice-filled glass. Stir and garnish with the lime wedge.

Suggested Reference Books

Artisanal Cocktails,
by Scott Beattie

Southern Cocktails: Dixie Drinks, Party Potions, and Classic Libations,
by Denise Gee

The Ultimate Bartender's Guide,
by Fred DuBose

and other beverages

✦ ✦ ✦

Wine, beer, and cocktails may get a lot of play, but they aren't your only beverage options. Water (both sparkling and still), juices, spritzers, punch, mulled wine or cider, and hot or iced coffee and tea should round out your repertoire.

H_2O. It's customary to serve water, either still or sparkling, with lunch or dinner. Use tap or bottled water depending on your water quality. You don't have to go with a fancy, imported variety either—sparkling water produced locally may not have the same cachet as imported, but it's easier on the pocketbook and on the carbon footprint.

Juices. Fruit or tomato juices are traditionally served at breakfast and brunch. Go for fresh-squeezed juice whenever you can. There's a rainbow of color and flavor out there: pomegranate, cranberry, orange, mango, guava, papaya, apple, pineapple, grape, and grapefruit, to name a few.

Spritzers. Even the name sounds fun! Mix wine, fruit juice, or syrups with sparkling water for a refreshing pick-me-up.

Punch—grown-up style. You loved it as a kid; now it's all grown-up. Our favorites are sangria and Pimm's Cup. For a nonalcoholic version, mix fruit juices, cut-up fruits, and sparkling water, and top with a sprig of mint or a slice of lemon or lime. (See recipe, page 114.)

Hard lemonade or cider. Alcoholic versions of these two classics are popular on hot summer days.

Mulled cider or wine. Hot spiced cider or wine will quickly warm up fall and winter parties. Make your own spice mix (cloves, allspice, cinnamon, nutmeg, and orange peel are a nice combination) and invest in a supersized tea ball for steeping.

Lemonade and iced tea. In the summer, big pitchers of lemonade, iced tea, or Southern-style sweet tea are front and center at all of our parties. Homemade is best, and honey adds a different kind of sweet. Some guests like to make an Arnold Palmer—half lemonade, half iced tea—while others make lemonade spritzers with sparkling water. Garnish with lemon slices and mint sprigs.

Coffee and tea. Whether hot or iced, coffee and tea are staples at every meal. Offering guests a cup of coffee or tea is a gesture of welcome the world over.

BEVERAGES TO SERVE WITH MEALS

Breakfast	Coffee, tea, cocoa, milk, freshly squeezed fruit juices, tomato juice
Brunch	Coffee, tea, milk, fruit juices, tomato juice, soft drinks, iced tea, sparkling water, white wine, beer, Bloody Marys, mimosas
Tea	Tea (hot or iced), coffee (hot or iced), sherry
Dinner	Still or sparkling water, aperitifs, wines, beer, coffee, tea, after-dinner drinks

pimm's no. 1 cup

**According to Wikipedia, this is the original recipe.
Makes 1 drink**

1 part Pimm's No. 1
2 to 3 parts lemonade
Borage leaves, mint leaves, and lemon, orange,
   strawberry, and apple slices

Into a tall glass over ice, pour the Pimm's and
the lemonade. Infuse with borage leaves, mint
leaves, and slices of lemon, orange, strawberry,
and apple.

Note: Popular variants include using half
lemonade and half lemon-lime soda, or using
just ginger ale and garnishing with a cucumber
slice.

red sangria

Serves 4 to 6

½ cup water
½ cup sugar
½ cup brandy
1 cinnamon stick
1 bottle light-bodied dry red wine
1 cup fresh orange juice
1 small orange, sliced into thin rounds
1 green apple, thinly sliced
1 lemon, sliced into thin rounds

Bring the water, sugar, brandy, and cinnamon
stick to a boil. Turn off the heat, cover, and let
steep, cooling to room temperature. Add the
remaining ingredients and chill. Serve cold, over
ice if you like.

HAPPY NEW YEAR

COME ON OVER

when
Saturday · July 10, 2010
8 p.m. to ?

where
Sophia & Andrew's Loft

why
It's Summertime!

rsvp
415. 555. 2341 or
summercocktails @ gmail.com

MAX IS 3!

JOIN US FOR A ROARIN' GOOD TIME
SATURDAY, JULY 10TH AT 1:00 PM

MAX'S HOUSE
1245 OAK STREET, NO.2
SAN FRANCISCO, CALIFORNIA

RSVP TO JULIETTE
JBENDEL@GMAIL.COM

Natalies 4th Birthday

IN HONOR OF STEPHEN BLAKE'S

50TH BIRTHDAY

JENNIFER AND FAMILY
INVITE YOU TO A BIRTHDAY CELEBRATION
SUNDAY, SEPTEMBER 23RD, 2012
AT SIX O'CLOCK
196 UPPER TERRACE
SAN FRANCISCO, CALIFORNIA

KINDLY REPLY BY THE TENTH OF SEPTEMBER

To JENNIFER AT 415.422.8764

VALET PARKING
WILL BE PROVIDED

MARCH 15, 2008

Invitations. *Printed, handwritten, or fill-in, the invitation reveals the style of your party. Be as creative as you wish with shapes, colors, fonts, and images. Invitations also serve as keepsakes from your party, a delightful reminder of a wonderful time!*

Place cards. Place cards let your guests know where to sit at the table. Think beyond the traditional cream or white tent card. Tags in a variety of shapes and colors can be attached to pears or pinecones. Write directly on seashells, mini pumpkins, or tiny flowerpots. Prop the cards against holiday ornaments. A place card can also double as a favor or gift for guests to take home when paired with a picture frame or a sweet treat.

Maxine

Daphne

Mr. John Lee
Ms. Gina O'Brien
Dr. Lea Martin
Ms. Ava Brooks
Mr. Henry Wu
Art

Simple place setting. *From left to right, this simple place setting includes a salad fork, dinner fork, plate, dinner knife (with blade set toward the plate), and a dessert spoon. Glasses (water, left, and wine, right) are set at about a 45-degree angle above the knife. Here, the napkin is folded decoratively on the plate.*

Formal place setting. *Formal place settings lend grace and utility to more elaborate meals. As with a simple setting, use only what is needed for the courses served. Additional elements include a place card, bread plate, butter knife, soup spoon, salad knife, dessert fork, and spoon set at the top of the place setting, and a second wineglass.*

Three simple centerpieces. *Centerpieces are all about artistry and creating a mood for your meal. Candlelight is cozy and intimate. Displays from nature, such as fruit, branches, river rocks, or beach glass can be whimsical or elegant, simple or elaborate. Flowers are the most popular option and offer so many ways to express your personal style. Wow your guests with a stunning, classic floral centerpiece or delight them with a more modern look—tiny bouquets or individual blossoms at each place.*

Your simple flower arrangements. *Keep it simple by using just one type of flower, or experiment with a burst of different colors and textures for a big impact. So guests can see each other across the table, save tall arrangements for side tables and front halls. And don't forget the powder room—a lovely place to find a posy.*

Wineglasses. *Wineglasses come in all shapes and sizes, not to mention styles. If your glasses have nontraditional shapes, use the larger, rounder ones for water and red wine, and the smaller ones for white wine and aperitifs. Stemless glasses are the modern version of the classic wine tumbler used throughout France.*

Barware. *Simple and elegant barware turns any drink into party fare. A good set includes, from left to right, margarita, highball, pilsner, martini, and old-fashioned glasses. Add bar basics such as an ice bucket and tongs, a jigger, and a martini shaker along with fun cocktail recipes and you'll be shaking and stirring in style.*

Jewelry for cocktails. *Garnishes such as rimming sugar or salt, citrus peels, slices of fresh fruit, onions and olives, small edible flowers or herbs are a surefire way to turn simple cocktails and punches into something special for your guests. Left to right: classic martini and olive, Pimm's champagne punch with rose petal, manhattan with cherry, blood orange mimosa with mint sprig (back), salt-rimmed fresh juice margarita on the rocks with lime slice (front). Don't forget coasters.*

Cocktail snacks and hors d'oeuvres. *A simple offering of hors d'oeuvres whets the appetite for the meal to follow. Offer a variety of tastes and textures to satisfy different palates, and choose hors d'oeuvres that can be eaten with one hand and in one or two bites. Leaving the green stems on radishes makes them more visually appealing (and easy finger food). Olives and nuts are favorites at any party. Meats and cheeses, accompanied by honeys, jams, mustards, tapenades, and specialty breads, round out a great hors d'oeuvres table.*

Charcuterie. *Charcuterie is French for cured meats. Offering a selection of salumi, prosciutto, soppressata, cappicola, and pâtés with a few accompaniments such as cornichons, caper berries, mustards, and grilled breads allows guests to mix, match, and try new flavors.*

Cheese plate. *Cheese is a favorite before and after dinner, or as a course on its own. Offer a selection from one or a variety of milks, and an assortment from mild to sharp in flavor and soft to hard in texture. Fruits, nuts, marmalades, and honeys make great accompaniments.*

Cupcakes. *Loved by all ages and perfect for any occasion from children's birthdays to wedding showers, cupcakes offer endless variety. Dress them up and serve them individually on dessert plates to cap off a formal dinner party, adding a whimsical, lighthearted touch.*

✦

it's party time!

CHAPTER NINE

classics
with a twist

Cocktails and cocktail parties are back in style. The martini, the cosmo, the manhattan, and the simple gin and tonic are fast becoming part of every host's repertoire, while cocktail parties now top the casual entertaining list. The beauty of the cocktail party is its versatility: It can be as large or small, as simple or elaborate as you wish, from a word-of-mouth "Come over for drinks" gathering for a few friends to a full-scale holiday gala complete with mailed invitations. Unless you're including a buffet, state the start and end times on the invitation: "Cocktails from 6:00 P.M. to 7:00 P.M.," rather than "Cocktails at 6:00 P.M." Otherwise, your guests may expect some sort of dinner or stay the evening (and believe us, they will!). It's always a good idea to include an RSVP with a phone number so you'll know how many to plan for.

✦ ✦ ✦

Compared to a dinner party, a cocktail party requires less preparation, is usually less expensive, and allows you to entertain more people in a small setting. It's the perfect way to introduce new acquaintances to your friends or to reciprocate other casual invitations. Just remember, whether you go fancy or casual, the operative word is *fun*.

how many to invite?

✦ ✦ ✦

The cocktail party is one event where even a tiny apartment can absorb a large number of people. Why? Because most people stand and mingle and don't expect to sit, so you only need a relatively small number of chairs. That said, you also need to take care not to overcrowd your place to the point where your guests are uncomfortable. Before you try to cram thirty people into your studio apartment, consider whether a group that size will be able to move about without spilling their drinks or smushing their hors d'oeuvres. Noise level—both the chat and the music volume—is a factor, too: You want your guests to be able to hear each other.

Note to Self

Don't greet guests at the door with a drink in your hand—it looks tacky.

planning the party

✦ ✦ ✦

The classic cocktail party stars drinks and hors d'oeuvres, a little glam, lots of chat, and a great playlist. Some of your choices in these areas may depend on whether you're doubling as bartender. It's simply not realistic to be the host and the bartender for more than six people—you'll be spending way too much time tending bar instead of tending to your guests. If you don't want to hire a bartender, call on your spouse, partner, or a good friend to fill the job. Or you can mix the first drink for each guest and then invoke "summer rules," inviting everyone to refill as they wish.

As for the yummies? Think finger food—or any hors d'oeuvre that can be eaten easily. One-bite foods, dips, mini appetizers, and anything on a toothpick are perfect choices. Just be careful to keep hot foods hot and cold foods cold. Sushi, for example, may be the perfect "bite," but it must be absolutely fresh and kept cold (do you have room in your fridge?) and not left out on a platter or you risk making your guests ill.

Always start the party with something guests can help themselves to—a simple bowl of toasted nuts or a dip with pita chips will do the trick. Passing a tray or two of hors d'oeuvres yourself once everyone has arrived is hospitable, even if you plan on offering that appetizer as a self-serve for the rest of the evening; it's a nice to way to welcome everyone and provides an opportunity to circulate quickly. Open with tiny one-bites and a few things for the ravenous, then graduate to more substantial fare if you choose. You can also go the stationary buffet route with small plates, or serve a combination of passed and stationary hors d'oeuvres.

Designated Drop-Off

If you don't have any help, set aside some kitchen counter space as a drop-off center for used glasses and plates and be sure to have readily accessible bins for trash and recyclables. That way you and any helpful guests will know just where to put the discards, keeping the party area neat and attractive.

Where to Put Those Toothpicks?

Include a small cup or glass on any tray that has picked hors d'oeuvres and put one toothpick in it so that guests get the idea. The same goes for olives, shrimp, or nuts with shells: Provide a small dish for the pits, tails, and shells. No one wants to be stuck holding a fistful of those!

Even the best multitasker will have a hard time holding a plate and napkin in one hand and a glass in the other, eating the hors d'oeuvre and maybe even shaking hands at the same time. If you're using small plates, have tables or other landing spaces available to put them down on.

Also provide lots of cocktail napkins, receptacles for cocktail picks, and a tray or designated spot for discarded glasses, plates, and napkins.

In addition to providing cocktails and hors d'oeuvres:

+ Choose and set up a bar area—with ample space in front of it—out of the way of traffic flow.
+ Check on seating—a few small groupings for a large party, enough seats for all at a small party.
+ Decide whether to hire help.
+ Check your bar and bar supplies, ice bucket, tongs, wine bucket, glasses, and serving plates.
+ Purchase cocktail napkins and picks.
+ Stock up on ice yourself or plan to have it delivered about an hour to an hour and a half before the party. Trust us: You can never have enough!

the self-serve bar

✦ ✦ ✦

A self-serve bar will free you up to visit with guests and see to your hosting duties. You don't have to offer a full bar selection—you can limit the offerings or serve a signature drink (Appletini, cosmo, Champagne cocktail, margarita) plus wine, beer, and nonalcoholic choices. Another option is to mix a big pitcher of sangria or serve a drink that can be spiked by the glass or not, like a spiced pomegranate punch. If you offer a signature drink, do a taste test to make sure it's mixed well. It's better to have too much in the bar than too little; you can always use it again at another time, and some liquor stores will take back unopened or unchilled bottles.

one bar or two?

✦ ✦ ✦

One bartender can handle twenty to thirty people easily. Any more than that, and you might consider setting up a second bar. In this case, you don't necessarily need to hire a second bartender: Simply designate one bar as a cocktail bar and the other a self-serve bar for wine, beer, and nonalcoholic drinks. Don't forget to set up lots of ice, glasses, napkins, lemons, and limes at your second bar. Locate the two bars in separate areas to prevent overcrowding.

A COCKTAIL PARTY TIMELINE

Four weeks:	Hire any professionals and other help.
Three weeks:	Send invitations; plan menu and decor.
Two weeks:	Purchase all nonperishables: liquor, beer, wine, seltzers, sodas, napkins. Order special ingredients and arrange for any rental items—set the delivery date one day before the party.
One week:	Organize music, prepare grocery and to do lists, pick up any nonperishable decor items, order flowers.
Two days:	Shop for groceries.
One day:	Clean house, prep guest bathroom, set up coat area, prep food, pick up flowers, arrange flowers, make "day of" timetable.
Day of party (morning):	Assemble flowers and decor; assemble or have ready to assemble all hors d'oeuvres; prep serving platters with utensils. Label dipping bowls or platters; set up bar and glassware; chill wine, beer, and mixers.
Two hours ahead:	Get yourself ready.

continued on next page

One hour to 45 minutes ahead:	Begin setting out hors d'oeuvres on platters; preheat oven for heated hors d'oeuvres; set out coasters.
Half hour:	Turn on music (test volume); give guest bathroom and party area a final check; finish setting bar with ice, mixers, and garnishes; finish hors d'oeuvres.
During:	Replenish hors d'oeuvre platters; heat and serve any hot hors d'oeuvres.

the cocktail buffet: hearty hors d'oeuvres

The cocktail buffet is a cocktail party that doubles as a light dinner. There's plenty of food, so guests won't have to make dinner plans and can linger longer at the party. Your invitation should indicate that it's a cocktail buffet or say "Hearty Hors d'Oeuvres." (Another option is to say "Serious Hors d'Oeuvres.") Just listing a starting time on your invitation is also a signal to guests that you're expecting them to stay and that they can expect plenty to eat.

Your menu can be simple, but it should be substantial. If you don't want to deal with plates, serve hearty finger food: skewered chicken or beef satay, jumbo shrimp, sliced ham or cold steak with mustard or aiolis, and little rolls or biscuits for mini sandwiches. Hot items, like Swedish meatballs, hot artichoke dip, or crab cakes, call for small plates. Set up a buffet table so guests can help themselves, and be sure to keep the table and platters tidy and refreshed. You can end the evening with cookies and coffee—a nice way to indicate that the party is wrapping up.

FIVE COLD HORS D'OEUVRES

Chilled Cucumber Soup Shooters
(served in shot glasses)

Tomato and Basil Bruschetta

"Stand-up" Salad with Green Goddess Dip
(page 197)

Smoked Salmon Toast Points with Crème
Fraîche, Chives, and Capers

Prosciutto-Wrapped Melon, Pears,
or Asparagus

FIVE HOT HORS D'OEUVRES

Canellini Bean Puree on Grilled Bread with
Olive Oil, Pine Nuts, and Herbs

Mojo Shrimp Skewers
(page 124)

Crab Cakes

Stuffed Mushrooms with Spinach, Bacon,
and Aged Gruyère

Spiced Lamb Riblets
(page 124)

EASY-TO-PREPARE HORS D'OEUVRES

Crostini with:

Goat Cheese and Olive Tapenade

Cream Cheese and Chutney

Blue Cheese and Toasted Walnuts

Prosciutto and Fresh Figs

Butter, Radishes, and Sea Salt

Avocado and Cilantro with Lime

Ham and Honey Mustard Butter

DIPS

Hummus with Endive Spears and
Pita Toasts

Greek Yogurt with Celery and
Cucumber Spears

Blue Cheese with Hearts of Romaine

SKEWERS

Pineapple Skewers with Chile and Lime
(page 125)

For cocktail recipes, see Chapter 8, Delicious
Drinks, page 95.

mojo shrimp skewers

Mojo sauce is as much a condiment in Cuba as it is a marinade, often found right on the
dining table and splashed onto just about anything. It also makes a delicious marinade for
chicken or seafood. Serves 12 (approximately 2 each)

½ cup extra virgin olive oil

10 garlic cloves, minced

1 tablespoon chili flakes

2 teaspoons ground cumin

¼ cup freshly squeezed orange juice

¼ cup freshly squeezed lime juice

¼ cup roughly chopped parsley

1 pound large (21 to 30) raw shrimp, peeled and
deveined, tails left on

1½ teaspoons salt

1. In a medium saucepan over medium-high heat,
heat the olive oil until hot but not smoking. Carefully
add the garlic, chili flakes, and cumin, and cook,
stirring occasionally, until golden but not brown.
Remove from the heat. Add the orange juice, lime
juice, and parsley—be careful as this may bubble
violently. Transfer to a bowl and cool to room temperature before using.

2. Preheat a gas or charcoal grill until very hot.
Toss the shrimp in the salt and let sit for 3 to
5 minutes. Add the marinade and let sit for at
least 10 but no more than 20 minutes. Skewer
the shrimp and grill over high heat for 2 minutes
on each side until cooked.

spiced lamb riblets

These chops also make a great dinner party main course. Serve 3 to 4 chops per person,
with Salsa Verde (page 161) on the side, accompanied by Garlic Mashed Potatoes (page 84)
and Roasted Fall Vegetables (page 83). Serves 4 (approximately 4 ribs per person)

1 tablespoon olive oil

2 teaspoons ground fennel

2 teaspoons ground coriander

½ teaspoon ground cloves

½ teaspoon ground cinnamon

5 teaspoons kosher salt

Finely grated zest of 1 large or 2 small lemons

2 racks of lamb, about 1½ pounds each, frenched
(see Note)

1. Heat the olive oil in a small pan over medium heat and add the spices. Toast for several minutes, stirring constantly, until fragrant. Remove from the heat and add the salt and lemon zest. Let cool completely.

2. Cut the lamb into individual chops, cleaning any remaining bits of sinew off the bone if necessary.

3. Preheat a gas or charcoal grill until very hot. Rub the spice mixture into both sides of each chop, keeping the bones wiped clean. (You may rub in the marinade an hour or two before grilling and set aside, but no more than 2 hours.) Grill over high heat until medium-rare—about 2 minutes on each side depending on the size of the chops and how hot the grill is.

Note: Chops that have been frenched have the meat and tough residual tissue scraped clean from the bones. You can ask the butcher to prepare them for you.

pineapple skewers with chile and lime

This festive hors d'oeuvre is inspired by street food in Mexico, where vendors sell all kinds of fruit and vegetables on sticks seasoned with chile and lime. Light, colorful, and intriguingly flavored with sweet, salty, tart, cool, and hot—sure to get partygoers' attention.

Makes 18 to 20 skewers, serving 8 to 10

1 medium pineapple
¼ cup unblended medium-hot powdered
    red chile

¼ cup kosher salt
3 limes, cut into 6 wedges each
20 (8-inch) thin bamboo skewers

1. Cut the top and bottom off the pineapple. Then cut in half crosswise. Stand each half up on the cut end and carefully cut off the skin in strips, working from top to bottom. Remove any remaining "eyes" (the little brown divots) with the point of a paring knife. Quarter each piece lengthwise into 4 wedges and remove the tough core from the edge of each wedge. Then slice the quarters crosswise into ½-inch fan-shaped pieces.

2. Skewer the pineapple, sprinkling a few of the skewers with the powdered chile and salt as you go. Place the skewers on a platter. Scatter the lime wedges around the pineapple. Place the extra salt and chile in little ramekins and place on the platter.

3. Provide a tall glass for the spent skewers and a little plate for the used lime.

Note: You may provide little salt spoons for the chile and salt or instruct guests to sprinkle. Provide plenty of cocktail napkins!

the cheese party

❖ ❖ ❖

Artisanal cheese makers in the United States can stand up to anything Europe has to offer. And since we're Vermonters we'll shamelessly plug the Green Mountain State's finest. But whether you're a fan of Jasper Hill Farm's Bailey Hazen Blue from Greensboro, Vermont, Great Hill Blue from Marion, Massachusetts, or The Original Blue from Point Reyes Farmstead Cheese Co. in Point Reyes Station, California, the whole idea is to search out *your* local cheese makers. Anna found a locally produced Brie made with raw goat's milk that's now her "house cheese." Goat, sheep, or cow; fresh or aged—there's a whole universe of cheese to discover. Start by scouting out local cheeses in farmers' markets and restaurants that feature local produce, or go online—great artisanal cheese is just a click away on the Internet.

There are several ways to present a selection of cheeses at a party. To keep the palate from being overwhelmed, offer three to six cheeses. In making your selections, consider a cheese's milk source, texture, and age. You could offer cheeses made from a variety of milks—cow, goat, sheep, buffalo, or mixed—or select a variety of cheeses made from

just one type of milk. Texture and age provide even more variables: fresh-ripened, bloomy rind, semisoft, washed rind, hard or blue.

Round out your platter with fruits like grapes, figs, peaches, pears, and apples or honeys and fruit jams. Brie with Champagne grapes, Gorgonzola with pears, and aged Cheddar with apples are classic pairings that shouldn't be missed.

If you're looking for beverages to pair with cheese, fruity wines, artisanal beer, and cider make great soul mates. Think young light wines like Chenin Blanc or Gavi with fresh soft cheeses. Spicier and lusher whites like Chardonnay, Riesling, and Viognier pair well with double and triple cream cheeses such as Brie and St. André, washed rind cheeses like Taleggio and fontina, and hard aged cheeses like St. George or Vermont Shepard.

One of our all-time favorite cheese experiences was in Italy, tasting a local sheep's cheese in three stages of aging. First was *pecorino fresco Toscano* (fresh Tuscan sheep cheese and Anna's favorite) served with a light honey; then *pecorino medio stagionato* (medium-aged) with a hot-pepper marmalade; and to finish *pecorino stagionato* (aged over three months) with a deep, dark, rich chestnut flower honey. Incredible!

To serve the cheeses, group them on a platter or plate them individually with their accompaniment. (See How to Compose an Attractive Cheese Board, below.) Label each cheese and provide the right cutting tool—a sharp knife or wedge for hard cheeses like Parmesan and Cheddar, a sharp knife for semisoft cheeses like Edam or Bel Paese, a "soft" knife for bloomy rind cheeses like Brie, and a spreader for very fresh cheeses like chèvre. Have several pieces started so guests know how to proceed.

how to compose an attractive cheese board

+ A wood cheese board looks attractive and is actually a practical choice if you're going to be cutting any firm cheeses or fruit like apples and pears.
+ We often build our cheese boards by placing several boards in a large flat basket lined with white linen napkins or, in summer and fall when we can find them, grape leaves.
+ The cheese is placed on the boards, with hard cheeses sliced in small slices and attractively fanned next to a larger whole piece of the same cheese. This way, the shape and rind of the cheese are nicely displayed.
+ Garnish with toasted or spiced nuts. Dried fruit like dates, apricots, or figs (cut them in half and pit; arrange cut side down), even strawberries or cherries can all be scattered on the board. Tiny clusters of grapes or fresh figs also make an attractive edible garnish.
+ Herb bundles are inserted between the boards and the perimeter of the basket.
+ Chutney, *membrillo* (quince paste), olive tapenades, olives, and honey should be offered in little bowls. These bowls can be placed in the spaces between the boards, as can the bread, either fresh or toasted, and crackers, so that the entire presentation is self-contained.

creating an antipasto platter

✦ ✦ ✦

While cheese can be savored on its own, it can be part of an antipasto platter, too. We like to build combination platters for parties where we include:

✦ Cheeses: soft, semiaged, and blue or aged

✦ Nuts and dried or fresh fruit

✦ Salumi like prosciutto, sopressata, salami

✦ Pickled vegetables: caper berries; gherkins; pickled green beans, beets, or other seasonal vegetables; roasted red peppers; giardiniera

✦ Toasts, made from a baguette, brushed with olive oil

Cheese Pairings

Many of these accompaniments work with a number of cheeses. The idea is to present a cheese with one or two accompaniments, such as jams or honeys, toasted nuts, fresh or dried fruit, and little toasts, and expand to include additional cheeses and a larger board.

CHEESE TYPE	VARIETIES	SERVE WITH	WINE PAIRING	CUT WITH
Fresh, unripened	Cream cheese Ricotta Mozzarella Mascarpone Fresh goat Burrata	Honey, chutneys, and jams Fruits: berries, pears, figs, apples, grapes, dried cherries Toasted nut breads	Viognier Vermentino	Spreader

CHEESE TYPE	VARIETIES	SERVE WITH	WINE PAIRING	CUT WITH
Fresh, ripened	Chèvre Crottins Humboldt Fog	Grapes, apricots, figs, berries Toasted grainy breads	Rosé Beaujolais Lager Pinot Grigio Dolcetto	Spreader
Bloomy rind	Brie Camembert St. André	Grapes, apricots, plums Chutneys Olive tapenades Sourdough bread	French Chardonnay Sparkling wine Pale ale	Knife or spreader
Semisoft: firm with a natural rind, aged a minimum of 60 days	Gouda Monterey Jack Bel Paese Fontina Taleggio	Tomatoes Apples Pickled vegetables Toasted nuts (Taleggio pairs well with honey)	Beaujolais Spanish Riojas Riesling Viognier Tokay d'Alsace	Sharp knife or slicer

Hard: aged over
60 days
	Cheddars
	Manchego
	Pecorino
	  Toscano
	Parmesan
		Apples, pears
		Fruit jams
		Hot pepper
		  marmalade
		Toasted nuts
		Dates, dried figs
			Chianti
			Rosso di
			  Montepulciano
			Cider
			Dark ale
			Sparkling wine
			(with Parmesan)
				Knife or wedge;
				use a vegetable
				peeler for long,
				wide shavings

Washed or brushed rind	Epoisses Morbier	Prosciutto Pickled vegetables Fruit spreads	Sangiovese Barolo Dark ale	Sharp knife

continued on next page

Cheese Pairings

CHEESE TYPE	VARIETIES	SERVE WITH	WINE PAIRING	CUT WITH
Blue	Roquefort Rosenberg Gorgonzola	Dates Figs Honey Walnuts Arugula Walnut wheat toasts	Shiraz Gewürztraminer Port	Knife or cheese scoop

More About Cheese, Please

For more information about cheese, we recommend reading:

The Vermont Cheese Book, by Ellen Ecker Ogden

Cheese Essentials, The All American Cheese and Wine Book, and
The New American Cheese, all by Laura Werlin

Cheese & Wine: A Guide to Selecting, Pairing, and Enjoying,
by Janet Fletcher and Victoria Pearson

the wine party

✦ ✦ ✦

With wine's popularity at an all-time high, and vineyards popping up in every nook and cranny of the world, becoming wine savvy can feel like a daunting proposition. A wine party is a fun way to learn about new wines and sample vintages that ordinarily might be out of your price range. Although there's no reason why a wine party can't be large, they tend to be more intimate—a smaller party lets everyone have a say about the wines they're sampling. You can throw a wine party one of several ways. You can host and provide all the wine and food, or it can be a group effort—you provide hors d'oeuvres, say, and each guest or couple brings a bottle of wine to share.

But which wines should you concentrate on? Here are several interesting ways to customize your wine tasting.

✦ **VERTICAL TASTING:** Tasting one wine, different vintages

✦ **HORIZONTAL TASTING:** Tasting one year, one wine, different producers

✦ **PRICE-BUSTER TASTING:** Your best $10 to $15 selection of wine

✦ **ONE WINE VS. ANOTHER:** Merlot and Cabernet (place each in a brown bag and let people take notes)

✦ **BLIND TASTING:** Choose a wine and provide bottles in a wide price range, from the inexpensive to one expensive wine. Wrap all bottles in brown bags—it's fun to see how people rate the cheapest and costliest bottles. Either the host purchases the costliest wine or the group divides the total costs evenly among the participants.

✦ **WORLD CUP TASTING:** Same varietal, different countries: Australia vs. Chile; Spain vs. Portugal; Italy vs. France; United States vs. South Africa; Germany vs. Hungary; Oregon Pinot vs. French Burgundy.

Become buddies with your local wine merchant. She'll be a terrific resource not just for wine recommendations, but for helping to organize your tasting as well.

party notes

✦ ✦ ✦

A professional wine tasting is serious business: One doesn't so much drink the wine as take a sip that's swirled in the mouth but not necessarily swallowed. It involves "spit cups" and palate and nose cleansers (see Tasting Like a Pro, below). For most of the rest of us, a wine-tasting party is an occasion to actually drink wine and have fun learning, comparing, and experiencing how wines pair with foods.

Tasting Like a Pro

Spitting, rinsing, dumping, priming—it sounds, well, gross, but at a true wine tasting, you do all of these things with aplomb.

✳ **SPITTING:** Learning to spit is a fine idea if you plan to taste several wines. It will keep your palate from being overwhelmed and *you* from getting woozy. Each taster should have his or her own cup to spit in. After you've tasted the wine, just hold the cup up to cover your mouth and spit.

✳ **RINSING:** Before tasting the next wine, rinse your glass with water, usually provided in pitchers on the table.

✳ **DUMPING:** A "dump bucket" is a must at a real tasting. That's where tasters pour out the water used to rinse their glasses between wines.

✳ **PRIMING:** Priming is what prepares your glass for the next wine. True aficionados do it like this: After rinsing and dumping with water, pour a small amount of the next wine to be tasted, swirl, dump, refill, and proceed to taste.

Of course, you don't have to do all that priming and rinsing at your wine party. You can be casual but still correct simply by providing a pitcher of water for tasters to drink between wines.

You can throw a dinner party where your wines are featured and paired by course, or serve wines paired with various hors d'oeuvres or small plates. In the latter case, you'll want to provide enough food to balance the wine. Have lots of glasses for this party—one per person for each wine. Even if you don't want to invest in just the right glass for each wine, provide good, all-purpose white and red wineglasses—one per guest for each wine to be tasted. Have enough glasses for at least two rounds—you can always rinse them in between in a pinch.

tips on serving
and enjoying wine

✦ ✦ ✦

+ At dinner, set a glass for each wine to be served.
+ If you're having several wines, serve whites before reds and dry before sweet.
+ Fill wineglasses to the widest point of the bowl; this will let the wine breathe.
+ At dinner, plan on one bottle of wine per person (but adjust according to your knowledge of your guests).
+ Pouring red wine into a decanter, a vessel, usually glass, with a large bowl and a narrow neck, exposes a large surface area of the wine to oxygen. This is also called "letting the wine breathe" and allows the full flavor of the wine to be released.

+ Finish wine within a day or two of opening; otherwise, use the leftover for cooking. The same oxidation that develops the wine's flavor will also cause it to deteriorate over time. Vacuum pumps are great for this reason—they really do extend the drinkability of the wine.
+ Shop around. Prices vary greatly from store to store. You can find some great deals on the Internet; some sites even include free shipping. Many stores offer a 10 percent discount when you buy a case (twelve bottles) of wine—mixed or single label.
+ Store wine in a cool, dark place, preferably on its side.

chillin'

✦ ✦ ✦

White wines and Champagnes should be served chilled—at about 45°F. It can take more than two hours to chill a bottle of wine in the fridge (use the lower shelves; they're colder), so plan ahead. In a pinch, place the wine or Champagne in a bucket and add half ice, half water. It will be chilled in twenty to thirty minutes. The freezer isn't the answer: There's a good chance that you'll overchill and damage the flavor (not to mention forgetting it's in there and having it explode!).

red with red and white with white?

✦ ✦ ✦

Not so long ago it was tradition to only serve red wines with red meat dishes and white wines with chicken and seafood—and why not? They do a really good job of complementing each other. Today, there's more interest in creative wine and food pairings. For example, a Pinot Noir pairs well with chicken, and a dry Riesling goes nicely with pork. When choosing a wine, don't let cost, color, or where it came from be your only guide. It's more important that the flavor complements the food and that it's pleasing to the palate.

hors d'oeuvres
for a tasting party

✦ ✦ ✦

This tasting follows the progression from whites to reds to sweet wines. Remember to have plenty of water—still and sparkling—and bread available in baskets on the tasting table. Each of these hors d'oeuvres can pair with several wines. Taste and see what you like best!

Crab Cakes, or Smoked Salmon Toast Points, Crème Fraîche, Chives, and Capers
with Sauvignon Blanc or Champagne

Prosciutto-Wrapped Melon, Pear, or Asparagus
with Sauvignon Blanc, Pinot Grigio, or Viognier

Tomato and Basil Bruschetta
with Sauvignon Blanc or Rosé

Mojo Shrimp Skewers
(page 124)
with Chardonnay, Sauvignon Blanc, Pinot Grigio, or Rosé

Curried Cashew Chicken in
Cucumber Cups
(page 183)
**with Riesling, Gewürztraminer,
or Viognier**

Canellini Puree on Grilled Bread
with Olive Oil, Pine Nuts,
and Garden Herbs
**with Chardonnay, Rosé, Beaujolais,
or Sangiovese**
*(This is a "bridge" hors d'oeuvre to go with
white or a lighter red.)*

Stuffed Mushrooms with Spinach, Bacon,
and Aged Gruyère
with Pinot Noir, Sangiovese, or Merlot

Horseradish-Crusted Hanger Steak with
Roasted Garlic Aioli on Crostini
(page 198)
**with Cabernet, Merlot, Barbera,
or Chianti**

Spiced Lamb Riblets
(page 124)
with Zinfandel or Syrah (Shiraz)

Blue cheeses: a selection of
Great Hill Blue, Gorgonzola, Stilton,
and toasted walnuts
**with Late Harvest Sauvignon Blanc,
Sauternes, or Port**

Little Chocolate Spice Cakes
(page 199)

with Port or Late Harvest Reds

CHAPTER TEN

your signature dinner party

the dinner party is our favorite way to entertain. As the host, you create an entire evening as a gift to your guests: from the music to the menu, the table setting to the atmosphere. Whether it's an informal meal with a few friends or a showstopping four-course dinner for eight, the dinner party is the ultimate entertaining event. While it can be the most involved party, we think it's the most rewarding. The day is done, work is over. There's nothing to distract your focus and enjoyment of time spent with good friends, old or new.

✦ ✦ ✦

What makes a dinner party a fabulous success? The four main ingredients are:

+ Guests who mix well

+ A fresh, interesting, balanced menu, well prepared and created to please

+ A beautifully set table

+ Relaxed, gracious, and attentive hosts

Add your personal style and creativity along with a detailed game plan, and it's sure to be a success.

party notes: planning your dinner party

✦ ✦ ✦

Dinner parties are usually composed of three acts: predinner hors d'oeuvres and/or cocktails, the dinner itself, and after-dinner drinks and conversation. The menu generally consists of four courses: a starter, entrée, salad or cheese course, and dessert. It's perfectly fine to serve only two or three courses. If you're confident, you can certainly serve five or six. It's better to pull off a small party perfectly than to find yourself overwhelmed trying to tackle a large dinner party or a complicated menu.

As with any party, your planning begins with:

+ Stating your purpose: "just because" or a celebration

+ Choosing your style: casual or formal

+ Deciding how many to invite

+ Planning your menu and the number of courses

+ Deciding how you'll serve it: passed, plated, semibuffet, or family style

+ Creating a timetable for the evening

Often, the purpose of your party influences the other choices you have to make. Dinner with three or four close friends might be more casual than a party in someone's honor. You may find that hosting a sit-down dinner for four to eight guests is manageable on your own, depending on your experience and comfort level. But with nine or more guests you'll enjoy your party more if you can enlist a completely dedicated partner— friend or spouse—to give you a hand or hire extra help, either for the cooking, serving, or both.

Chart of Courses

	2-COURSE	3-COURSE	3-COURSE	4-COURSE	5-COURSE	6-COURSE
1st	Main course	Main course	Appetizer/ Soup	Appetizer/ Soup	Appetizer/ Soup	Appetizer/ Soup
2nd	Dessert	Salad	Main course	Main course	Main course	Soup /Fish
3rd		Dessert	Dessert	Salad/Cheese	Salad	Main course
4th				Dessert	Cheese/Fruit	Salad
5th					Dessert	Cheese/Fruit
6th						Dessert

invitations

Dinner party invitations run the gamut from e-mail to a phone call to a written invite. Whatever you choose, the invitation should clearly indicate the style of your dinner party, be it dressy, casual, or something in between to give guests an idea of what to expect and what to wear.

For a casual dinner, to which guests should be invited at least five days to a week ahead, phone and e-mail work well. Mailed invitations imply that you're planning something more special, so send these out three to four weeks ahead, or even five to six weeks ahead for a holiday party.

Use your invitation to get your guests in the mood before the party begins. One of the best invitations we ever received came in a little box. Inside was a bottle filled with sand and a message: SURPRISE LOBSTER BIRTHDAY PARTY FOR JAY! We could hardly wait. (For more on invitations, see Chapter 4, The Invitation Tells All, page 35.)

Dinner Party Checklist

- ☐ Hire or arrange for help
- ☐ Invitations
- ☐ Check the outdoors
- ☐ Clean your house or party space
- ☐ Decorations, flowers
- ☐ Linens: laundered and pressed
- ☐ Tableware (glasses, dishes, flatware): sparkling
- ☐ Atmosphere: lighting, music, fire in fireplace
- ☐ Menus and recipes
- ☐ To do lists
- ☐ Shopping lists
- ☐ Timetables
- ☐ Seating plan

"places, please"

✦ ✦ ✦

Be prepared to answer the question "Where should I sit?" *before* your party starts; otherwise, just when you're preparing to serve dinner, you'll have to stop and come up with a seating plan on the spot. Of course, place cards answer the problem completely, but even if you don't use them, have a plan in mind—preferably on paper. As a handy reference for you, draw a diagram of your table, placing guests' names where you'd like them to sit.

The goal of a good seating plan is to honor any special guests and pair up other guests so the conversation will flow. Here are a few tricks to make that happen:

- ✦ Usually, the host and hostess sit at each end of the table.
- ✦ Seat any honored guests at the host or hostess's right: the man on her right and the woman on his right. If you have other honored guests, they sit at the host and hostess's left.

- Don't worry about "boy-girl-boy-girl." If you have an uneven number of men and women, simply space them as evenly as possible.
- If you have more than one table, the host sits at one and the hostess at the other.
- In general, split up married couples and close friends—they tend just to chat with each other, and the point is to visit with people you might not see all the time. Seat any newcomer near the host and hostess, and place someone with similar interests on his or her other side. Of course, you don't want to make people miserable—it's fine to seat couples together who are newly dating, engaged, or married.
- Consider interests and temperament. Pair people who have similar interests. Pair shy types with outgoing types. If two of your guests are on the polar opposite end of any spectrum, try to seat them at opposite ends of the table. You want conversation, not a heated argument.
- Consider special needs. Seat a lefty on a corner so that he's not throwing his left elbow at his dinner partner. A person who's hard of hearing may be more comfortable with her best ear to the conversation or seated next to someone who speaks clearly.

Timeless Advice from Emily

The endeavor of a hostess when seating her table is to put those together who are likely to be interesting to each other. Professor Bugge might bore you to tears, but Mrs. Entomoid would probably delight in him; just as Mr. Stocksan Bonds and Mrs. Rich would probably have interests in common. Those who are placed between congenial neighbors remember your dinner as delightful—even if both food and service were mediocre; but place people out of their groups and seat them next to their pet aversions and wild horses could not drag them to your house again!

—Emily Post, *Etiquette*, 1922

place cards

✦ ✦ ✦

Place cards solve the whole problem of guests shuffling awkwardly to the table. Place cards should reflect the style of your table. For a formal dinner, place cards are written on folded white or cream card stock. For a less formal affair, use colored papers and inks to complement your color scheme, decorate with shells or leaves, and prop against mini vases of flowers or wrapped chocolates—whatever you have on hand.

For a formal dinner, use titles and first and last names: Mr. Smith, Ms. Wang, Judge Stevens. Use first names only if two people have the same last name: Mr. Tucker Smith, Mr. Adam Smith. Among friends, use first names and add a last initial if needed: Caroline P. and Caroline B.

the dinner party game plan

✦ ✦ ✦

Just as you need a timetable to do your shopping, cleaning, and cooking, it's important to create a game plan for your actual party so that the evening's events flow smoothly. If you end up serving dinner two hours after your guests arrive, there's a good chance they'll be (1) starving, or (2) too full of hors d'oeuvres and (3) too full of cocktails. Begin by dividing the evening into three acts: gathering and cocktails, dinner, and after dinner. The following sections approximate times for each part of the evening and each course of the meal:

Gathering, cocktails, and hors d'oeuvres: Plan on forty-five minutes to one hour from the time guests arrive. During this time you'll greet guests, take coats, make introductions, serve drinks and hors d'oeuvres, finish any dinner preparations, and prepare food for service. (It's probably the busiest hour of the party.)

Dinner: Depending on the number of courses, dinner itself lasts about forty-five minutes to an hour or an hour and a half, including clearing and serving. The following is a guide for the approximate timing of each course. (Clear the table only when *everyone* is finished with each course.)

First course (soup or appetizer):

10 to 15 minutes

Main course: 20 to 30 minutes

Salad/cheese course: 10 to 15 minutes

Dessert: 10 to 15 minutes

If you've done a particularly good job with your guest list and seating plan, lively conversation may extend these times. Just take it as a compliment to your hosting skills!

After dinner: This is the time to serve coffee, tea, and after-dinner drinks such as cordials, Port, brandy, or single malt Scotch, perhaps accompanied by special chocolates or walnuts for cracking. It's the cozy time to continue conversation and begin to wrap up the evening and lasts anywhere from a half hour to late into the evening.

So, to recap, if you invite guests to arrive at 7:00 P.M., plan on:

Serving dinner between 7:45 and 8:00

Dinner lasting until 8:45 or 9:15, depending on the courses

Guests departing between 9:45 and 11:00 (or later!)

It goes without saying that the evening can certainly be extended if your guests are having a great time. How many times have we looked at the clock to see that it was after 11:00 and the party was still lively? If you really have to call it a night, however, it's up to you, as the host, to gently guide the party to its end. (See Chapter 2, Producer, Director, and Star, page 15.)

spring dinner party for 8, in 3 or 4 courses

FIRST COURSE

Louise's Spring Pea Soup
(opposite)

and/or

SECOND COURSE (OPTIONAL)

Composed Salad
(a plated—as opposed to tossed—salad, such as sliced tomatoes, mozzarella, and basil)

MAIN COURSE

Grilled Wild Salmon Garnished with
Lemon and Parsley

Cold Asparagus with Champagne Vinaigrette
(page 12)

Garlic Mashed Potatoes
(page 84)

DESSERT

A Trio of Sorbets and Little Cookies

A Bowl of Strawberries or Cherries
(to eat out of hand while lingering)

(For a fall dinner party menu, see page 80.)

After-Dinner Cigars

To some, this is one of the world's great pleasures; to others, it's repulsive. Only the host should suggest an after-dinner cigar, as he or she sets the house rules regarding smoking in general. Most at-home cigar smoking is an outdoor activity—a screened porch or chairs in the backyard—which makes it friendlier for nonsmokers to join in as well. Cigar smokers should take care to sit downwind of nonsmokers and dispose of butts in a proper ashtray and not simply toss them on the ground.

louise's spring pea soup

This is our dear friend Louise Roomet's version of an Elizabeth David classic. While it's simply delicious as a chilled soup, it's just as wonderful served hot. The vibrant green makes it the perfect soup for Christmas dinner. This soup is easily adaptable for vegetarians.

Serves 4 to 6

1 medium-size head iceberg lettuce
1-pound bag frozen peas (baby peas are
    sweetest) or 1¾ pounds fresh peas in the pod
2 tablespoons butter
3½ cups water

2 teaspoons salt
1 to 2 lumps (teaspoons) of sugar (optional)
Optional garnishes: Mint sprigs, pea shoots,
    edible flowers, black sesame seeds

1. Remove the tough outer leaves of the lettuce. Wash and cut the lettuce into quarters, then into fine strips, ¼ to ½ inch wide. Shell the peas if using fresh.

2. Melt the butter in a large saucepan over medium heat. Add the lettuce strips and the peas. Cover and cook gently for 10 minutes, stirring occasionally, as the lettuce begins to cook down. Add the salt and sugar to taste.

3. Add the water. If using fresh peas, cook further until the peas are tender. No further cooking is needed if using frozen peas.

4. Using a blender, puree the soup (in batches, if necessary).

5. Refrigerate, or return to the pan to heat to serving temperature.

6. Serve in bowls and garnish with mint sprigs, pea shoots, or edible flowers, or sprinkle with black sesame seeds.

serving it up

✦ ✦ ✦

There are two basic ways to serve at a dinner party—the seated meal and the buffet—and each has variations. Pick the one that best fits your needs and style. Each style is adaptable, and we like to mix it up. Generally, we plate the first course—soup or appetizer—and have it on the table when guests come in to dinner. When everyone is finished with the first course, we remove the plates and invite guests to serve themselves the main course from the buffet. Then we clear the main course, plate the dessert, and serve guests individually at the table.

serving at the table

When guests are seated at the table, there are three ways to serve the meal:

Served. This is the most formal style. Servers bring the food on platters and serve each guest each course individually. This is hard to do alone—you'll need to hire help or enlist a partner or a good friend. Each platter or dish is presented to the guest's left, starting with the guest of honor on the host's right, continuing counterclockwise around the table, ending with the host.

Plated. The food is arranged on plates in the kitchen and then served to each guest. This works for a small number of guests and is the most attractive way to present your dinner. Think logistics, though. One person can't handle more than three trips carrying two plates before the first plates start to cool off. Ask your partner or a guest to help bring the plates to the table. Women are usually served before men. Remember to serve on the left (LL—leave left).

Family style. This is the least formal style. The hostess passes platters at the table and each guest serves herself, or the hostess prepares each plate from platters on the table and then the plates are passed around the table. You'll then need to put the serving dishes on a warming tray on a sideboard or in the kitchen.

serving buffet style

Semi buffet or seated dinner with buffet service. Food and plates are set out on a buffet table. Guests serve themselves and then proceed to the table or groupings of smaller tables. Drinks, salad, and dessert courses are usually brought to guests at the table. This style adapts itself to large groups and outdoor parties nicely. We also love it because guests can choose their own portions and pass up foods they can't eat or don't care for without having to say, "No, thank you."

Buffet with casual seating. This is the classic buffet. Everything necessary for the meal—plates, napkins, silverware, food, condiments, and beverages—are all set out on a buffet table or tables. Guests help themselves and then sit where they please: living and dining rooms, family room, or patio. It's perfect for a crowd—just be sure to have plenty of seating and tables where guests can place glasses or cups and saucers. (See Chapter 6, Setting the Stage, page 59, for more on buffets.)

when to start?

✦ ✦ ✦

Guests wait for the host or hostess to lift his or her fork and take the first bite (a holdover from the very old days when guests needed assurance that they weren't going to be poisoned) or to say, "Please begin." At a big party, the guest of honor's soup might be stone-cold by the time everyone is served—so don't keep your guests waiting! For any more than six guests, invite them to begin eating as soon as three or four have been served, especially if it's a hot dish. Once everyone is served, you can interrupt for a moment to offer a toast or blessing or otherwise welcome guests to your table.

the passing lane

✦ ✦ ✦

If you're the one to start passing something, the convention is to offer once to the left and then pass to the right, serving yourself in between. It's more convenient for right-handed people, but honestly, what's more important is that dishes move in only one direction so they don't cause a traffic jam. Here's what's passed at the table:

Salt and pepper, usually together

Bread, if not already on bread plates

Chargers

You see them everywhere in magazines, home entertaining catalogs, and bridal registries, those large, gorgeous plates that give drama to a table setting. The charger, also known as a service plate, is basically an underplate for the plate holding the first course. Do you actually *need* chargers? In a word, no, but they can add a touch of elegance, festivity, and formality to your table. When using a charger, the first course is either served to guests at the table or it's already on the service plate when guests come to the table. Remove the first course and the charger, and then serve the main course on its own plate. The charger does not appear again.

Butter, if not already on bread plates

Sauces and condiments, each in a dish with a saucer and a serving utensil

Main-course dishes or salad are passed the same way, except that the person on the left holds the platter so the person on his right can serve herself.

would anyone like a little more?

✦ ✦ ✦

It's always a good idea to have enough food for second helpings. Seconds are usually offered for the main course, the salad (if it follows the main), and the dessert. (Offering seconds on a first course could throw a monkey wrench into the timing of your main course.) Keep an eye on your guests and begin offering seconds when about three-quarters of them have finished the first course. You can bring a platter or dish to the table and serve each guest individually, or pass the dish around the table and let each guest help himself. If it's a buffet, invite guests to help themselves to more food.

Keep an eye on wine and water glasses, too. Replenish as needed, either by passing carafes, pitchers, and bottles or by pouring for your guests.

clearing the table

✦ ✦ ✦

Make clearing between each course as efficient as possible, because after you clear, you also need to prep and serve the next course. Ahead of time, ask your partner or a close friend to assist if you haven't hired servers (you don't want all your guests jumping up to help). Take a tip from professional waitstaff: Never enter or leave the kitchen empty-handed. Here are some of the finer points of clearing the table:

✦ Wait until *everyone* has finished the course before clearing.

✦ Remove two plates at a time, but don't stack them.

✦ Remove from the guest's right side (remember RR—remove right.)

✦ Remove both the plate and the used and unused utensils for that course, as well as any condiments for the course.

Finger Bowls: Retro Chic

Finger bowls—little glass bowls filled with cool or lukewarm water—are meant for cleaning your fingers. You rarely see them anymore except at formal dinners, but they are practical—especially if your main course involves messy finger food, such as artichokes, ribs, or lobster. They're brought in on a dessert plate after the main course has been cleared and just before dessert is served. One hand at a time, diners dip and swish their fingers gently in the water, carefully shake off the excess, and dry them with their napkins. It takes just a second or two. When finished, the diner lifts the finger bowl (and the doily if there was one) and moves it to the upper left of the place setting. Dessert is then served on the dessert plate. For an extra touch try using rose- or orange-scented water, or add a slice of lemon, a sprig of mint, or a floating flower. If you're eating ribs outside, instead of using finger bowls you can distribute warm, wet rolled-up cotton napkins with a pair of tongs, à la airplane service.

- Clear the deck before dessert is served. Remove all salts, peppers, bread plates and knives, bread baskets, condiments, and predessert utensils that weren't used.

- At the end of the meal, clear the dessert plates and blow out the candles. Finish the rest of the table-clearing duties after your guests leave.

  In the kitchen, have a place to scrape and stack plates and a container of soapy water for utensils. Save the true washing up for after your guests leave.

when it's business

✦ ✦ ✦

There's a good chance that you (and your partner) may be invited to a purely social evening with a boss, colleague, or client. While most business entertaining takes place in restaurants, an at-home dinner party can be the perfect vehicle for doing a little social networking.

Since this is a social occasion, all the usual rituals of host and guest apply. There's only one thing you should do differently: Limit yourself to one drink. You're not being a party pooper; you're being smart. Even though business may never be discussed—and at a purely social evening it shouldn't be—you'll want to present yourself at your best. After all, these are people you either do business with or *want* to do business with, and as such it's still a professional occasion.

✳

a breath of fresh air

down in the sunny South, entertaining alfresco is a way of life. In the chilly North, it's a short-lived but much-loved season between Memorial Day and Labor Day. Our summer schedule in Vermont is crammed with invitations to barbecues (Lizzie's favorite), lawn parties, clambakes, and picnics. But that doesn't mean we huddle indoors the other three seasons. Fall is great for tailgating parties and a game of touch football, and picnics during brisk leaf-peeping hikes. Winter skating parties, bonfires to celebrate the solstice, or an afternoon of snowshoeing followed by a hearty chili dinner keep spirits up on long, dark winter days. Spring in Vermont means maple "sugar on snow" parties (fresh hot syrup poured over snow with a side of pickle, definitely an acquired taste) and dinner parties featuring the first peas and asparagus from local gardens.

◆ ◆ ◆

An outdoor party can take the brakes off your guest list, giving you room to invite more guests than your house or apartment alone can handle. With a few adjustments, any party can be held in the open air. About the only thing that might rain on your parade is . . . rain! Outdoor entertaining calls for a foolproof backup plan if Mother Nature chooses not to cooperate.

Most outdoor entertaining tends to be casual in nature, but that doesn't mean you can't plan an elegant midsummer's night dinner party under an apple tree or a dressy cocktail party on the patio. Twinkling lights strung between trees and the starry sky above are all the decoration you need.

sharing the wealth

✦ ✦ ✦

Backyard parties are great opportunities to gather a crowd, with everyone pitching in. Usually, the hosts provide the main event—the steak, burgers, ribs, and vegetables for grilling—and the beverages, while guests bring sides and desserts. It's up to you to ensure that the menu is balanced. Before you start making phone calls or sending invites, determine which dishes you need to round out your meal. It's okay to be specific: "Tanya, could you please bring a salad?" Or divide your list alphabetically: A–Ms bring a side and N–Zs bring dessert.

How Much Should I Make?

When cooking for a potluck, calculate your servings on half the guest list. So, for twenty guests, make ten servings. Why? Because when there's so much yummy food, guests tend to sample each dish and no one takes a full serving.

the table

✦ ✦ ✦

For a sit-down outdoor dinner party, linens, china, and glassware are great, but for a barbecue or large crowd, paper or reusable alternatives like bamboo, tin, or melamine plates, cups, and utensils is the practical way to go. (You don't want the "good stuff" getting lost or broken.) Find vintage tablecloths at a thrift shop, or purchase sturdy, easy-to-clean oilcloth (available by the yard in colorful patterns) and pretty cotton or paper napkins—all suitable for outdoor dining. Just be sure that whatever you choose will stand up to what you're serving. Anything that requires a knife and fork, such as steak or chicken, will need a sturdy plate and heavy-duty knives.

the alfresco menu

✦ ✦ ✦

Outdoor barbecues tend to feature hearty, soul-warming, nonfussy grilled foods such as ribs, chicken, steak, burgers, hot dogs, and fish, with sides like corn on the cob, salads (especially potato or pasta), coleslaw, and baked beans. Foods dressed with olive oil dressings like grilled vegetables and grainy salads like bulgur wheat, wild rice, and couscous all hold up extremely well and can be made in advance. Beer, cider, and wine all complement the informality of a barbecue, as do big pitchers of margaritas, sangria, lemonade, iced tea, and iced coffee. Hors d'oeuvres are of the simple and easy variety: chips and dips or salsas, deviled eggs, and vegetable crudité platters. Don't forget the condiments—ketchup, mustard, hot sauce, BBQ sauces and mayo; relish and pickles; chutneys, Romesco, and tapenades—but serve each in a dish with a serving utensil, never directly from the jar. Cakes, cookies, cupcakes, brownies, pies, fruit salad, or sweet summer watermelon round out the menu.

safety first

✦ ✦ ✦

Outdoor entertaining means that food will be served and sometimes even cooked outside. You'll need to take extra precautions so that food doesn't spoil in the heat and isn't attacked by insects. Set up all food stations in the shade and provide mesh covers for dishes if insects are a problem.

Have lots of coolers on hand. To keep foods cool, especially those with a mayonnaise base, set bowls in larger bowls filled with ice or on wrapped cold packs. It's better to use smaller platters that you refresh often than to leave a larger one wilting in the heat. If cold is a problem, use Crock-Pots, hot trays, or thermoses.

cooking outdoors: the backyard barbecue

✦ ✦ ✦

Easy and fun, the backyard barbecue is a quintessentially all-American way to entertain. (Don't have a backyard? Check to see if a local beach or park can accommodate you.) You can host it yourself or, as is often the case, arrange a potluck or assign contributions. No matter what you cook—potatoes or a crock of beans baked in the coals, a pig roasted in a pit, s'mores toasted over a bonfire, or chicken sizzling on the grill—a barbecue takes any picnic to the next level.

The critical element to successful outdoor cooking is *timing*—not just the kind of timing that brings the whole meal together so it can be served, but the kind of timing that saves a beautiful steak from becoming a charcoal briquette. But since cuts of meat vary in thickness and some like it rare and some like it done, how do you know when to take it off the grill? Here are tried-and-true tips for successful grilling from our dad, Peter, and from Chef Peter (of the Jimtown Store in Healdsburg, California).

grilling 101

✦ ✦ ✦

✦ Purchase an instant-read thermometer. Test it for accuracy in a measuring cup filled with boiling water (it should read 212°F). Use it to test meat for doneness (see the chart).

✦ Keep your grill clean. Let any residue burn off and use a steel brush to clean the racks. At the very least, brush the racks after you preheat the grill.

✦ Brush the grill with oil, or before lighting spray the racks with cooking spray like PAM or a spray made for grills.

✦ If you're not using a barbecue sauce or marinade, season the meat or fish ahead of time with salt and let the salt soak in. Pat the meat or fish dry before putting on the grill, to prevent sticking. Or, try rubbing a little olive oil on the meat or fish.

✦ Start the meat on high heat to sear the outside and create a seal that locks in moisture.

✦ Once it's been seared, turn the heat to medium or, if using charcoal, move to a cooler section of the grill.

✦ Use the instant-read thermometer, inserting it in the center of the thickest part of the meat. Pay attention to the temperature, and take the meat off the grill when the thermometer reads 5 degrees lower than your desired doneness. Let it "rest" on a platter, covered with foil, for 5 to 10 minutes. It will continue to cook for a bit.

Beef and Lamb:		
rare: 125°F	medium: 135–140°F	well: 155°F
Pork:	medium: 150°F	well: 160°F
Chicken:	breast: 165°F	thigh: 175°F

✦ If you didn't baste with barbecue sauce, sprinkle a little more olive oil on the meat along with freshly ground pepper. Add salt only after you've tasted a slice to see if it's needed. Add a spritz of lemon juice on steak, lamb, pork, or veal as a finishing touch.

the grill

✦ ✦ ✦

A grill is a wonderful thing—simple food cooked over an open fire in the great outdoors. Grilling is an art to master, whether it's over a real or a gas fire. Here are several grill varieties and the pros and cons of each:

Charcoal grills. The kettle grill and the hibachi use charcoal and are the most inexpensive. Lighting can be tricky. Get a canister fire starter or make your own out of open-ended, large no. 10 cans. Shred cardboard and paper on a little pile of coals, and light. It's like starting a campfire, and healthier than using lighter fluid. These grills are the best for achieving a "charcoal flavor" or for adding mesquite or other hardwoods for a smoky flavor. They're also portable—great for the beach or balcony (check your lease first!). Never use inside.

The Tuscan grill. This is an insert for an indoor or outdoor fireplace. Basically, it's a frame with a single rack that can be positioned at two to three levels above the coals. Outdoors you can use hardwood or charcoal; indoors you *must* burn hardwood, since burning charcoal

indoors can cause carbon monoxide poisoning. Start cooking when you have glowing coals, not an active flame. This may take up to an hour. Cooking over hardwood gives food an incredible flavor; in fact, some claim it's the only way to grill!

Gas grill. A stand-alone gas grill is pricey—$200 to $500 depending on the model. Gas grills use propane canisters that are refilled or traded for filled ones—another ongoing expense. They're extremely convenient to use and are the best for controlled cooking. If you have propane service at your house, a service professional can hook up a line to the grill, eliminating the canisters. (We recommend you also buy models with a shut-off timer, just in case you forget to turn it off.)

The outdoor cooking center. This is the *sine plus ultra* of cooking alfresco. It's basically an outdoor kitchen, a combination grill, rotisserie, stovetop, and oven, and often sink and storage. It's a hefty investment, but if you live in a warm climate, it could pay off over the long haul.

outwitting mother nature

✦ ✦ ✦

Not every day is a clear, sunny 76 degrees. Rain is the obvious outdoor party spoiler. If you can't accommodate your guests in your house or at another nearby location, a tent is the best way to provide weather insurance. Besides rain, you'll want to factor in heat, cold, wind, and even insects. As the party day approaches, keep an eye on the weather forecast to be prepared if Mother Nature throws you a curveball. Here are some ways to bat a thousand, no matter the weather conditions:

HEAT	COLD	WIND	INSECTS
Entertain in afternoon or evening, when it's cooler	Space heaters	Secure tablecloths, furniture, and flowers	Citronella, repellent candles, or tiki torches with citronella oil
Umbrellas, fans, awnings, tents	Warm, spicy food	Replace stemware with tumblers	Have insect repellent sprays or towelettes for guests
Paper fans	Candles, warm colors	Don't use umbrellas, balloons	Use pop-up mesh food covers
Have extra ice, water, and nonalcoholic offerings	Tea, hot chocolate, soup	Set up in the "lee" (nonwindy) side of a house, garage, or fence	
Serve salads, cold foods	Hand warmers, blankets	Nix any fires or candles	
Sunscreen			

lighting

✦ ✦ ✦

Evening parties call for extra outdoor lighting, and twinkle lights aren't just for the holidays. Festooning trees and shrubs with little white lights gives instant sparkle to nighttime parties. Luminarias and candles in hurricane lamps or canning jars are great for lighting pathways and tabletops. Kerosene lamps provide extra drama when hung from porches or branches. Just be careful of open flames near buildings or on windy evenings. Designate someone to be in charge of lighting and extinguishing and to keep an eye on the flames.

restroom

✦ ✦ ✦

Does your location have restroom facilities? This isn't always the case at public beaches and parks. Check it out ahead of time. At your house, make it clear where the guest bath is located, and leave the lights on to guide the way. Renting a portable toilet is another option, especially if you're having a large party and your septic system may not be equipped to handle the extra activity.

A Pretty Privy

The not-so-attractive portable toilet can be gussied up with flowers or a wreath on the door, flowers by the sink, a bunch of lavender or rosemary, scented soap, pretty paper hand towels, a wastebasket, and spray air freshener.

neighbors

✦ ✦ ✦

It's all a matter of perspective: Your fabulous party with the awesome sound track could be your neighbors' nightmare. Think about whether parking or noise will be a problem for them. If you can, it's a great idea to invite your neighbors to a big outdoor party—it does a lot to keep possible complaints to a minimum. However, be respectful of any noise ordinances in your town, and be prepared to tone it down if a neighbor complains. If parking is an issue, consider hiring a licensed high school or college student to valet park cars within a two-block radius. (Make sure he knows that you will pay him and tip him, and that your guests are not expected to do so: "Thanks, Mr. Hemley, I'm already taken care of.")

Lizzie's barbecue menu

An outdoor barbecue is Lizzie's favorite way to entertain. She's the queen of the grill, and her gatherings are famous not only for her spicy cuisine but also for the perfect playlist. Let the good times roll!

MIXED GRILL

Grilled Italian Sausage with Salsa Verde
(*page 161*)

Post Family Favorite Marinated and
Grilled Chicken or Shrimp
(*page 160*)

Bourbon-Marinated Flank Steak

SIDES

Buttermilk Coleslaw
(*page 160*)

Potatoes Tossed in Romesco Sauce
(*page 162*)

Fresh Corn, Cherry Tomatoes, Mozzarella,
and Basil with Extra Virgin Olive Oil

Cornbread with Ancho Chile Butter
(*page 163*)

DESSERT

Strawberry Shortcakes and
Whipped Cream

post family favorite marinade

This works well with chicken, pork, shrimp, or lamb kebabs. Makes enough for
2 pounds of meat or shrimp

Juice of 2 lemons

1 garlic clove, mashed to a pulp

¼ cup olive oil

2 tablespoons grated onion

3 teaspoons salt (or less)

1 teaspoon ground chile peppers (or to taste!)

2 teaspoons curry powder

1 teaspoon ground coriander

1 teaspoon powdered ginger

Combine all ingredients. Store in a glass bottle in the fridge for up to a week.

buttermilk coleslaw

Serves 6 to 8 generously, depending on the size of the head of cabbage

Dressing

2 cups buttermilk

1 cup mayonnaise

½ teaspoon celery seed

¼ teaspoon caraway seed

4 teaspoons salt

¼ cup sugar

¼ teaspoon freshly ground black pepper

3 tablespoons apple cider vinegar

Whisk all ingredients together in a bowl.

Slaw

1 large head green cabbage

½ cup shredded carrot

¼ cup chopped scallions

¼ cup red onion, thinly (julienne) sliced

1 tablespoon chopped fresh parsley

Toss all these ingredients together, then add the dressing and toss thoroughly. Serve chilled within 24 hours.

salsa verde

This Italian staple is incredibly versatile—delicious with grilled or roasted meats, vegetables, seafood, or just some good crusty bread. The variations on this sauce are as numerous as its applications, but certain ingredients are a must. The base of salsa verde consists of good olive oil, garlic, capers, anchovies, and loads of fresh herbs. Using this recipe as a base, have fun and experiment with the sauce to suit the dish it is accompanying. This sauce should always be served the day it is made and never refrigerated, to ensure bright clean flavor and color.

Makes approximately 1 1/2 cups, enough to serve 6 to 8

1½ cups roughly chopped fresh parsley

½ cup roughly chopped fresh oregano

½ cup roughly chopped fresh mint

3 scallions, finely chopped

2 teaspoons finely chopped rosemary

1 teaspoon Dijon mustard

2 tablespoons rinsed, dried, and roughly chopped capers

3 anchovy fillets, chopped into a paste

2 teaspoons red wine vinegar

½ teaspoon crushed red pepper

4 garlic cloves, minced

1 cup extra virgin olive oil

Combine all the ingredients except the olive oil in a food processor. Repeatedly pulse the motor while drizzling in the olive oil in a steady stream. Alternately, place everything but the oil in a large bowl (you may want to chop the herbs a little finer if using this method). While whisking, drizzle in the olive oil. Taste and add a pinch of salt or a splash of vinegar if you think it needs it.

romesco sauce

A nubbly, ruddy emulsion, thickened with bread crumbs and almonds, not egg yolks, Romesco sauce is bold yet suave. Serve it with sausages and grilled vegetables, spread it on sandwiches, or use it as a dip for crudités. A smaller batch is a little tricky to make, but Romesco freezes well. Small, quick-thaw quantities are good to have on hand. Makes about 4 cups

1 cup fine fresh bread crumbs

1 cup whole unblanched almonds, about
   4½ ounces

½ teaspoon crushed red pepper

2 garlic cloves, peeled and chopped

3 cups seeded chopped red-ripe plum tomatoes
   (from about 1 pound whole)

1 (7¼-ounce) jar roasted red peppers, drained
   (about 1 cup), see Note

6 tablespoons red wine vinegar

½ teaspoon best-quality sweet Spanish or
   Hungarian paprika

½ teaspoon fresh lemon juice

½ teaspoon sugar

½ teaspoon kosher salt

½ teaspoon freshly ground black pepper

1 cup extra virgin olive oil

1. Position a rack in the middle of the oven and preheat the oven to 400°F.

2. In a shallow metal pan, toast the bread crumbs, stirring them once or twice, until they are golden brown, about 15 minutes. Remove from the oven and cool.

3. In a food processor, combine the crumbs, almonds, crushed red pepper, and garlic. Process until the almonds are fairly evenly chopped. Add the tomatoes, peppers, vinegar, paprika, lemon juice, sugar, salt, and pepper and process briefly. With the motor running, gradually add the olive oil through the feed tube, stopping once or twice to scrape down the work bowl. Transfer to a storage container and refrigerate for at least 24 hours to allow the flavors to develop.

4. The Romesco can be refrigerated for up to 1 week or frozen for up to 2 months. Return it to room temperature and adjust the seasoning before using.

Note: Freshly roasted red pepper can certainly be substituted. One meaty, medium-large pepper should yield about 1 cup chopped flesh.

ancho chile butter

A delicious addition to cornbread! Or, serve with warm tortillas.

Makes approximately 1 pound

1 pound unsalted butter, at room temperature

1 tablespoon Ancho chile powder

¼ cup honey

Whisk all the ingredients together until smooth. Serve at room temperature. Leftovers can be stored in the refrigerator for up to 2 months.

Lizzie's playlist
FOR A HOT SUMMER NIGHT

Inspired by the movie *The Divine Secrets of the Ya-Ya Sisterhood*, Lizzie chose three artists from the sound track to set the mood for a sultry summer's night—Ann Savoy with her Cajun flair and bluegrass-folk sound, Jimmy Reed for a soft, vintage backyard sound, and legendary blues artist Taj Mahal.

Ann Savoy

"C'est Si Triste"

"Lulu Revenue dans la Village"

"C'est un Péché de Dire un Mentire"

"Mélodie au Crépuscule"

"The Very Thought of You"

"Getting Some Fun out of Life"

"Ces Petites Choses"

"It's Like Reaching for the Moon"

"Si Tu Savais"

"The Way You Look Tonight"

Jimmy Reed

"Big Boss Man"

"Baby What Do You Want Me to Do?"

"You Got Me Dizzy"

"I Ain't Got You"

"Shame, Shame, Shame"

"Goin' to New York"

"Ain't That Lovin' You, Baby"

"Found Love"

Taj Mahal

"Hesitation Blues"

"You've Got to Love Her with a Feeling"

"Lovin' in My Baby's Eyes"

"Queen Bee"

"Sittin' on Top of the World"

"Nobody's Business but Your Own"

"Early in the Morning"

"Come on in My Kitchen"

"Lonely Avenue"

the perfect picnic

✦ ✦ ✦

An alfresco picnic makes us feel liberated, free from the conventions of the table. A picnic always has an element of adventure and spontaneity, whether it's an elaborate feast in a field of wildflowers or a simple lunch in a public garden, a romantic evening on the beach or an afternoon under a shady tree with the Sunday paper. Let your imagination go wild: You're limited only by how much you can transport and how well it will travel. Ideally, everything should be ready to serve when you happen upon your ideal picnic spot.

Half the fun of preparing a picnic is foraging for yummy ingredients, something special you don't eat every day. One of the simplest picnics, in the European tradition, consists of little more than a loaf of bread, cheese, some olives, salami, fruit, and a bottle of wine. If you take care to pick the best of these ingredients, you'll have a spectacular, but still affordable, feast. If you want to expand it further, you can add a tomato and basil salad or a curried chicken salad (ready to serve from a container) or soup (hot or cold in a thermos to be poured into mugs). To up the elegance factor, pack chutney, honey, or jam to go with the bread and cheese, opt for prosciutto instead of salami, and finish with a fruit tart or pastry and sparkling wine.

Picnic Gear

✳ Blanket, tablecloth, oilcloth, or ground cloth ✳ Cushion(s) or folding chairs ✳ Umbrella (if there's no shade) ✳ Glassware, mugs, plastic or paper cups ✳ Enamel, melamine, bamboo, or paper plates ✳ Cutlery or reusable utensils ✳ Cloth or paper napkins and/or WetNaps ✳ Salt and pepper in shakers ✳ Knives for cutting bread, cheese, and meat ✳ Cutting board or plate ✳ Corkscrew and/or bottle opener ✳ Thermos for hot and/or cold drinks or soup ✳ Cold packs ✳ Bottle of water—just in case ✳ Flashlight, lantern, or candles in tall jars ✳ Jar for flowers ✳ Bug spray ✳ Sunscreen ✳ Matches in a waterproof bag ✳ Tea towels or paper towels ✳ Plenty of garbage bags ✳ Basket, tote, backpack, or cooler to transport food, beverages, and picnic gear

four seasonal picnics

SPRING

Louise's Spring Pea Soup
(page 145)

Smoked Salmon, Goat Cheese, Black Pepper,
Red Onion, and Capers on Baguette

or

Melon Seed Pasta Salad with Roasted
Asparagus and Prosciutto
(page 166)

Asparagus with Champagne Vinaigrette
(page 12)

Cherries and Almond Dream Cookies
(page 169)

SUMMER

Cold Grilled Chicken or Large Shrimp

Salad of Cherry Tomatoes and Fresh Corn
with Mozzarella and Basil

or

Green Bean and Potato Salad with
Caesar Dressing
(page 13)

Baguette

Strawberries and Shortbread Cookies

FALL

Ham and Brie Sandwiches with Honey
Mustard Butter on Baguette

Bulgur Salad with Dried Cherries
and Pumpkin Seeds
(page 167)

Grapes, Apples, Figs

Little Espresso Brownies
(page 170)

WINTER

Creamy Mushroom Soup with Sweet
and Hot Paprikas
(page 168)

Roast Beef Sandwiches with Fresh
Horseradish Sauce

Orange and Fennel Salad with Olive Oil
and Red Onion

Grappa and Biscotti

melon seed pasta salad with roasted asparagus and prosciutto

In springtime we think of this fresh, pink-and-green salad. Made with our favorite pasta (which is indeed shaped just like melon seeds, but you can also substitute orzo), it's the perfect foil to slightly crisp asparagus and soft, salty prosciutto. Lemon zest and plenty of fresh black pepper provide the punctuation. Serves 8

½ pound medium-thick fresh asparagus, tough stem ends snapped off
7 tablespoons extra virgin olive oil
Kosher salt
1 pound dried semolina melon seed (semi de melone) or orzo pasta
3 tablespoons fresh lemon juice (see Note)
Freshly ground black pepper

¼ pound thinly sliced prosciutto, cut into ½-inch squares
1 tablespoon finely chopped lemon zest
1 tablespoon finely chopped fresh flat-leaf parsley, plus more for serving (optional)
Butter (Bibb) lettuce leaves, arugula, or mesclun, for serving (optional)

1. Position a rack in the middle of the oven and preheat the oven to 500°F. Line 1 or 2 half-sheet baking pans with parchment paper. On the paper, toss the asparagus with 3 tablespoons of the oil and 1 teaspoon of salt. Spread the asparagus in a single layer. Bake, stirring once, until the asparagus is just crisp-tender, 6 to 8 minutes. Do not overcook; the asparagus will continue to cook on the pan after they come out of the oven. Cool to room temperature. Cut the asparagus diagonally into 1-inch pieces.

2. Bring a large pot of lightly salted water to a boil. Add the pasta and cook according to the package directions, stirring once or twice, until barely tender, about 8 minutes. Drain, rinse under cold water, and drain again.

3. In a large bowl, whisk together the remaining 4 tablespoons of oil, the lemon juice, ½ teaspoon of pepper, and ½ teaspoon of salt. Add the pasta, asparagus, prosciutto, lemon zest, and parsley and toss well. Adjust the seasoning—we like lots of black pepper. (Depending on the saltiness of the prosciutto, additional salt may not be needed.)

4. Serve immediately, or cover tightly and refrigerate for up to 24 hours. Return the salad to room temperature, adjust the seasoning once again, and toss just before serving.

Note: To serve as a first-course plated salad, line 8 salad plates with the greens and divide the pasta evenly among the plates, mounding it in the center. Garnish with an additional sprinkling of chopped or plucked parsley.

bulgur salad with dried cherries and pumpkin seeds

Nutty, crunchy, moist, and wholesome, this salad is attractive, too, with red cherries, scallions, and pumpkin seeds in colorful polka dots. Since it travels well, take it along with sandwiches on a picnic or put out a big platter on a buffet. (Tuck some watercress, baby lettuce, or frisée around the edges when you do this, and be sure to use the maximum amount of orange juice in the dressing to keep it moist.) Serves 6 to 8

2½ cups boiling water

2 cups medium-grain bulgur (cracked wheat)

½ cup raw pumpkin seeds

¾ cup chopped cilantro

½ cup coarsely chopped tart dried cherries

¼ cup diagonally sliced scallions (tender tops included)

4 to 6 tablespoons fresh orange juice

3 tablespoons extra virgin olive oil

2 tablespoons finely chopped orange zest

Kosher salt

Freshly ground black pepper

1. In a medium heatproof bowl, pour the boiling water over the bulgur. Let stand, stirring once or twice, until the bulgur is cool and has absorbed all the water. (If it remains watery after 45 minutes, drain it for a few minutes in a strainer.) Fluff the bulgur with a fork, spread it on a sheet pan, and let stand uncovered at room temperature to dry out. (It won't become bone-dry, but it shouldn't be soggy.)

2. Meanwhile, in a small, heavy skillet over medium heat, toast the pumpkin seeds, stirring often, until they are lightly colored and beginning to pop, 6 to 8 minutes. Remove from the skillet immediately and cool to room temperature.

3. In a large bowl, combine the bulgur, cilantro, pumpkin seeds, cherries, scallions, 4 tablespoons of orange juice, the olive oil, orange zest, 1 teaspoon of salt, and ¾ teaspoon of pepper. Toss to combine. Adjust the seasoning (add the additional orange juice if you think the salad needs it) and toss again.

4. The salad can be held for several hours, covered, at room temperature or it can be refrigerated overnight. Return it to room temperature before serving.

creamy mushroom soup
with sweet and hot paprikas

Serves 6 to 8

5 tablespoons unsalted butter

1 cup chopped leeks (white and pale green
  parts of 2 medium leeks)

1 cup chopped shallots

½ cup chopped celery

2 garlic cloves, peeled and finely chopped

¼ cup unbleached all-purpose flour

2 tablespoons hot paprika

2 tablespoons sweet paprika

5 cups chicken stock or reduced-sodium canned
  chicken broth, preferably organic

2 pounds brown (cremini) or white cultivated
  mushrooms, trimmed and thinly sliced

Kosher salt

½ teaspoon freshly ground black pepper

1⅓ cups sour cream, whisked until smooth, plus
  additional sour cream for serving

2 tablespoons finely chopped fresh dill, plus
  additional dill for serving

1. In a large pot over medium heat, melt the butter. Add the leeks, shallots, celery, and garlic. Cover and cook, stirring once or twice, for 10 minutes. Sprinkle the flour and paprikas over the vegetables, lower the heat, and cook, stirring and mashing often without browning or burning (the mixture will be dry), for 3 minutes. Gradually whisk in the stock, then add the mushrooms, 1 teaspoon of salt, and the pepper. The soup will look impossibly thick at this point, but persevere. Bring to a simmer, partially cover, and cook, stirring once or twice, until the mushrooms are tender, about 20 minutes. Remove from the heat and cool slightly.

2. In a food processor, puree half the soup (or, for a smooth soup, puree all of it). Return the pureed portion of the soup to the pan. The soup can be prepared to this point up to 3 days ahead. Cover and refrigerate.

3. Set the pan of soup over low heat. Whisk in the sour cream; stir in the dill. Heat, stirring often, until steaming; do not boil or the sour cream will curdle. Adjust the seasoning. Ladle the soup into bowls, top each portion with a small dollop of sour cream and a sprinkle of dill, and serve hot.

almond dream cookies

These are Carrie Brown's version of meltaways, eggless confectioners' sugar–based cookies popular in the fifties. They're fun, easy cookies to make with children. Makes about 40

¼ cup blanched slivered almonds
2¼ cups sifted cake flour, not self-rising
½ teaspoon salt
½ teaspoon ground cinnamon
2 sticks unsalted butter, softened

½ cup sifted confectioners' sugar, plus extra for dusting the cookies
1 teaspoon almond extract
1 teaspoon vanilla extract

1. Position a rack in the middle of the oven and preheat the oven to 400°F. In a shallow metal pan, toast the almonds, stirring them once or twice until they are crisp, fragrant, and lightly browned, about 7 minutes. Remove from the pan immediately and cool.

2. Onto a piece of wax paper, sift together the flour, salt, and cinnamon.

3. In a medium bowl, with an electric mixer on medium speed, beat the butter until smooth. Add the sugar and cream until fluffy, then add the almond and vanilla extracts and blend in well. Add the dry ingredients and mix on low speed until incorporated.

4. Drop by teaspoonfuls onto parchment-lined or ungreased baking sheets, spacing about 1 inch apart (the cookies don't spread much). Top each cookie with an almond sliver. Bake until firm on top and lightly browned on the bottom, about 8 minutes.

5. Transfer the cookies to wire cooling racks. Dust the cookies with confectioners' sugar, using a fine-mesh sieve to sift it over them. The cookies can be eaten immediately, stored in an airtight container at room temperature for up to 1 week, or frozen for up to 1 month. Layer them in the storage container between layers of parchment or wax paper and dust them again with confectioners' sugar if necessary just before serving.

little espresso brownies

Fudgy and moist, not too sweet, these brownies allow the dark chocolate flavor to shine. They're chock-full of toasted walnuts and a hint of espresso for grown-up complexity. Full-sized, they make extravagant picnic sweets, while cut into more manageable morsels, they star on cookie platters or dress up a dessert of ice cream or sorbet. For the ultimate sundae, top with a scoop of vanilla ice cream and warm chocolate sauce.

Makes 16 large (2 1/4" x 3 1/4") or 30 small (1 1/2" x 2 1/2") brownies

2 cups walnuts

1 cup unbleached all-purpose flour (measure it by scooping the cup into the flour container and then sweeping it level)

1/4 cup plus 2 tablespoons unsweetened good-quality cocoa powder, preferably Sharffen Berger or Valrhona

1 tablespoon powdered instant espresso, such as Medaglia D'Oro

3/4 teaspoon salt

6 ounces unsweetened chocolate, chopped (use the best available, like Sharffen Berger)

1/2 pound (2 sticks) unsalted butter, cut into 1/2-inch chunks

5 large eggs, at room temperature

2 1/2 cups sugar

1/2 cup sour cream

2 teaspoons vanilla extract

1. Position a rack in the middle of the oven and preheat the oven to 375°F. Lightly butter a 9- by 13-inch rectangular metal baking pan. Line the bottom of the pan with parchment paper; lightly butter the parchment.

2. In a shallow metal pan, toast the walnuts, stirring occasionally, until crisp, lightly browned, and fragrant, 8 to 10 minutes. Remove from the pan immediately, cool to room temperature, and coarsely chop. Increase the oven temperature to 400°F.

3. Sift together the flour, cocoa, espresso powder, and salt.

4. In a medium bowl set over a pan of simmering water, combine the chocolate and butter. Heat, stirring once or twice with a wooden spoon, until melted and smooth. Remove the bowl from the hot water and let stand on a rack while preparing the rest of the batter.

5. In a large bowl with a hand mixer on medium-high or in the bowl of a stand mixer on medium, beat the eggs until light and foamy. Using the same speed setting, gradually beat in the sugar. Increase the speed to high and beat for 18 minutes with a hand mixer or 15 minutes for a stand mixer. Reduce the mixer speed to low, add the sour cream and vanilla, and beat until just incorporated. Add the chocolate mixture and mix on low until just barely blended into the batter. Add the dry ingredients and mix until just moistened. Fold the nuts into the batter by hand. Scrape the dough into the prepared pan and level it with a spreader.

6. Bake for 18 minutes. Reverse the position of the pan on the oven rack from front to back and continue to bake until the top of the brownies just begin to pull away from the sides of the pan, another 10 to 12 minutes (monitor closely). The top will be set and feel firm while a tester inserted into the center will come out with a few crumbs still clinging to it. Your kitchen will smell fragrant with chocolate. Cool the brownies in the pan on a rack to room temperature. Wrap the pan tightly with plastic or foil and refrigerate until cold, at least 2 hours and up to 24 hours. The brownies can also be frozen in the pan for up to 1 month. Thaw in the refrigerator before removing from the pan and cutting.

7. To cut the brownies, carefully run a knife around the edges. Flip the pan over onto a cutting board; the brownies will drop out. (Give the bottom of the pan a rap if the brownies seem reluctant.) Lift away the pan and peel off the parchment paper. Flip the brownies back over (right side up). With a long, thin-bladed knife, wiped occasionally between cuts with a damp kitchen towel, trim the slightly drier edges off the brownie if desired (save these for kitchen nibbling). Cut the brownies into quarters and then evenly divide each quarter into 4 rectangles. We use a ruler to accomplish this.

8. Serve cold or at room temperature. Individually wrap leftover brownies in plastic wrap and refrigerate for up to 1 week.

Minding Your Picnic P's and Q's

✳ Be respectful of private property—don't trespass. Always ask permission and leave the area just like (or even better than) you found it.

✳ Be respectful of public picnic areas—clean off tables, and leave cooking areas clean and neat.

✳ Remember the hiker's rule: Pack it in, pack it out, or "take nothing but photos, leave nothing but footprints."

✳ "Fluff" the ground you sat on so it isn't matted down.

✳ Bring a trash bag and be responsible for your own trash. Some picnic areas offer trash cans, but if they're full, take your trash with you and dispose of it later.

✳ Never leave a fire unattended and *be absolutely sure* it's out before you leave.

traditions and special occasions

When we look back at our calendars, we see celebrations not just of official holidays, but also of personal milestones like birthdays and anniversaries, and the traditions we establish ourselves— an annual trip to the lake with friends or our Aunt Sara's annual lobster party. As we peruse these calendars, over and over we see good food as the cornerstone of any celebration. For instance, Anna hosts an early Thanksgiving every year to celebrate with friends, and Lizzie always celebrates Mardi Gras with cocktails, beads, and hors d'oeuvres. Choose a reason to celebrate that has meaning for you, and then turn it into a tradition.

✦ ✦ ✦

sunday dinner:
an old tradition in a new light

✦ ✦ ✦

Our parents like to regale us with stories of the Sunday family dinner "back in the day." Our mom, wearing her Sunday best, went to her grandparents' after church for a sit-down meal with a roast—something that her grandfather carved perfectly at the table. At our dad's, the 2:00 P.M. Sunday family dinner was followed by a second ritual, as the family piled into the station wagon and drove to the city for a New York Rangers hockey game. The Sunday dinner table was where you really learned about your family—their history, hopes and worries, stories, jokes, and personalities. The meal was pretty special, too—something that had been cooking all morning while the family was at church, food that was delicious, comforting, and made with love.

We're happy to see that Sunday dinner is making a comeback. When you think about it, it's an ideal way to entertain: long, lazy afternoons with friends and relatives gathered together around the table. Think uncomplicated comfort food like roasts, braises, and casseroles. The event doesn't have the formality of a Saturday night dinner party—it's more of a community effort and a chance to decompress. Since Sunday night is a "school night," an afternoon or early evening meal covers both lunch and dinner and lets everyone get home in time to prepare for the upcoming week. And like the Sunday dinner of old, it's an opportunity to bring multiple generations of friends and family together around the table.

tips for a successful sunday dinner

+ Keep the atmosphere casual, warm, and relaxing: You want the focus to be more on spending time with your guests than on an elaborate menu.
+ Invite as many people as you can comfortably fit around your table.
+ Be open to guests who ask if they can bring someone.
+ Invite guests to arrive between one and four in the afternoon.
+ Keep the menu simple and seasonal, but have plenty of everything.

- Say yes to help—with the prep, the food, the cleanup, the works.
- Serve the food family style, buffet style, or a combination of both: You could sit everyone down to a plated first course, then serve family-style platters. Or enlist helpers to plate each course. It's all about lingering.
- Have an activity available before or after the meal: Play board games, do Sunday crossword puzzles, take a walk, play croquet or bocce, watch a movie or a ball game, or just plain chat.
- Consider hosting Sunday dinners on a regular basis. You'll be surprised at how easily the idea catches on.

the communal table

✦ ✦ ✦

Having everyone at one table creates a sense of family, so make the table your focal point. It's up to you how you set your table but for this occasion, simple is best. Unless it's the dark of winter, candles aren't really necessary. Instead, a simple arrangement of fresh flowers, fruit, or greens is inviting without being too formal. Since this is a cozy group, place cards aren't needed either—but do have a seating plan in mind if you've invited more than six guests.

A Word on Blessings

When everyone is served and seated, the host may raise his glass in welcome—a nice way to put the focus on the meal and the company around the table. On certain occasions, such as Thanksgiving, or in certain traditions, it's customary to offer a blessing before the meal. As host, you may invite your guests to say grace, a prayer, or a blessing with you. However, you can't demand and should never put a guest who doesn't wish to participate on the spot. As a guest, if you choose to refrain, simply sit quietly and respectfully until the blessing is finished. You don't have to fold your hands in prayer. If everyone holds hands around the table, join the circle as a courtesy to the others.

the sunday dinner menu

✦ ✦ ✦

This is one time when you can skip the hors d'oeuvres if you choose, or offer just a few olives or something simple like radishes, butter, and salt; or pickled vegetables, toasted nuts, and a few slices of salami, like sopressata, along with a welcome glass of wine, beer, dry sherry, or a nonalcoholic drink.

SPANISH-INSPIRED SUNDAY DINNER MENU

Start with some roasted Marcona almonds and a glass of sparkling Cava or Manzanilla sherry.

Green Salad with Sherry Vinaigrette and
Shaved Manchego

Basque Chicken Ragout with Sausages and
Sweet Peppers
(opposite)

Rustic Bread

Rice Pudding or Flan

TRADITIONAL SUNDAY DINNER MENU

Crab or Shrimp Cocktail with Scallions, Avocado, and
Extra Virgin Olive Oil

Chicken Cobbler with Cheddar-Dill Biscuits
(page 179)

Peppery Greens and Golden Beets with
Grainy Mustard Vinaigrette

Apple Tart Tatin

basque chicken ragout with sausages and sweet peppers

Cider, sweet or hard, makes an especially good pairing. Serves 8

¼ cup fruity, good-quality olive oil

1 pound cooked spicy sausage, such as Spanish chorizo or andouille, angle-cut into ¼-inch slices

1 medium-large yellow onion (about ¾ pound), peeled and thinly sliced

6 garlic cloves, peeled and chopped

2½ pounds (6 to 8) large sweet peppers, preferably a mixture of red and yellow, stemmed, cored, and cut into ½-inch-wide strips

1 cup dry white wine

1 (28-ounce) can plum tomatoes with their juices

Kosher salt

2 teaspoons hot Spanish pimentón or Hungarian paprika

1 teaspoon freshly ground black pepper

½ teaspoon sugar

6 cups All-Purpose Shredded Roast Chicken (page 178)

2 tablespoons finely chopped fresh flat-leaf parsley

1. In a large, deep skillet over medium-high heat, warm the olive oil. Add the sausage and cook, stirring once or twice, until lightly browned, 8 to 10 minutes. With a slotted spoon, remove and reserve. Do not discard the oil or clean the skillet.

2. Set the skillet over low heat. Add the onion and garlic and cook, uncovered, stirring occasionally, until the vegetables have softened and are beginning to brown, about 10 minutes. Add the peppers, raise the heat to high, and cook, uncovered, stirring occasionally, until the peppers begin to brown, about 15 minutes. Stir

in the wine and bring to a simmer, scraping the browned deposits from the bottom of the skillet. Lower the heat. Add the tomatoes, thoroughly breaking them up with the side of a metal spoon, and their juices. Stir in 2 teaspoons of salt, the pimentón, black pepper, and sugar, then the chicken and chorizo and simmer 10 minutes. Adjust the seasoning.

3. The ragout can be prepared up to 1 day ahead. Cool, cover, and refrigerate, rewarming it over low heat until steaming. Serve hot in soup plates or bowls, topped with a generous sprinkling of parsley, with rustic crusty bread.

all-purpose shredded roast chicken

This is an easy way to prepare chicken for casseroles such as the Basque Chicken Ragout with Sausages and Sweet Peppers (page 177) and the Chicken Cobbler with Cheddar-Dill Biscuits (opposite). It's a completely unattended method (no basting required), which is great when you're cooking in volume, and the moist, tasty meat it produces is always a pleasure. While so simple a process can hardly be considered a chore, and extra meat freezes well for future meals, for a small home quantity you might prefer instead to roast a couple of on-the-bone chicken quarters—a combination of light and dark meat makes for the best flavor. Makes 4 cups

1 roasting-frying chicken, about 4 pounds, preferably organic or at least free range (see Note)

1 teaspoon fresh thyme or ¼ teaspoon dried crumbled thyme

Kosher salt

Freshly ground black pepper

1. Position a rack in the middle of the oven and preheat the oven to 400°F.

2. Remove the giblets and reserve them for another use (except for the livers, giblets can go into the chicken stock). Set the chicken up on its tail end and with a long, sharp knife, cut downward along both sides of the backbone, through the ribs. (Save the backbone for stock, too.) Make a shallow cut in the breastbone from inside the chicken, then press hard with both hands to crack the breastbone and flatten or butterfly the bird (this enables the meat to cook more evenly).

3. Lay the chicken, skin side up, on a half-sheet baking pan (lined with parchment paper if you like, for easier cleanup). Sprinkle with the thyme, plus salt and pepper to taste.

4. Set the pan in the oven and bake until the chicken thighs, when pricked at their thickest, yield clear yellow juices, about 1 hour. Cool to room temperature. Remove and discard the skin. Pull all the meat from the bones and shred it with your fingers. Save the bones, if desired for stock. The shredded chicken can be used immediately, wrapped well and refrigerated for up to 2 days, or frozen for up to 1 month.

Note: Chickens have gotten huge these days, and if all you find is a 6- or 7-pounder (or you just like the idea of having plenty of cooked chicken on hand), merely extend the roasting time, about 10 minutes for each pound over 4 pounds.

chicken cobbler with cheddar-dill biscuits

When we were growing up, creamy chicken served over biscuits or cornbread was our idea of perfect comfort food. Here's Carrie Brown's grown-up version, sure to be a hit for Sunday supper. When making this with Thanksgiving leftovers, Carrie calls it Gobbler Cobbler.

Serves 8

1 (10 ounce) basket white pearl onions

Kosher salt

¾ pound (2 or 3 medium) red-skinned potatoes

1½ sticks (¾ cup) unsalted butter, softened

1 cup chopped yellow onion

3 garlic cloves, peeled and finely chopped

5 cups chicken stock or reduced-sodium canned chicken broth, preferably organic

3 carrots, peeled and angle-cut into 1-inch pieces

3 celery ribs, trimmed and angle-cut into 1-inch pieces

Freshly ground black pepper

1½ cups heavy cream

½ cup unbleached all-purpose flour

5 cups All-Purpose Shredded Roast Chicken (opposite)

1 cup fresh or thawed tiny peas

1 cup fresh or thawed corn kernels

1 tablespoon finely chopped fresh dill

½ teaspoon crumbled dried thyme

½ teaspoon hot pepper sauce, such as Tabasco

Pinch of freshly grated nutmeg

1 recipe (about 24) unbaked Cheddar-Dill Biscuits (recipe follows)

¼ cup buttermilk, for brushing biscuits

1. With a sharp paring knife, mark a small X in the bottom of each onion. Bring a small saucepan of water to a boil. Add the onions, salt the water, and cook for 2 minutes. Drain, rinse under cold water, and cool. Peel the onions.

2. In a medium saucepan, cover the potatoes with lightly salted cold water. Set over medium heat and bring to a brisk simmer. Cook, uncovered, stirring once or twice, until the potatoes are just tender, about 20 minutes. Drain and cool. Cut the potatoes into ½-inch pieces.

3. In a large pot over medium heat, melt ½ stick of the butter. Add the onion and garlic, cover, and

cook until the vegetables are tender, stirring occasionally, about 10 minutes. Add the stock, carrots, celery, 2 teaspoons of salt, and 1 teaspoon of pepper. Bring to a simmer, lower the heat, and cook, partially covered, for 15 minutes. Stir in the cream, raise the heat slightly, and cook, uncovered, stirring once or twice, until the vegetables are tender, another 10 to 15 minutes.

4. Meanwhile, in a small bowl, mash together the remaining 1 stick of butter and the flour to form a smooth paste. Lower the heat slightly and whisk the flour paste into the vegetable mixture bit by bit. Stir in the chicken, potatoes, onions, peas, corn, dill, thyme, pepper sauce, and nutmeg.

Partially cover and simmer until thick, about 10 minutes. The filling can be prepared to this point up to 1 day ahead. Remove from the heat, cool, cover, and refrigerate. Rewarm over medium heat just until hot before proceeding.

5. Position a rack in the middle of the oven and preheat the oven to 450°F. (If your oven is very fast or hot, set the temperature to 425°F.) Butter a rectangular 9- by 13-inch glass baking dish or any attractive ovenproof serving dish with a 3-quart capacity.

6. Spoon the hot chicken mixture into the prepared dish. Arrange the biscuits over the chicken mixture, spacing them evenly. Brush the chilled biscuits with the buttermilk. Set the pan on the baking rack (with a parchment- or foil-lined sheet pan on the rack below to catch drips).

7. Bake until the biscuits are puffed and golden brown, about 20 minutes.

8. Let the cobbler rest on a rack for 5 minutes. Serve hot.

cheddar-dill biscuits

Though they make the perfect topping for Chicken Cobbler, these biscuits are also good on their own. Serve them piping hot with eggs and bacon at breakfast or enjoy them at supper. Mini biscuits can be split while still hot, filled with a sliver of good ham and a dollop of honey mustard and passed as a terrific country hors d'oeuvre.

Makes about twenty-four 1 1/2-inch biscuits

3 cups unbleached all-purpose flour, plus flour for the work surface
4 3/4 teaspoons baking powder
1 1/2 teaspoons sugar
3/4 teaspoon baking soda
3/4 teaspoon salt
4 1/2 tablespoons chilled butter, cut into small pieces

3 tablespoons chilled shortening, cut into small pieces
1 1/3 cups buttermilk, plus extra for brushing the tops (see Note)
2 tablespoons finely chopped fresh dill
1 cup shredded sharp Cheddar cheese

1. Position racks in the upper and lower thirds of the oven and preheat the oven to 450°F.

2. Into a large bowl, sift together the flour, baking powder, sugar, baking soda, and salt. With a pastry cutter blend in the butter and shortening until the mixture resembles coarse meal. Add the buttermilk and dill and stir until the dough just begins to come together. Stir in the cheese. Turn the dough out onto a lightly floured work surface.

Knead it 10 or 15 strokes, until the surface is smooth. Pat the dough out ¾ inch thick. With a 1½-inch round cutter, form as many biscuits as possible, spacing them 2 inches apart on 2 half-sheet baking pans. Gather and reroll the scraps and cut them out as well. Refrigerate the biscuits on their pans for 30 minutes.

3. Bake the biscuits, exchanging the position of the pans on the racks from top to bottom and front to back at the halfway point, until they are puffed and golden, 12 to 15 minutes. Serve hot or warm.

Note: For biscuits with pretty golden tops, brush them with about ¼ cup buttermilk after they have been cut out. The biscuits can be prepared up to 1 week ahead and frozen. Arrange unbaked biscuits on a sheet pan and freeze. Store the frozen biscuits in a plastic freezer bag. Two hours before baking, remove the biscuits from the freezer, arrange them on a sheet pan, and thaw them in the refrigerator. You can bake them frozen—they just might take a little longer. Use the thawed biscuits to top the Chicken Cobbler.

birthdays for grown-ups

✦ ✦ ✦

Funny, we all loved our birthdays . . . until a certain age. Then it somehow became more fun to celebrate someone else's birthday instead. No matter someone's age, birthdays are a great excuse for a party, so celebrate every birthday you can! The big ones—the 5s and the 0s—get the most attention, usually with a cocktail party or dinner party. But we like celebrating the not-so-important years, too, usually by going out to brunch, lunch, or dinner with a group of friends and treating the birthday boy or girl.

birthday party hosting tips

+ Consult the honoree about the guest list.

+ It's understood that guests are supposed to bring gifts to a birthday party unless you specify "No gifts, please" on your invitation.

+ Phone, e-mail, or mail invitations at least 2 to 3 weeks ahead.

+ Bake or order a cake or cupcakes (or other cake-worthy equivalent) and buy birthday candles.

+ Have Champagne, sparkling wine, and sparkling water on hand for toasts.

Surprise!

There's nothing like a successful surprise party. There's a shared sense of purpose— and fun—between guests and host that brings people together long before the event. To plan one you have to be a little devious at heart, as well as quick on your feet if the "surprisee" starts to get suspicious. A few guidelines for would-be surprisers:

* Make sure you have a willing victim—some people just don't like being surprised.
* Send the surprisee a fake invite for a similar event in the same time slot so she knows what to wear.
* Hold the party a week or more *ahead* of the surprisee's actual birthday.
* Ask guests to arrive a half-hour before the honoree is due to show and make sure they know it's a surprise!
* Park cars on another block.
* Try to act normally and casually and, whatever you do, *don't spill the beans.*

Anna's birthday lunch

Anna's birthday is in June, when the garden is a riot of peonies and local strawberries are just appearing. If it's nice weather, we'll dine in the garden. Otherwise, we re-create the garden indoors, with peonies on the table and throughout the house.

Elderflower Mimosas
(page 109)

Louise's Spring Pea Soup
(page 145)

Curried Cashew Chicken on Bibb Lettuce
(opposite)

Whole Grain Toasts

Birthday Cake or Buttermilk Feather Cake
with Nutmeg
(page 85)

Whole Strawberries

curried cashew chicken

Serves 4 as a main-course salad

4 boneless, skinless chicken breasts

1 tablespoon kosher salt

2 tablespoons good-quality fresh curry powder

1 cup roughly chopped toasted cashews

¼ cup roughly chopped raisins or currants

⅓ cup full-fat yogurt, preferably Greek yogurt

¼ cup roughly chopped fresh cilantro

¼ cup finely sliced scallions

Juice of ½ lemon

1. Preheat the oven to 350°F.

2. Rub the chicken with the salt, then rub in all of the curry powder. Place on a lightly oiled or parchment-lined baking sheet pan and bake until just cooked through (160°F), 10 to 15 minutes. Let cool to room temperature. Cut the chicken into ¼-inch dice, and, in a medium bowl, mix in the remaining ingredients. This may be done up to 24 hours in advance.

3. To serve as a salad, place ½ cup or more of the chicken on a bed of butter lettuce. Garnish with cucumber slices, slices of peeled orange, additional cashews and raisins, or any combination of the above.

4. To serve as an appetizer, serve on crostini or in cucumber cups. To make cucumber cups, peel lengthwise stripes into the skin of a hothouse or English cucumber. Cut crosswise into ½-inch-thick slices. Using a small spoon or melon baller, hollow out the shallow center of each slice, being careful not to scoop through to the other side. Lightly salt each cup and fill with several teaspoons of chicken salad. Garnish with plucked cilantro or chopped scallions.

showers

✦ ✦ ✦

Whether they're held to honor a new baby or a bride, showers are a lovely tradition. Friends and family of the happy couple or the expectant parents literally shower them with gifts for their new home or child. Showers range from simple and casual to elaborate—and while they were once for girls only, these days guys are often included as well. They're meant to be adaptable to busy schedules, and can be held almost any time of day—even after dinner. Anyone can host a shower, but guests should be limited to family and close friends of the honoree. Most baby showers are held a month or so before the mom's due date, although some people prefer to wait until after the baby's safe arrival.

Wedding and baby showers usually last 1½ to 2½ hours, enough time for refreshments, gift opening, and perhaps games. Match the food to the time of day, but lighter fare is the norm. The gift opening is the main event, with everyone oohing and aahing as each present is unwrapped. Some honorees find it overwhelming to be the

Thoughtful Showers

All first time parents—couples, single, or adopting—can benefit from a shower to help welcome the new addition to their family. It's okay to have showers for second and even third children, but be sensitive and limit the guest list to family, close friends, and new friends—you don't want to overtax anyone's generosity.

center of so much attention, so it's fine to stagger the gift opening with refreshments, a game, or conversation. As for the refreshments, you may opt to skip alcohol if it's a daytime event. Serve iced tea or lemonade, or make punch or spritzers with a pretty fruit garnish. Nuts, crudités, and little tea sandwiches make a great start and cookies or cake a lovely finish. Cupcakes, whether homemade or store-bought, offer room for lots of creativity with the frosting.

shower invite smarts

+ Consult with the honoree(s) about the guest list.

+ Send out invitations 4 to 6 weeks ahead of the party. Shower invites are usually mailed, but e-vites and even phone invitations are fine.

+ Include the honoree's name, the date and time, where the shower's being held, and RSVP contact info.

+ Add directions to the host's house.

+ For a wedding shower, list the theme: kitchen, bar, lingerie, monogram. For a baby shower, list nursery colors or *boy* or *girl* if known.

+ *Never, never, never put specific gift requests or registry information on the invitation!* You always want to keep the focus on the people, not the gifts. Since showers are a gift occasion, it's fine to include a separate note with registry info. As the host, keep a list of what the honoree might need or like, and share it with guests who inquire when they RSVP.

Saying Thanks

All wedding and baby shower gifts must be acknowledged with a thank-you note, even if the honoree thanked the participants in person. You can help your honoree by:

✳ Asking a guest to be a recorder, writing down each gift as it's opened, along with a short description ("onesie" alone won't give her a clue whether Aunt Christine gave her the pink one or the blue) and the name of the giver. This list is critical, especially if a card gets separated from a gift.

✳ Providing her with names and addresses of all the guests. Note: It's tacky to have guests preaddress their own thank-you notes, no matter how "efficient" that might seem. A handwritten note is a handwritten note, envelope and all.

welcome!

✦ ✦ ✦

Celebrate your new or renovated house or apartment with a housewarming party for friends and neighbors. Plan to spend time giving tours, unless you're comfortable letting your guests explore on their own. Needless to say, everything—even closets—should be in tip-top shape. People's curiosity knows no bounds, and at a housewarming it's considered fair game to look anywhere and everywhere. (Items such as bills, prescriptions, and underwear should be out of sight—for everyone's sake!) If you're planning on being the tour guide, designate a partner or friend to greet guests at the door.

A housewarming is often a cocktail party or cocktail buffet, as simple or as elaborate as you wish. Or it can be "Drop by for minestrone, bread, and salad on Sunday afternoon." Phoned, e-mailed, or informal written invitations all work well for this kind of event, but be sure to issue them two to three weeks ahead. Because a housewarming is similar to an open house, add a start and end time to your invitation. Three to four hours is a typical time frame, with guests coming and going. If you're inviting a small group, include only a start time and expect the party to last two to three hours.

Presents for You

It's traditional for guests to bring gifts to celebrate your new digs, a birthday, or an anniversary. If you have a small group and everyone brought a gift, open them at the party and thank the giver in person. Otherwise, save them to open later and send a thank-you note. By the way, rule or not, a thank-you note is always appreciated.

happy anniversary

✦ ✦ ✦

Young couples celebrate early anniversaries on their own or with a small cocktail or dinner party with friends. The guest list can include family members and their children, members of the couple's wedding party, and friends.

hosting away from home

✦ ✦ ✦

You might decide to host certain parties—like a significant birthday or your parents' anniversary—at a club or restaurant. There are definite advantages to this, especially if you'd like to invite more people than you can fit comfortably into your home, or if the honoree lives far away and you're hosting the party in their town. If you do this, the one guideline you absolutely must follow is that you *cannot* ask your guests to help pay the bill. (See Who Pays?, page 188.)

The key to a successful party away from home is to arrange everything with the club or restaurant manager ahead of time. Once you've secured your date and sent out invitations, meet the manager to discuss the menu and beverage options. If you have a cocktail hour you can either offer an open bar and run a tab, or offer a signature cocktail, wine, beer, and nonalcoholic options. It's fine to select a red and a white wine to serve with dinner (and a Champagne or sparkling wine for toasts). You can either choose one meal that's served to all, or create a mini menu from what the venue offers. This second option lets guests choose among a limited number of appetizers, entrées, and desserts. If all the items are in a similar price range, it makes it easy to stay within your budget while still offering choices. For a nice flourish, print your chosen menu on card stock and set the menus at each place setting so guests can check out their choices before the waitstaff takes orders (they make nice keepsakes, too!).

Who Pays?

You wouldn't ask your guests to pay for dinner at your home, so don't ask them to do so if your party's held elsewhere. When you're the host, you pick up the tab. Better to host a smaller or less elaborate party at home than risk insulting guests with an invitation asking them to pay $50 a head. Worse would be to invite guests simply to celebrate Tim's birthday, say, and then—surprise!—expect them to split the bill when it arrives.

If a group decides to host the party together, then splitting the cost is fine—but everyone should agree on the concept and the details ahead of time. Invitations are then sent to the honoree(s) and any other guests (who, of course, are *not* required to pay anything). Include the names of all the hosts on the invitation, so guests know who to thank.

group gifts

✦ ✦ ✦

A popular idea these days is the group gift, where family and friends pool their resources for a big-ticket gift, like a baby stroller or an anniversary trip. While this is a fine idea in theory, group gifts can run into etiquette problems if they're not handled carefully. A few tips to keep in mind when going this route:

✦ Remember, the choice of gift is always up to the giver. If someone chooses to opt out of a group gift in favor of giving something else, that's her prerogative.

✦ Gift information should be on a separate enclosure with the invitation, not on the invitation itself.

✦ Refrain from asking people for a specific amount. Instead, be willing to accept (and keep anonymous) all contributions. Deliver the gift (or the check) with a card that includes the names of everyone who contributed, so the giftee can send a thank-you note to each person.

giving toasts

✦ ✦ ✦

If you're hosting a special occasion like a birthday or an anniversary, it's your privilege, if you wish, to offer a toast to your guest of honor. No need to be intimidated: The best toasts are short and come from the heart. A simple "To Susie: May each birthday find you among good friends" will fit the bill. Or you can share reminiscences, tell a story, or speak to your guest of honor's best qualities.

You don't need a special occasion to make a toast, however. No matter what kind of party it is, if the mood is right, it's lovely to give an informal toast to good friends around the table.

toasting tips

✦ At a dinner party, it's the host or hostess's prerogative to give the first toast.

✦ If the hosts don't offer a toast, a guest may propose a toast saluting the hosts.

✦ Typically, toasts are proposed as soon as wine or Champagne is served—usually at the beginning of the meal or just before dessert.

✦ The person proposing the toast stands or raises a glass and gathers everyone's attention before launching into the toast itself.

✦ At the conclusion of the toast, everyone except the honoree(s) stands or raises their glasses and drinks.

✦ The honoree doesn't rise or drink the toast; instead he or she simply smiles, nods, and enjoys. After the toast or toasts are drunk, the honoree rises and drinks to his or her toasters in return with a "Thank you" or his or her own toast.

✦ No need for everyone to drain their glasses during a toast—a sip will do just fine.

✦ You don't need an alcoholic beverage to propose or drink to a toast. Any liquid will do, but we think it's more fun if the drink is something bubbly: Champagne, sparkling wine, sparkling water, fruit juice spritzers, or ginger ale. (See Chapter 8, Delicious Drinks, page 95, for more on Champagne and sparkling wine.)

when the party's all about you

✦ ✦ ✦

If you're the lucky honoree at a shower, birthday, anniversary, farewell, or other party, you know you have some pretty good friends. Sometimes, though, it's hard to be the center of all the attention. Just remember that people are making a fuss because they care about you and want to celebrate your milestones with you. So do your very best to jump into the spirit of the event with a smile, and go along graciously with everything your hosts have planned.

Be respectful of your host's budget if you're asked for any special requests, and stay within your limit if you're asked to provide a guest list.

Whenever you're feted, it's traditional to thank your hosts with flowers or some other gift either the day of or the day after the party. And of course, your hosts should get a handwritten note from you as well, as should anyone who gave you a gift.

✳

celebrate!
holiday parties

Starting with Thanksgiving and lasting through New Year's, the holiday season is a whirl of celebrations—Hanukkah, Christmas, Kwanzaa. This is the time of year when entertaining is at its most fabulous and frenetic. It's a blizzard of celebratory elements: holiday traditions, glittering decor, traditional holiday foods, and the coming together of family and old friends. Communities celebrate with tree or menorah-lighting ceremonies, carol sings, and potluck dinners, and most businesses host an annual party. This is the time of year when we want to connect with everyone. We send cards, letters, and photos to those far away, and even greet strangers with "Happy holidays!" A holiday party is a special gift to friends—a chance for everyone to eat, drink, and be merry at this most joyous of seasons.

✦ ✦ ✦

start early!

✦ ✦ ✦

The spirit of the season is infectious, and calendars fill up fast during holiday time. For your party to make it on this year's calendar, start planning early: Believe it or not, mid-October is not too early to book vendors or locations. You'll want to be sure that any hired help—caterer, servers, a bartender—is lined up before you send invitations. Mail holiday invitations up to six weeks ahead of time, (that's two weeks earlier than the norm) especially for a party on a Friday or Saturday evening in December. If you're inviting relatives to stay during the holidays, extend your invitation as far in advance as possible so they can make travel arrangements.

We may laugh seeing commercial holiday decorations appear before Thanksgiving, but it's a good reminder to have your house cleaned and decorated a good week before your party. Putting up seasonal decorations can be a big job, and you don't want to leave it to the last minute. Besides, it'll put *you* in the holiday spirit, which will make the rest of your party prep much more fun.

While Christmas is a focus for many, it's only one aspect of the holidays. It's just as easy to be

Let It Glow

Even if you keep your decorations simple, bumping up the lighting will instantly create a warm, festive atmosphere during dark December days.

✳ Light candles on mantels, dining tables, and sideboards.
✳ Light your Christmas tree, even if it's not decorated yet. (If you're having a big Christmas party, you'll want to display a decorated tree. For a simpler event, just the lights will provide atmosphere if you don't have time to hang ornaments.)
✳ Wrap garlands (faux or real) with strings of little lights. Drape over window and door frames or wrap a banister.
✳ Put battery- or solar-powered candles in windows.

festive without a Christmas tree, wreaths, and everything red and green. Capture the spirit of the season with lights, generosity, family, community, peace, and goodwill. Add touches of blue and silver for Hanukkah or feature red, green, and black for Kwanzaa. White, gold, and silver are great holiday colors in general. To celebrate winter, decorate your space with masses of candles and showcase white flowers, either in arrangements or pots of forced bulbs, like amaryllis and narcissus. (You can grow these yourself, but you'll need to start the bulbs five to eight weeks ahead. Purchase bulb kits or ask a florist for directions.)

fa-la-la-la-la—la-la-la-la

✦ ✦ ✦

There's enough holiday music out there to suit everyone's style: Traditional, chill, soul, hip-hop, jazz, Bing Crosby, Nat King Cole . . . what's your style? What will your guests enjoy? Most likely it's a mix of styles, so put your CD player on random or create your own mix. Label it "Holiday 20__" and start a tradition—a new mix each year.

the scent of the season

✦ ✦ ✦

We don't mean spraying your house with "Eau de Noel." Your tree may do the trick, but adding fresh greens around the house—tucked behind pictures and mirrors or added to flower arrangements—lends another subtle layer to the holiday atmosphere. No access to holiday spruce? Find candles with a hint of northern forest or spiced berries. Simmer mulled cider or wine on the stove . . . you can even cheat and boil spices such as cinnamon sticks and cloves in water for a steam potpourri.

Holiday Party Checklist:

- ☐ Hire professional or nonprofessional help.
- ☐ Extend invitations up to six weeks ahead.
- ☐ Put in orders for flowers and greens.
- ☐ Put up seasonal decorations (inside or outside).
- ☐ Trim your Christmas tree with lights—and ornaments if you're having a gala event. (Check water daily.)
- ☐ Polish, polish, polish. (You want your home to really sparkle!)
- ☐ Check outdoor lighting. Does your home look inviting?
- ☐ If you live in the snowbelt, make sure your entryway is cleared of ice, snow, and slush.
- ☐ Prepare adequate room for coats, wraps, hats, and boots.
- ☐ Check the hanger supply if using a coatrack.
- ☐ Check the guest bathroom.

holiday open house

✦ ✦ ✦

An open house is the perfect party for the holiday season. Open houses usually last from three to five hours, with guests coming and going at different times. Most guests stay for about an hour to an hour and a half. This means you can invite far more people than would normally fit into your space and have enough time for people to really visit.

holiday party particulars

- ✦ Send personal invitations on informal cards or fill-ins. Shop early for the best selection. You can also find lots of fun downloadable invites on the Internet that you can personalize and print from your computer.
- ✦ Invitations follow the usual form but should include a specific start and end time.

- With a large guest list, you may be tempted to use "regrets only" and just tally the no's. We say requesting RSVPs is the way to go: You'll get a more accurate headcount, essential if you're using a caterer or a bartender.
- Make sure you greet every one of your guests either at the door or by circulating at your party.

holiday party menu tips

- If food is being passed, keep it simple. Stick to finger foods or foods that just need a cocktail pick to eat.
- Pass hot hors d'oeuvres so you don't have to worry about them staying warm.
- Have lots of four-inch plates when serving buffet style or using food stations.
- Put out bowls of candied or spiced nuts, such as pecans, a delicious and sophisticated touch.
- Toward the last third of the party, add in or switch to dessert-type bites: sugar-frosted grapes, strawberries dipped in chocolate, chocolate truffles, holiday cookies, or little cakes, such as cupcakes, sliced loaf or Bundt cakes, fruit and spice loaves, or petits fours.

- Use small platters and refill often to keep them looking fresh. Have a buffet table or distribute platters throughout your party space.
- Have extras of everything: small plates, glasses, napkins, cutlery.

Festive Attire?

We hate ambiguous dress codes on invitations! Yes, "festive" means wearing something to do with the season, but is it dressy or not? Other than "black tie" and "white tie"—which come with their own rules—it's difficult to communicate a dress preference. Nowadays, there are so many options that even if your invitation style screams formal, guests still have cause to wonder, *What should I wear?* So, it's perfectly okay to be direct. If your open house is a laid-back affair—jeans and sweaters, say— put "casual" on the invitation. If it's an "Ooh, let's all wear our silk, satin, and pearls," write "dressy." You may still get some phone calls, but you've narrowed the field.

holiday open house buffet

A buffet works perfectly at a holiday open house, where people are coming and going at different times and it's important to have plenty of food available throughout the party. Here is a delicious buffet menu created by food writer and caterer Carrie Brown for a holiday open house buffet:

ANTIPASTI BOARD

A selection of cheeses, cured meats, pâtés, olives, and nuts; special condiments such as membrillo (quince paste), fig cakes, chutney, preserves, and honey; a variety of toasts, crackers, crostini, and nut breads. (This may also be divided in two food stations: a cheese board and a charcuterie board, with cured meats and pâtés and pickled vegetables.)

"Stand-Up" Salad with Green Goddess Dip
(*opposite*)

Cannellini Bean Puree with Crostini

Whole or Sliced Ham with Grainy
and Honey Mustards, Herb Butter,
Cranberry Chutney, and Homemade Biscuits
or Purchased Rolls

Smoked Salmon Platter with Crème Fraîche,
Minced Shallots or Chives, Capers, and
Dark Rye Bread

IF PASSED HORS D'OEUVRES ARE AN OPTION

Stuffed Roasted Mushrooms

Crab Cakes with Romesco Sauce
(*page 162*)

Horseradish-Crusted Hanger Steak with
Roasted Garlic Aioli on Crostini
(*page 198*)

DESSERTS

Holiday Cookies and Biscotti

Little Chocolate Spice Cakes
(*page 199*)

DRINKS

Mexican Hot Chocolate

Mulled Cider or Wine

Eggnog

Champagne, Cava, Prosecco, or
Other Sparkling Wine

"stand-up" salad with green goddess dip

Among California's many contributions to the American salad lexicon, green goddess dressing must surely ra nk high. The potent and tangy concoction inspired this dip, which is featured in this unexpected but delightful stand-up hors d'oeuvre salad. Thinned with a little buttermilk, the dip becomes a very nice dressing for cold seafood, chicken, or vegetables. Serves 8

1 large egg

2 large egg yolks

2 tablespoons white tarragon vinegar

4 oil-packed anchovy fillets, chopped

1 tablespoon fresh lemon juice

2 teaspoons Dijon mustard

1 garlic clove, peeled and chopped

1 cup canola oil or other light oil

½ cup chopped fresh flat-leaf parsley

2 tablespoons chopped fresh tarragon leaves

¼ cup snipped chives

2 scallions, white and tender green parts, trimmed and chopped

½ pound plain, mild goat cheese, softened, or ½ cup buttermilk (see Note)

Kosher salt

3 Belgian endives, cored and separated

Tender inner leaves of 3 heads of romaine lettuce

1. In a food processor, combine the egg, yolks, vinegar, anchovies, lemon juice, mustard, and garlic and process until smooth. With the motor running, gradually add the oil through the feed tube; the mixture will thicken. Add the parsley, tarragon, chives, and scallions and pulse to blend into the sauce; do not overprocess—some flecks of green should remain. Add the cheese and pulse again until just blended. Adjust the seasoning, adding salt if necessary. Transfer the dip to a container, cover, and chill for several hours or overnight.

2. Spoon the dip into a bowl and set the bowl on a platter. Surround the bowl with the endive and romaine and serve immediately.

This is also a pretty way to display other crudités: Nestle in small bunches of radishes, carrots, or stringed snap peas. In warm weather, select a large, round serving basket and place small ice packs in the bottom. Cover with linen napkins or a tea towel, hiding the ice packs, and place the bowl of green goddess dressing in the center. Stand the larger, darker green romaine leaves around the perimeter of the basket. Continue to place the lighter green leaves around the bowl, with the smallest ones nearest the center. You may serve this simply with hearts of romaine or add Belgian endive, tucking them into the lettuce leaves. Be sure to stand all the leaves upright, core ends down. The entire presentation looks like a big green daisy.

Note: To use this as a salad dressing rather than a dip, omit the goat cheese and blend in ½ cup buttermilk instead.

horseradish-crusted hanger steak
with roasted garlic aioli

You may prepare all the components for this hors d'oeuvre in advance. But wait to assemble until you're ready to serve—you don't want the steak to turn brown or the crostini to get soggy! Serves 6 people (around 2 pieces each)

3 large unpeeled garlic cloves
1 teaspoon lemon juice
Salt
Freshly ground black pepper
½ teaspoon Dijon mustard
2 very fresh egg yolks
½ cup extra virgin olive oil, at room temperature
1 hanger steak (about 6 ounces)

1 tablespoon freshly grated horseradish or well-drained prepared horseradish
2 tablespoons olive oil plus additional for drizzling on the crostini
1 small baguette
Kosher or sea salt
1 bunch of arugula or watercress
Finely chopped chives, for garnish

For the Aioli:

Roast the garlic in a 350°F oven until very soft, about 15 minutes. When cool, peel and mash in a small bowl. Whisk with the lemon juice, ¼ teaspoon of salt, a pinch of pepper, and the mustard. Then whisk in the egg yolks. While whisking, drizzle the extra virgin olive oil into the egg yolks in a very thin, steady stream. Chill, tightly covered, until ready to serve. Serve within 8 hours.

For the Hanger Steak:

Season the steak with salt and pepper. Rub in the horseradish. Heat the olive oil in a sauté pan over high heat until nearly smoking. Carefully place the steak in the pan and sear on all sides until well browned and medium-rare (125 to 130°F). Rest on a rack or plate for at least 5 minutes, until ready to serve. This may be done up to an hour in advance.

For the Crostini:

Slice the baguette into very thin (⅛-inch) slices. Place in a single layer on a cookie sheet and drizzle with olive oil, then season lightly with kosher or sea salt and pepper. Bake at 300°F until dry and very lightly browned.

To Assemble:

1. Cutting across the grain, carve the hanger steak into thin slices. Cut the slices into pieces roughly the size of the crostini.

2. Spread a little aioli (¼ teaspoon or so) on a crostini. Place a small piece of arugula or watercress on the aioli and place a small slice of steak on top of the arugula/watercress.

3. Finish with a second, tiny dollop of aioli and sprinkle with chives. Serve right away at room temperature.

little chocolate spice cakes

These little cakes are as much fun to make as they are to eat—and they look terrific.
They don't require plates or utensils, and as such are a perfect end to a holiday cocktail party.
The spice notes and bittersweet chocolate also pair well with many red wines, particularly
reds with high fruit and low tannins. The recipe can be doubled easily.
Makes 24, serves 12 (2 each)

1 cup unbleached all-purpose flour

1 teaspoon baking powder

½ teaspoon ground cinnamon

¼ teaspoon ground cloves

¼ teaspoon finely ground black pepper

Pinch of salt

¾ cup cold water

5 ounces (1¼ sticks) unsalted butter

½ cup unsweetened cocoa powder

2 ounces semisweet chocolate chips

⅓ cup bourbon or whiskey

1½ teaspoons instant coffee (we use instant espresso)

1 cup sugar

1 egg, lightly beaten

Glaze

4 ounces unsweetened chocolate

4 ounces semisweet chocolate

4 tablespoons (½ stick) unsalted butter

1. Preheat the oven to 325°F. Spray 2 mini-muffin pans (approximately 1½-inch diameter, 12 in each pan) with nonstick cooking spray. Sift together the flour, baking powder, spices, and salt. Set aside.

2. In a heavy-bottomed saucepan, combine the water, butter, cocoa powder, chocolate chips, bourbon or whiskey, and coffee, and set over medium heat. Stir until the butter and chocolate have just melted. Transfer to a large bowl and whisk in the sugar. Cool to room temperature and whisk in the egg. Fold in the dry ingredients and mix gently until no lumps remain.

3. Fill each muffin cup two thirds full. Bake for 20 to 25 minutes, or until a toothpick inserted in the center comes out clean. Allow to cool and pop each one out, using a paring knife to gently loosen if necessary.

To Glaze:

1. In a double boiler, melt together the unsweetened chocolate, semisweet chocolate, and butter. Stir until just combined and cool for a few minutes.

2. Dip the top of each cake in the glaze, then place on a cooling rack until the chocolate sets. The idea is to have a nice glossy top, without chocolate on the sides, so your guests don't end up with chocolate all over their fingers!

Holiday Parties: Going Small

Can't manage a big party or prefer something more intimate? Opt for something simpler at a less popular time:

* **HOST A "WRAP IT UP" PARTY:** Invite guests to stop by on a weeknight after holiday shopping, for supper (soup, salad, quiche, or lasagne), holiday cheer (wine, beer, and spiced cider), and communal gift wrapping. Provide ribbon, wrap, and tags.

* **START A TRADITION:** Get a group together to go to a local production of *The Nutcracker* or other holiday show. Serve cocktails and small plates beforehand. Make it an annual event and rotate the hosting.

* **GO ON A TREE HUNT:** Gather friends at a Christmas tree farm or tree stand to find just the right one. Exchange tree ornaments and take photos.

* **HAVE A SKATING PARTY:** Buy tickets at a local rink and invite guests to join you for an hour or two of skating. Follow with soup and crusty bread, holiday cookies, cocoa, and hot cider back at your place.

when the party's at the office

✦ ✦ ✦

Thankfully, the days when the holiday office party was synonymous with wild behavior are passé. Today's party is more about socializing with coworkers and perhaps clients. Often spouses, significant others, and family members are included in the invitation as well. Whether the party is a casual get-together evening of cocktails and hors d'oeuvres at the end of the week or a formal dinner, treat this invitation as seriously as you would any social invitation you receive. Here are some tips for being at your office-party best:

- Check your calendar and respond to the invitation right away. If your invitation includes your spouse or significant other, let the organizer know if he or she will be coming and supply his or her name.
- Let your spouse or significant other know what to wear, and give him or her a heads-up on the names of bosses or colleagues who are likely to be there.
- Arrive—and leave—at the designated times.
- At the party, don't ditch your significant other and hang with your office mates. Introduce him or her to your colleagues and your boss, and include him or her in conversations.
- Try not to talk about work. It's a party!
- Keep the alcohol to a minimum, or stick to nonalcoholic options. It's tempting to overindulge, especially when the company is paying. You may not be working, but you are still in a position to be judged by bosses or colleagues and you don't want to draw negative attention to yourself.
- Thank your hosts and/or the organizer twice: once when you leave the party and again, with a note, the next day.

family holidays and parties

✦ ✦ ✦

It's important to involve children in family celebrations and traditions at an early age and to include them in the planning. Kids love having the opportunity to help. Preschoolers can make place cards using stickers; five-year-olds can fold napkins; seven-year-olds can help set the table. Don't go for perfection—believe us, your guests will all applaud their contributions. Kids will enjoy the party more if they know what's expected of them and what they can expect:

- Give your kids a heads-up on who will be at the party.
- Let them know what the basic schedule will be.
- Let them know if they have any particular jobs or responsibilities.

Even at a family party, where everyone shares child supervision, consider hiring a sitter to make the party more enjoyable for all.

kid-friendly holiday food

✦ ✦ ✦

Holiday parties often include the kids, so if you'd like them to come along, be sure to say so on your invitation. Consider, too, whether you want to hire a "kid wrangler" (see page 54), who makes sure that the little ones are fed and entertained—a thoughtful touch for moms and dads. Add some kid-friendly food and have it available at a low table or station just for them:

+ Small filled sandwiches, cut into shapes (use cookie cutters)

✦ Crudités and dip
✦ Cheese cubes and crackers
✦ Holiday cookies in the shape of stars, Christmas trees, bells, dreidels—with lots of festive sprinkles
✦ Clear juices like white grape or white cranberry (think spills), maybe mixed with ginger ale and topped with a maraschino cherry (all kids love the cherry!)

hostess gifts

✦ ✦ ✦

It's the giving time of year and you can expect some guests to bring a hostess gift. Decide ahead of time where you'd like to put these gifts—choose someplace safe where cards won't get lost—and save them to open later. Thank the giver when you accept the gift and thank her again with a short note:

Dear Nell,

So delighted you could make the party—you looked smashing! The lighthouse ornament is just charming—a great memento of our girls' weekend at the beach.

Thanks and cheers,

Beth

Why a thank-you for a thank-you? Since you didn't have a chance to open the gift and only offered a generic "Thanks," you need to acknowledge the actual gift personally, with a note. (Just don't send a thank-you *gift* for a thank-you gift, or the cycle will never end!)

hostess favors

✦ ✦ ✦

Favors for your guests are a sweet gesture, but by no means a must. Your gift to your guests is your party, so even if you're bursting with generosity and your budget can handle it, don't let your favors overwhelm. Keep them simple: a little bag of holiday cookies or spiced nuts, a two-truffle box of chocolates, an ornament painted with guests' names in glitter, candy canes, a $1 scratch-and-win lottery ticket (wrapped and ribboned).

post family traditions all year long

✦ ✦ ✦

Yes, Christmas and Thanksgiving get lots of attention as big family celebrations, but we make sure the rest of the year's holidays are occasions for highly anticipated family get-togethers. What we truly love is being able to be together and repeat the rituals and traditions that help bind us as a family. Here's how the Post family celebrates holidays all year long:

NEW YEAR'S EVE: We've been doing a "progressive" dinner party since 2000 with a group of four families who are close friends. Progressive dinner parties are movable feasts, where you travel from house to house as you go from course to course. First we head to Aunt Sara's for hors d'oeuvres, then to our close friends the Aronssons' for a lovely sit-down dinner with a gorgeously decorated table. (How they manage to fit all of us into her dining room, we don't know!) The last stop is at our parents' house for a New Year's Eve bonfire. That's when the party opens up to *everyone*—extended friends, *their* friends, kids, and dogs. All year long, people bring them scrap wood and add it to the pile. We light the bonfire around 11:00 P.M., make s'mores, and drink Champagne and hot cider. At midnight, we throw in The Box, a box filled with slips of paper inscribed with our wishes or our "be gones" for the New Year. Hugs, kisses, and many toasts follow "Happy New Year!" Meanwhile, back at the house, a buffet table is piled high with smoked ham, sliced baguettes, a smoked salmon platter, a cheese platter, grapes, clementines, and cookies. It's a great way to start the new year!

MARDI GRAS: For several years, Lizzie's apartment overlooked the local Mardi Gras parade route. She'd invite friends (and parents) to hang out the windows to watch the parade and catch beads, while treating us to some great New Orleans music, cocktails, and hors d'oeuvres.

EASTER: We celebrate this holiday at our grandmother's in New Jersey, a treat because it's usually spring there while Vermont is still mired in freezing mud. When we were small, we spent the day decorating eggs and hunting for jelly beans hidden by Poppa John, Dad, and Uncle David. These days, there are no little ones hunting Easter eggs, but it's a chance for all of our mom's family to come together, enjoy baked ham, fettuccine alfredo, and asparagus with

oceans of hollandaise sauce. Dessert is the incredible, edible "Egg:" a melon-shaped mold lined with ladyfingers and filled with chocolate mousse. Unmolded, it's covered with whipped cream and decorated with tiny violets and daffodils (our job). Fabergé, eat your heart out!

FOURTH OF JULY: This is our Post grandfather Poppy's birthday. On Martha's Vineyard, that means watching the Edgartown parade and then heading to the beach for a clambake or picnic with a red, white, and blue dessert—yearly variations of strawberries, raspberries, blueberries, whipped cream, and Poppy's favorite, vanilla ice cream. Fireworks are a must.

HALLOWEEN: We have a great friend who throws an annual potluck Halloween party—costumes required and prizes given. A former DJ, he plays amazing music, and pirates, mermaids, witches, and zombies shake the house down.

THANKSGIVING: This is our family's time to host. A while back, our grandmother Granny Pat gave Mom all the Thanksgiving plates, platters, and tablecloths she had purchased for her first Thanksgiving in 1950. She had a huge family, so our Thanksgivings can handle twenty-five people. When we were little, our job was to make place cards using stickers, leaves, acorns, and lots of little craft items. Mom has saved them all, and now we rummage in the box to find "Aunt Carroll," "Uncle David," and "Granny Pat." Mom and Dad cook the fresh Vermont turkey, Granny Pat makes the gravy—no one else does it quite as well—and the guests all bring their favorite sides and desserts. Anna makes her famous apple pie, which she mastered when she was about ten. Football or a classic movie round out the day.

And if that wasn't enough celebrating, Friday evening our parents host a leftover party. Friends bring their leftovers from Thanksgiving dinner along with their leftover visiting relatives—a great way to mix up the generations and get to know your friends' extended families.

CHRISTMAS: We celebrate Christmas with the Post family at our grandparents' house, North Hill, in Waterbury, Vermont. The "out of Vermont" relatives arrive a day or two ahead for skiing and visiting. On Christmas day, we gather at North Hill around 1:00 P.M. for the big present exchange, an annual draw by generations: parents to siblings and spouses, and cousins to cousins and spouses (a great way to simplify gift giving in a big family!). Then it's on to the roast feast: standing rib roast, gravy, green beans, and Poppy's famous onions in brown sauce, with pie and ice cream for dessert. China and wineglasses that belonged to our great-grandparents are lovingly used, hand washed, and put away until next Christmas.

it's time for cake

Children love parties! Their happiness and enthusiasm at celebratory events is infectious. For adults, watching kids eagerly dive into special occasions is a privilege and a joy. Besides being fun, children's parties are important because kids discover their social selves and learn about being gracious hosts and gracious guests and rising to the occasion.

✦ ✦ ✦

what kind of party?

✦ ✦ ✦

In planning a children's party, keep the following in mind:

✦ Whether a birthday, a holiday, or a special occasion, base the party on your child's interests. If your daughter likes circuses, set that as your theme and perhaps hire a juggler to entertain. If your son's into sports, have your party in a play space where he and his buddies can run around. Your kid's a fish? Think pool party or water park outing.

✦ Your child's age and temperament will determine the party details: how many guests to invite, how long the party lasts, and whether you host the event at home or not. Young kids like it simple—friends, fun food—with activities they can all enjoy.

✦ Don't be pressured into "keeping up with the Joneses." Yes, it's tempting to go all out for Johnny's birthday, but be realistic about what you can afford. Consider, too, the message an extravagant blowout sends to a child—what could you possibly do for an encore?

the birthday party

✦ ✦ ✦

Birthday parties are the primary school for learning how to be a good host and a good guest, give and receive gifts, and say thank you graciously. That's why it's good to involve your child in the planning from the start. It may be as simple as asking her whom she'd like to invite or what kind of cake she'd like to have (watch out— you may get stuck coming up with a chocolate cake with rainbow icing, as our mom did for Anna's fourth birthday), but let her know that her input is important. And don't worry if it's not what you had in mind. It's your job to be open and flexible but also realistic. Consider asking limited questions. Instead of "What would you like?" ask, "Would you like chocolate or vanilla?" Remember: It's her party. Base the party on your child's interests—dinosaurs, trucks, dolls, movie or book characters, or sports. Think about it from her perspective—even at a young age she may have a better handle than you do on what her friends would enjoy. After all, happy, entertained kids make your job that much easier! As your child gets older, involve her in more of the details of the guest list, activities, and menu. By the time she's eleven or twelve, she'll be well on her way to being a great hostess.

where's the party?

✦ ✦ ✦

Home is the usual place for a party for children under six. Most guests will have visited your home on playdates, making it a familiar space. Is there enough room for activities and play and an area to serve refreshments? Keep in mind that kids do better sitting down at a table (although a picnic on a big blanket on the floor is fun, too). Your yard is another option, but have a backup plan in case of bad weather.

If your apartment or house is just too small or your group is old enough, a destination party could be the perfect solution. You can rent out kids' play spaces or recreation centers, or hold the party in a park. Or take the group to a local site that hosts kid parties: movie theaters, roller- or ice-skating rinks, mini golf courses, science museums, art centers, and hotel pools. Some stores offer crafts—beading, pottery painting, or Build-A-Bear.

Surprise! Or Not?

Four reasons to avoid a surprise party with children:

1. It's difficult for young children to keep a secret. **2.** If the secret gets out, someone is sure to feel guilty. **3.** Much of the fun of a birthday party is the anticipation—it's a shame for the birthday boy or girl to miss that. **4.** If the birthday child doesn't like the party that was planned or the guests invited, there could be tears instead of smiles.

who's invited?

✦ ✦ ✦

The old rule of thumb of inviting age plus one is still a good one—although we've been to several kids' parties where the entire preschool class was invited. Of course, consider your child's temperament—a shy six-year-old may want to invite only one or two friends.

As with any party, keep the basics in mind:

✦ **THE TYPE OF PARTY YOU'RE PLANNING:** An indoor supper may restrict the number of kids you can invite. An outdoor picnic supper may open the opportunity to invite more.

✦ **YOUR SPACE:** How many kids will fit comfortably in your space—for refreshments, play, and activities?

✦ **YOUR BUDGET:** Can you afford four or fourteen? You may be able to invite more kids to a party at home than to a party space off-site, where you'll be charged not only for the use of the space but for each child.

inviting the whole class

✦ ✦ ✦

It's a question everyone asks: Do you invite the whole class to the party or can you omit a few? Whether it's a school class, team, or scout troop, when inviting a group the most important thing is to invite *everyone*. Your child needs to understand that "everyone" includes children she may not get along with—and that she needs to greet her not so favorites as enthusiastically as she does her best friends. To exclude one or two—for whatever reason—is *not* an option.

On the other hand, when your child is entertaining a smaller group of friends, it's important for him to learn how to spare others' feelings—that there are ways to have a party without making others feel bad. Here's how:

✦ Use clear-cut groupings, such as just the T-ball team or ballet class, or all girls or boys.

✦ *Don't* have your child pass out invitations at school: Either send invitations through the mail or make calls to invite individually.

What to Do with Brothers and Sisters?

Most kids don't want to miss their brother or sister's party. We were always a part of each other's birthdays. Here are some other tips to consider:

✳ Enlist an older sibling to help out with games or serving cake. ✳ If your siblings are close in age, by all means let the brother or sister invite a playmate to the party so he or she doesn't feel left out. ✳ Younger children may need a sitter who can whisk them away if they get partied out too soon. ✳ Be sure to have party favors for siblings, too.

✦ Let your child know that he shouldn't discuss his get-together at school or in front of those who aren't invited or feelings will get hurt.

✦ When parents RSVP, you can clue them in that "it's going to be a small party" so they can avoid talking about it in front of other parents.

how long?

Probably the key to a successful children's party is defining how long it should be. Younger kids obviously have lower thresholds. Don't forget: Your little party host or hostess will be wound up in anticipation of the big event—it's only natural. Try to factor in extra rest time and nutritious meals or snacks, or schedule the party for after nap time. Even so, the added excitement may put him into sensory overload. Keeping the event short will help prevent party burnout.

As a parent, take a look at your child and the guest list and be realistic. Here's what's reasonable for different ages:

✦ 1 to 2   1 hour
✦ 3   1½ hours
✦ 4 to 5   2 hours
✦ 6 to 8   2½ hours
✦ 8 to 10   2 to 3 hours

"let's play..."

✦ ✦ ✦

You can never plan too many activities for your kids' parties. Better to have more than enough to do and not enough time to do it than to find yourself desperately casting about midparty for something to entertain the kids. Children five and under have relatively short attention spans, so you can't count on keeping them occupied with one activity for the entire party. As one mom told us, "At one of the first birthday parties I had for my child, the activity I'd planned was over in ten minutes." (Of course, if it's a hit, don't call a halt!)

Plan a schedule for the entire party, with several types of activities. Start with unstructured activities to occupy guests until everyone arrives, basically something that's easy to join in—coloring or sticker

---

The Spider Web

This is a fun activity—inside or outside.

FOR EACH CHILD YOU'LL NEED:

✳ A ball of string or yarn ✳ A goody bag (the birthday child can help assemble them).
✳ A stick (Popsicle or Mother Nature's finest) labeled with the child's name

Secure the string to the goody bag. Hide it and then start unraveling the string, wrapping it around trees and bushes outside; furniture, door handles, and other stationary objects, high and low, inside. Weave the string over and under, creating a maze. Make sure you end your weaving at a common starting point. Attach the string to a stick. Repeat with each bag, weaving a tangled, giant spider web.

TO PLAY:

Give each child a stick and tell them to wind up their string to find their prize.
Be sure to take pictures!

---

books, blocks, Legos, a dress-up box—then move on to more active or structured games or activities like freeze tag, pin the tail on the donkey, or scavenger hunts. Always have a couple of backup activities as well—a few good storybooks to read aloud, coloring books to draw in, chalk for the sidewalk, or a movie the kids can watch. Schedule time for refreshments and opening gifts (*if* you plan to open presents at the party; some parents make that a postparty activity—see Opening Gifts: During the Party or Later?, page 218).

celebrating with spongebob

✦ ✦ ✦

Does your child love Clifford the Big Red Dog? Or Dora the Explorer? Go to the Web to find entire parties built around book, movie, or TV characters, including activities and decorating ideas. At **www.pbsparents.org** you'll find a wealth of information on hosting theme parties based on PBS characters, all focused on what's age appropriate. For just about everything else, there's the Birthday Express catalog, also online at **www.birthdayexpress.com**, where you can order entire party kits, including paper goods, decorations, masks, party bags, and more—all featuring a favorite character or theme.

max the magician

✦ ✦ ✦

It may seem like the perfect solution to keeping the kids entertained—but before you hire a clown or magician, think about your age group. Most four- or five-year-olds won't last through a forty-five-minute magic show, and people in costumes, no matter how friendly, can be scary. That said, a storyteller or craftperson might suit your group perfectly. (We've seen kid-friendly jugglers thrill tiny guests by teaching them to balance plates on a stick!) *Note:* Be sure to check references before hiring anyone who works with children.

getting help

✦ ✦ ✦

At parties for one- to three-year-olds, parents or caretakers often stay for the duration of the party to keep separation issues at bay. But by age four, children are usually dropped off and left until the end of the party. Having another adult or two to help you with games, serving, cleanup, or a guest who might need a little extra attention will make the party go more smoothly. Pay the sitter, but give a relative or friend a gift and a thank-you note instead. Start by thinking about one additional adult for every four kids and adjust that number depending on:

✦ The age and number of kids in attendance
✦ The site of the party
✦ The length of the party
✦ The activities planned

Note: If the party is held at a site where there's water, for safety reasons it's imperative that a sufficient number of adult swimmers or a certified lifeguard is present. Make sure your invitation lets parents know that swimming will be involved.

childproof your party area

✦ ✦ ✦

For the younger set, make sure breakable items are out of reach and the play area is safe. Very young children—four and under—may have a hard time sharing toys with party guests. Simply put away favorite toys during the party. If you plan to be outside, make sure the yard is clear of rocks and branches, tools and grills have been put away, standing water has been emptied, and play equipment is in good condition.

As much as your pet is a member of the family, sometimes it's easier if Max or Fluffy isn't in attendance at the party. Some children have pet allergies, are afraid of animals, or don't know how to behave around pets. Plus pets can distract your attention when it needs to be on the kids. Arrange for your pets to visit a friend, go to doggie (or kitty) day care, or be confined in a place away from the party.

birthday cake...and more

✦ ✦ ✦

For most kids, birthdays are all about the cake! By three years old, it's time to ask your child what kind he'd like. If you're not a baker, don't despair. Your local supermarket bakery can provide a cake in almost any size and flavor and even decorate it to match the theme of the party, from trucks to movie characters. Since most kids go for the icing, try to have enough "roses" (or other icing decoration) to go around. Ice cream usually accompanies cake, and having a choice of flavors will make it easy to satisfy all.

For older kids, it's fun to do "make your own sundaes" with sprinkles, candies, sauces, whipped cream, and cherries; it's messy but memorable. Milk, ginger ale, or punch rounds out the refresh-ments. Yes, it's usually a sugar extravaganza—which is why refreshments are served at the *end* of the party.

Depending on the time of day or the party, you might want to add a meal. If you want the focus to be on the big finale (cake!), keep the meal simple and easy to eat:

✦ Sandwiches
  ✦ Cut in shapes (triangles, rectangles, diamonds, stars, hearts—cookie cutters make it easy!)
  ✦ Egg or tuna salad, turkey, ham, cream cheese and/or jelly
✦ Grilled cheese
✦ Wraps

Low-Sugar Treats

When you want to cut back on the sugar, serve:

✳ Cheese bites and apple wedges with whole grain crackers ✳ Pretzels ✳ Bread sticks ✳ Popcorn ✳ Hummus and toasted pita chips ✳ Mild guacamole or mild salsa and tortilla chips ✳ Ranch dip and carrot sticks ✳ Fruit cups with pineapple, watermelon, grapes ✳ Celery sticks filled with cream cheese ✳ Mini muffins (choose low-sugar ones) ✳ Oatmeal cookies and milk ✳ Fruit smoothies (keep the portions small)

- Pizza
    - Cheese and/or pepperoni
    - Make your own on English muffins
    - Add your own toppings
    - Cut the pizza into small pieces that children can handle with ease
- Hot dogs and hamburgers
- Fruit: strawberries, grapes, apple or melon wedges
- Little cheese crackers (these come in all shapes—fish, bunnies—and fill out the plate)

other yummy
kid-friendly party food

- Macaroni and cheese
- Spaghetti and little meatballs or just meatballs in sauce with French bread or garlic bread
- Mild chili with grated cheese and sour cream
- Quesadillas: The cheese can be a blend of jack and Cheddar
- Tacos: shredded chicken or ground beef with sliced romaine lettuce, sour cream, shredded cheese, mild salsa

- Cheesy twice-baked potatoes
- Cheese fondue with bread cubes, apples, and little potatoes for dipping
- Chocolate fondue with strawberries and cake squares
- Cake, cupcakes, cookies, and ice cream sandwiches

Allergy Alert

* Provide information about food on the invitation, so parents can plan meals or let you know of any allergies. Mention the basic menu, such as "Join us for pizza—and cake and ice cream!"
* You can also ask parents about allergies when they RSVP.
* Because of the prevalence of peanut allergies, skip the PB and J.

party favors—or not?

Favors aren't a must, but they are popular at birthday parties—and if it's a tradition in your neighborhood, it's probably a good idea to follow suit. Party favors certainly don't need to be expensive or elaborate—in fact, most parents agree that extravagant favors are out. Simply put together a goody bag with treats and a couple of little toys, or something more lasting, like a T-shirt or hat, a mini flashlight, crayons, jump ropes, or simple kites. One host we know handed out real but quite inexpensive harmonicas—a huge hit! If the party occurs around a holiday, such as July 4 or Halloween, include favors and toys around those themes.

Putting together goody bags is also another way to involve the birthday child in the preparations (see Fabulous Favors, below). Decorating the bags with markers or stickers and filling them will keep him busy before the party. Favors can be put at each child's place at the table, or the birthday child can give them out when saying thank you and good-bye to each guest at the end of the party.

fabulous favors

Take your child to the dime store or a toy store and give him a budgeted amount to spend on each bag. This is a great way for you and your child to get creative with your goody bags. Among the fun, inexpensive toys and favors you can find:

+ Fun erasers
+ Stickers
+ Disguises: fake mustaches, wax lips
+ Anything miniature: tiny art supplies, mini notebooks and pencils, little games or books
+ Tiny windup animals or little rubber ducks
+ Surprise balls
+ Noisemakers, party poppers
+ Glitter vials or pens
+ Sponge capsule animals
+ Candy: at least one piece of wrapped and lollipops for little ones (ages 3+)

opening gifts:
during the party or later?

✦ ✦ ✦

There's no definitive rule of thumb regarding this issue. Here are some things to consider, especially for children less than six years of age:

open at the party

pros:

+ Kids get to see the birthday boy open the present they brought.
+ The birthday boy thanks everyone in person at the time he opens the gifts.

cons:

+ The guests get bored.
+ The guests want to play with the presents right away, before the birthday boy has his turn first.
+ The birthday boy goes into sensory overload and has a meltdown in front of his guests.
+ There's the potential for fights or jealousy.

things to consider:

+ Bring some order to present opening by having everyone sit in a circle so they can see and hear what's going on.
+ Remind the kids they'll be getting their own party favors later.
+ Put the new toys or gifts away and out of sight until after the party.

open after the party

pros:

+ The emphasis is on the party and everyone having a good time and not on the gifts.
+ Your child has the chance to open the gifts slowly and appreciate each, one at a time.
+ You avoid any negative comments about gifts either from the birthday boy or the other guests.

cons:

+ The guests don't get to make the connection between their gift, the joy of giving, and the reaction of the birthday boy.
+ The birthday boy doesn't have the opportunity to thank the giver right there in person—an important skill to be learned.

things to consider:

+ As guests arrive, have your child thank them for the gift—unopened—and put it away on a shelf or table out of reach and even out of sight.
+ Write thank-you notes with your child as he opens gifts. Some parents won't allow their kids to play with the gifts until the note is sent!

the perfect combination: pizza-putt and a birthday

✦ ✦ ✦

Mini golf, pizza parlors, pool venues, movie theaters, roller- or ice-skating rinks, and craft centers often offer children's parties. No mess, no fuss, and kids over six love them! Here are some tips to make it a success:

+ Be sure the facility can accommodate your group.
+ As the host, you're responsible for all costs: tickets, equipment, supplies, and food. (Call ahead to see if there are all-inclusive group rates.)
+ Choose the menu or arrange for the food ahead of time.

+ Get an accurate head count—you'll be charged for the number of participants you contract for.
+ Have enough adult supervision—one adult for every four kids.
+ If you aren't providing transportation, **make sure each child has reliable transportation to and from the party site.**
+ *Always* carry contact information for parents or caregivers.
+ Save gift opening for later—even though that means a thank-you note for each gift.
+ Stay on-site until the last child is picked up.

perfect party manners:
how to help your child be a gracious host and guest

✦ ✦ ✦

Birthday parties are a great training ground, both for the birthday child and her guests. Parents can use these opportunities to help their children absorb and learn good party manners—which are really nothing more than everyday manners bumped up a notch, or a chance to use *all* our manners at once. Here are your goals:

the good host or hostess

✦ Is ready and greets everyone at the door.

✦ Includes everyone in the activities.

✦ Offers refreshments.

✦ Says "Good-bye" and "Thanks for coming" to each guest as they leave the party.

✦ Sends a thank-you note for presents that weren't opened at the party or if thanks weren't given in person.

the good guest

✦ Replies to the invitation right away. (Parents, you may have to help out here, but be sure to involve your child.)

✦ Arrives—and leaves—on time.

✦ Is prepared to join in, whatever the activity.

✦ Is careful and respectful with the host's house and belongings: no jumping on couches or feet on furniture; no touching of electronic equipment or objects on display.

✦ Follows the directions of any adults at the party.

✦ Lets an adult know if something spills or is broken.

✦ Gives—and *leaves*—a birthday present for the birthday boy.

✦ Says "Good-bye" and "Thank you" at the end of the party.

gifts and thank-yous

✦ ✦ ✦

Except for one- or two-year olds, all kids should be able to accept a gift and say "Thank you." You'll say it for your one- to two-year-old, and you'll prompt your three- to six-year-old, if necessary, but a seven-plus should be able to say thanks automatically. And what if your child receives a gift he doesn't like or already has? For the brutally honest three- to five-year-old, you'll have to be vigilant and nip any comments in the bud—stopping them at "Thank you." Before the party, talk to your six- to eight-year-old about how to react to a gift he doesn't like: Tell him to think of one positive thing to say about the gift, and be sure to say thank you! "Thanks for the sweatshirt. I really like this color blue."

kids' parties: avoid the most common parent pitfalls

✦ Don't ask guests to pool for an expensive gift, like a swing set.

✦ Follow up on invitations. Speak with each parent before the party to review some basic information:

  ✦ Drop-off and pickup times—be very clear!

  ✦ Phone number where they can be reached during the party.

  ✦ Any issues, like allergies.

✦ Call anyone you haven't heard from or anyone who's left a "yes" on your voice mail.

✦ Have enough food for unexpected guests (like an older or younger sibling of one of the guests).

Anna and Lizzie's
HOLIDAY TEA

One of our favorite childhood parties was a mother-daughter holiday tea in December. We each invited four friends, who in turn were asked to bring their mothers and favorite dolls. We baked holiday cookies and made lemon cake. While the moms had real tea in the dining room, we each had our own little table with a tea set for our friends and dolls. (Instead of tea, we had hot chocolate with tiny marshmallows.) This party was such a hit it became a tradition until we outgrew dolls!

- Don't invite all the parents. They end up partying and not helping. Usually, you'll want about one adult for every four kids.
- Be prepared for a meltdown—whether from a guest or the birthday girl.

- Have a backup plan in case a parent doesn't show up on time to pick up her child:
  - A phone number where parents or a caregiver can be reached.
  - Quiet activities for the kids.
  - Plans for a meal or a nap.

mrs. pettigrew's lemon cake

From *Tea, Recipes & Table Settings*, by Tricia Foley.
Makes one 7-inch round cake or 8-inch loaf

2 lemons
¾ cup sugar
8 tablespoons (1 stick) salted butter or
   margarine, softened

2 large eggs, beaten
¾ cup all-purpose flour
6 tablespoons milk
3 tablespoons sugar, for topping

1. Preheat the oven to 325°F. Grease and line a 7-inch round cake pan or 8-inch loaf pan with parchment or wax paper.

2. Grate the lemon rinds and set aside. Combine the juice of 1 lemon with 3 tablespoons of the sugar in a bowl and set in a warm place until the sugar dissolves and forms a syrup with the juice.

3. Cream the butter or margarine and the rest of the sugar together until light and fluffy. Add the beaten eggs, a little at a time, beating well after each addition. Stir in the grated lemon rind and flour; beat again thoroughly (the longer you beat, the softer the cake). Add the milk and beat again.

4. Pour into the prepared pan and bake for at least 1 hour; the cake should spring back when pressed gently in the center.

5. Immediately upon removing the cake from the oven, prick the top with a long-tined fork or thin skewer and pour the lemon juice–sugar syrup all over the top until completely covered.

6. Cool in the pan to allow the syrup to be soaked up and create a moist and tangy cake. Sprinkle with the 3 tablespoons sugar.

When we make this, we always use the loaf pan, dust the cake with confectioners' sugar, and slice it thinly to serve. It will serve about 8 when sliced ¾ inch; more if thinly sliced.

✳

hosting houseguests

having a guest stay in your home overnight is a chance to have a more personal visit. You can share your morning coffee, enjoy laid-back dinners or sophisticated nights out, or spend an afternoon by the pool catching up on each other's lives and sharing the good old days. A weekend with a good friend may be the ideal houseguest scenario, but in reality you're just as likely to find yourself hosting family members or your significant other's friends and family.

Successful visits hinge on communicating expectations. Clear communication between host and guest makes the visit a success, while ambiguity can cause tension and awkward moments.

✦ ✦ ✦

arrival and departure

✦ ✦ ✦

As the host, ask your houseguest when he plans to arrive and leave. Otherwise, saying, "Stay as long as you like!" may be taken literally. It's not rude to set boundaries; it's practical. "Of course you can come for the weekend! I'm booked for Friday; can you plan to arrive on Saturday morning? Will you need to be home Sunday night for work on Monday?" This direct approach lets both guest and host know what to expect—the host isn't left wondering if she needs to plan another day's worth of meals and activities. Conversely, if you're a guest and your host doesn't set a date or time, be sure to ask, "What dates would work for you?" or "When's your next free weekend?" Regardless of who sets the date, avoid extending your stay beyond what's been put on the calendar.

Once you've agreed on dates and times, follow up with an e-mail or a note to prevent any confusion. This is the time to let guests know what, if anything, you have planned for their stay. That way they can pack appropriately for a day of hiking, say, or dinner at a nice restaurant.

If your guests are coming by car, give them solid directions. Write the directions down and send them in advance—or provide your street address and zip code for a MapQuest or Google search or GPS coordinate. If guests are arriving by train or plane, discuss the options for getting to your house—being picked up by you or a car service, or taking a taxi or public transportation.

tour guide, chef, and innkeeper?

✦ ✦ ✦

As the host, you're the inside source on what activities and attractions are available in your area. The best agenda is a mix of things that both you and your guests enjoy. Have some ideas in mind before your guests arrive, rather than just saying, "What do you want to do?" when they show up. Local points of interest, parks, beaches, hikes, and bike rides are all things you can enjoy together or your guest can do separately. By suggesting options, you and your guest can create a schedule that includes "together time" as well as time for her to be on her own. Plan for some downtime too; guests will need it—and so will you!

Besides activities, plan your meals and make any restaurant reservations in advance. If you intend to cook, plan out your menus and stock your kitchen with whatever ingredients you need, and prepare as much food ahead of time as you can. This way, you'll be able to enjoy your guests rather than worry about what's for dinner.

The meal that's easiest to organize in advance is breakfast. One of the joys of a weekend away from home is being able to sleep late. Invite your guests to sleep in if they'd like, but if they're early risers, explain that they can just press the Start button on the coffeemaker and help themselves to cereal, toast, or any other breakfast items you have ready. Of course, if you're up before your guests, it's fine to go ahead and eat; just be there to greet them when they come to the table.

Set out the "help yourself" breakfast on the kitchen counter before you go to bed: Have all the bowls, plates, and utensils arranged like a mini buffet so your houseguests don't have to go rummaging through your cupboards. Write a little note: FRESH OJ AND MILK IN THE FRIDGE—HELP

YOURSELF! Something special like a coffee cake, favorite muffins, or a bowl of fresh strawberries makes breakfast more of a treat. If guests are staying two nights and leaving on Sunday, plan a real brunch as a send-off and ask if they'd like to join you at 10:00 or 11:00 A.M.

Lunch is also easy to organize. It can be as simple as arranging breads, meats, cheeses, lettuce, tomato, mayo, and mustards so that everyone can make their own sandwiches. You might buy lunch on the go if you're out exploring, or pack a picnic to take on a hike or a sail, to a park or the beach. (For picnic menus, see Chapter 11, A Breath of Fresh Air, page 151.)

That leaves dinner. Unless you wish, don't feel you have to cook dinner each night. Depending on when your guests arrive, it might be simpler to eat at a restaurant the first night, and plan something special at home for the second night. Often guests like to treat their hosts to a dinner out. If that's the case, thank them graciously, suggest some restaurant options, and offer to make the reservation for them. Otherwise, you can either treat your guests or split the bill, but this should be agreed upon ahead of time. If you're dining at home, choose a menu that won't keep you tied up in the kitchen all day. Stews, braises, lasagnes, and casseroles can be made ahead of time and reheated before serving. Add a salad and artisanal bread, a purchased pie or tart, and voilà, dinner practically takes care of itself.

Once your guests arrive, show them their room or sleeping area and the bathroom they'll use. If they're unfamiliar with your home, give them a quick tour: cabinets for towels and other items, light switches, the telephone, and kitchen appliances. Show them how to adjust the air conditioner or heater, if necessary. Then give them a chance to unpack and get settled. Also, let them know if they can use your washer and dryer, exercise equipment, bikes, TV, or Internet connection. Invite them to help themselves to snacks or beverages from the fridge during their stay, noting any foods that are off-limits: "Please help yourself to anything you see except the blueberries—they're for the pancakes tomorrow morning."

the guest room

✦ ✦ ✦

Getting a guest room ready is one of our favorite things to do—it's like wrapping a present for your guests. The best way to know how comfy and well equipped your guest room is, is to spend a night there as a guest yourself. There's nothing like firsthand knowledge to tell you the blind is broken, the mattress is sagging, or the closet door is squeaking. Here's a list of basics that every guest room should have, as well as a few extras that we think make guests feel especially welcome:

in the guest room or sleeping area

✦ A bed, sofa bed, futon, or air bed, made up with clean sheets and pillowcases
✦ An extra blanket at the foot of the bed
✦ A good reading light
✦ An alarm clock
✦ Good curtains or blinds on the windows
✦ A water carafe and glass on the night table
✦ A box of tissues on the nightstand
✦ An empty wastebasket
✦ Wooden coat hangers with bars or pressure clips for trousers; plastic hangers for dresses

in the bathroom

✦ Fresh bath towels, face towels, washcloths, bath mat
✦ Fresh soap
✦ Glasses for brushing teeth and drinking water
✦ New roll of toilet paper in the dispenser and an unopened one in the cabinet
✦ Box of tissues
✦ Shampoo, bath oil, bath powder, and hand lotion on the washstand
✦ New toothbrush, just in case your guest has forgotten her own, and toothpaste
✦ Headache and stomachache medications in the guest bathroom medicine cabinet; extra feminine supplies in a drawer or cupboard

nice touches

✦ A welcome note
✦ A small vase of flowers
✦ Candle and matches
✦ A plate of little cookies or a few chocolates
✦ A book you think your guest might enjoy— local history, fabulous gardens, short stories
✦ Current magazines

- Two pillows for each guest—one medium-firm and one soft
- A clothes brush, lint roller, and mini sewing kit
- A luggage rack
- A bathrobe and slippers
- A television with remote
- An area map
- A calendar
- Games and toys for kids

no guest room?

✦ ✦ ✦

If you live in a one-bedroom apartment or a house with no guest room, you can still play host. A sofa bed, futon, or air bed can be set up in the living room or den or, if the visit isn't lengthy, children can be doubled up to free up a room. Don't move out of your own room so you can give it to your guests, though—it could make them feel they're imposing.

You should also warn guests in advance that they won't have a separate room or will have to share. Some guests may be perfectly fine with sleeping on a sofa or air bed in the den, while others may decide to stay at an inn or hotel instead.

when you're the guest

✦ ✦ ✦

Being a guest in someone's home calls for a little extra sensitivity and awareness. Respect the agreed-upon arrival and departure times. While your host is sure to want you to feel at home, remember that it's *her* home: Don't use or borrow without permission, keep your room and bath tidy, and don't snoop. Be an enthusiastic participant and offer to help out, especially at mealtimes. And be a little self-sufficient—don't expect your host to entertain you every minute. It's a long-standing tradition that overnight guests bring or send a gift and follow up with a bread-and-butter letter (aka a thank-you note).

the golden rules for houseguests

✦ ✦ ✦

definitely do:

✦ make your visit short and sweet. Tell your host when you'll arrive and when you'll depart. Take cues from your host, but keep your visit to no more than three nights.

✦ bring your own toiletries.

✦ make your bed and clean up after yourself. Keep your bathroom tidy, especially if you're sharing it with other people. Clean up any ring in the tub, shaving cream residue in the basin, hair on any object or surface, or dirt on the soap.

✦ offer to help out, especially in the kitchen (unless your host objects).

✦ be adaptable. Be ready for anything—or for nothing. Whatever agenda the host sets, follow along happily.

✦ act like you're enjoying yourself.

✦ offer to pitch in for groceries if you're staying more than two or three nights.

✦ double-check to make sure you have all your belongings before you leave.

✦ bring or send a gift, or treat your host to a night out instead.

✦ send a handwritten thank-you note following your visit.

definitely don't:

✦ ask to bring your pet. If you must travel with your pet, inquire about a good kennel in the area or offer to stay in a hotel. This also gives your host an opening to invite your pet if she wishes.

✦ accept an invitation from someone else during your visit without first checking with your host.

✦ use your host's phone, computer, or any other equipment without asking.

✦ use more than your share of hot water.

✦ snoop.

✦ leave the toilet seat up.

how to leave the bed

✦ ✦ ✦

Remove the sheets, fold them, place them at the foot of the bed, and pull the blanket and spread up neatly so that the bed will look "made." This will make life easier for your host.

If you're close friends, ask for fresh sheets and make the bed. It's a nice gesture and it saves your host from having to do it later.

saying thank you

✦ ✦ ✦

Regardless of how you do it, giving a gift to your host is a must for any houseguest. For an overnight stay, something simple like a bottle of good wine is fine. A longer stay merits something a little more elaborate. You can bring the gift with you and present it to your host when you arrive, or buy it during your stay once you've gotten a better idea of what your host might need, or send it as soon as possible after you return home.

In lieu of a gift, you could also treat your hosts to a dinner out if you think they'd prefer it. If you decide to do this, let your hosts know in advance of your visit so it becomes part of the game plan. Let them suggest a restaurant; they can also make the reservation if that's more convenient for everybody.

The other must for overnight guests is to send a handwritten thank-you note afterward. An e-mail or a phone call once you've returned home is fine, as long as it's followed by the note.

Choosing the Perfect Gift for a Great Host

What does she like? Look around her house: What's her style? What colors stand out? What are her hobbies? If you enjoy shopping, look for a gift during your visit. Otherwise, think about what's easy to pack, or ship it upon returning home.

twenty-five great gift ideas
for your host

✦ ✦ ✦

You can take these gift ideas and adapt them according to the length of your stay. For example, you might give a houseplant in a pretty pot for an overnight stay, but bump it up to an orchid for a weekend visit. Give martini glasses and a shaker for a two- to three-night stay, and for a longer stay add gin (or vodka) and vermouth.

FOR AN OVERNIGHT STAY

Book of interest to the host

Set of nicely packaged herbs and spices or a selection of peppercorns and sea salts

Picture frame with a picture taken during your visit and sent later

Packages of cocktail napkins with a serving tray or wineglass charms

For an avid cook, a collection of specialized kitchen tools

Twelve-pack of the best local microbrew

Set of monogrammed soaps

For a golfer, a dozen golf balls

Houseplant in a permanent, decorative pot

FOR A WEEKEND STAY (TWO TO THREE NIGHTS)

Set of cloth napkins and decorative napkin rings

continued on next page

Themed gift basket, such as: playing cards, jacks, board game, crayons and paper, DVD movie, popcorn mix, a current best seller for a "rainy day" basket

Gift certificate to your hosts' favorite restaurant

Any locally made specialty from your area: Vermont maple syrup, Virginia peanut brittle, New Orleans chicory coffee or pralines, artisanal cheeses, specialty chocolates

Bonsai tree

Set of personalized note cards

Crystal or handmade wood or pottery nut/olive bowl

For an avid cook, a collection of specialized kitchen tools paired with a cookbook

(Monogrammed) linen hand towels

Twelve-pack of the best local brew with (monogrammed) pilsner glasses

FOR AN EXTENDED STAY OR FOR THE HOST WHO WENT ALL OUT

For someone with a cabin in the woods: supplies for your host's favorite outdoor activity such as fly-fishing, hiking, or camping

For someone with a beach house: (monogrammed) beach towels, hats, sunscreen and/or flip-flops, all packed in a sturdy, (monogrammed) tote bag

Lobster pot, lobster bibs, nutcrackers, corn holders, nice melamine or acrylic plates and utensils, along with a gift certificate to the local fish market

Spa gift certificate

Martini glasses and shaker paired with bottles of top-shelf gin or vodka and vermouth, your favorite martini recipe and the ingredients, and cocktail napkins, olives, nuts, or nibbles

Set of high thread–count sheets with monogrammed pillowcases to match

be invited back

Part of the fun of entertaining is that it's a reciprocal thing: You invite guests, and then your guests invite you in return. As important as it is to be a good host, it's equally important to shine as a guest. So here's a little polish for your partygoing manners. Being a good guest starts the minute you receive an invitation, whether it shows up in an envelope or in your e-mail inbox. Mais, oui, your party manners start even before the event.

◆ ◆ ◆

rsvp

✦ ✦ ✦

French for *Repondez s'il vous plaît* or, in English, "Please reply," these four little letters are the not-so-secret code signaling that your hosts want to know whether or not you can make their event. Most invitations have some sort of reply mechanism—an enclosed response card, a phone number, an e-mail address, or mailing address. Reply promptly, preferably within a day or two of receiving your invitation. It's a basic courtesy, and will be truly appreciated by your hosts.

is that your final answer?

Check your calendar carefully before you RSVP, because once you've sent your response you're committed. Changing a "yes" to a "no" is only acceptable if there's an illness or injury, a death in the family, or an unavoidable professional or business conflict. In such a case, call your hosts right away and explain. Canceling because you have a "better" offer is a surefire way to get dropped from *everyone's* guest lists, while being a no-show is just plain unacceptable. Changing a "no" to a "yes" is okay only if it won't upset the hosts' arrangements. Unless it's someone you know really well or you know it's a flexible kind

of party—cocktails or a buffet—it's better to stick with your "no" and hope you'll be able to make it next time.

"may I bring . . . ?"

Don't even ask! Invitations are extended to the people the hosts want to invite—and no one else. If you ask to bring a date, you may spoil her carefully chosen guest list. The biggest offenders in this area seem to be parents who think that their little darlings should be included in grown-up invitations. Here's the final word on "extras":

. . . a date? Some invitations tell you that you may bring a guest or date. When you reply, say, "I'd love to join you for dinner on the thirtieth. I'll be bringing Jim Alcott." (Your hostess is going to love you! Now she even knows your guest's name—handy for introductions and place cards.)

. . . my children? If they were invited, the invitation would have said so. If you can't get a sitter, it's best to decline the invitation. This is true not just for formal parties like weddings, but for informal get-togethers as well.

. . . my houseguest? If you're hosting a houseguest and get invited to a party, it's best to turn

HOW DO I RESPOND?

Mailed invitation with a phone number	Call and make sure to give your response in person (even if you left a message on a machine), as answering machines can be unreliable.
E-mailed invitation	Hit the Reply button.
E-vite	Follow the directions to reply, and don't stress out over trumping another guest's witty response. Most let you reply with a "Maybe" if you aren't sure—even that's a help to your host. (See Chapter 4, The Invitation Tells All, page 35, for more on e-vites.)
Phoned invitation	You can respond right away, or if you prefer not be put on the spot, say, "Let me check my calendar and get right back to you." Just be sure you do exactly that!
Mailed invitation with a response card	Fill in the card and return it in the enclosed envelope. Reply by the date indicated.
Mailed invitation with RSVP and no response card	Send a prompt handwritten reply to the host at the address on the envelope.
Regrets only	You only need to reply if you *can't* go. If your host doesn't hear from you, he's expecting you to be there!

the invitation down but explain the reason. This gives your host the option to extend the invitation to include your guests. If the event is casual and flexible, that's probably what will happen. If it's a more formal event, extras might upset the game plan.

Of course there are exceptions to every rule. If you receive an invitation addressed to you alone and you've recently become engaged or are in a serious relationship, it's okay to let your host know this. Again, it's best to decline the invitation and explain why, putting the ball in your host's court to offer to include your significant other. If your host had a restricted seating plan, he may want to invite another solo guest. If he can fit you and your significant other in as a couple, that's great—but you should leave this up to him.

could you please bring...

In some parts of the country, almost every acceptance is followed by "...and what can I bring?" Friends who entertain one another frequently usually keep things casual and may even share the cooking, even if one couple is officially hosting. At a potluck supper or family holiday dinner, you may be asked to bring a dish to share. The hostess is usually the organizer, and it's her job to see that the meal isn't heavy on salad and light on dessert. Your contribution may be left up to you—or you may be offered a choice ("Would you like to bring an appetizer or a dessert?") or given an assignment ("Could you please make your terrific mashed potatoes?"). In either case, accept graciously and follow through. Don't forget to ask your hostess how many people she expects your dish to serve. Bring your contribution in its serving dish, labeled with your name and phone number on the bottom. If you don't cook or are pressed for time, you can always offer to bring purchased items: cheese, bread, olives, pâté, a premade dish, cookies and ice cream, or a fruit tart from a favorite bakery.

allergies and other special conditions

✦ ✦ ✦

If you're invited to a cocktail party, large dinner party, buffet, or reception, it's probably not necessary to inform your host that you're a vegetarian, mildly allergic to milk, or diabetic, because there are bound to be a variety of foods to choose from. It's fine to ask about the ingredients in a particular dish. If it's a small dinner party, however, or if you're severely allergic to certain foods or pets, it's a good idea to let your host know up front when you respond to the invitation.

If you're allergic to dogs and your allergy can't be controlled by medication, you might have to forego an invitation to a house that has indoor dogs—there's only so much cleaning your host can do. Even if you can tolerate them, your host will want to know so that the dog can be kept in another room and extra care be taken when cleaning before the party.

If you have serious food allergies, again, let your host know when you first respond. More than the disappointment of serving a guest something he can't eat, it really is a question of your safety. Shellfish and nuts, for example, can cause severe, even deadly, reactions.

If your dietary restrictions are based on religious tenets, it may not be practical to accept some invitations. If the invitation is for a small gathering, you can explain to your hostess that you'd love to accept, but that you'll have to bring a dish you've prepared according to your dietary rules—provided that's acceptable to her. As a large part of entertaining is about being social, many hosts will encourage you to attend and bring your special dish.

If you don't drink alcohol, it's fine to ask for water, juice, or a soft drink instead. You don't have to give a reason unless you wish to. Never feel you have to have to drink alcohol, even if pressed by a host or another guest. The rudeness is theirs, not yours.

How exactly do you let your host know this sort of thing? Simply say, "I'd love to come, but I am completely allergic to shellfish"..."I'd love to come to the barbecue, but I should tell you that I'm a vegetarian. I could bring a tabbouleh salad if that's all right with you." Always give your host the option to accommodate you or not. In some cases it may not be possible, so don't take offense.

what to wear

✦ ✦ ✦

OCCASION	MEN	WOMEN
Black Tie	+ Black tuxedo jacket and matching trousers + Formal (piqué or pleated-front) white shirt + Black bow tie (silk, satin, or twill) + Black cummerbund to match tie, or a vest + Dressy suspenders to ensure a good fit (optional)	+ Formal (floor-length) evening gown + Dressy cocktail dress + Your dressiest little black dress

continued on next page

OCCASION	MEN	WOMEN
	+ No gloves + Black patent shoes and black dress socks + *In summer, in the tropics, or on a cruise:* White dinner jacket, black tuxedo trousers plus other black-tie wardrobe	
Creative Black Tie	+ Tuxedo combined with trendy or whimsical items, such as a black or other colored shirt, or matching colored or patterned bow tie and cummerbund	+ Formal (floor-length) evening gown + Dressy cocktail dress + Your dressiest little black dress + Fun or unique accessories
Black Tie Optional	+ Either a tuxedo (see Black Tie, above) or + Dark suit, white dress shirt, and conservative tie + Dressy leather shoes and dark dress socks	+ Formal (floor-length) evening gown + Dressy cocktail dress + A little black dress + Dressy separates
Semiformal	+ Dark business suit + Matching vest (optional) + Dress shirt + Tie + Dressy leather shoes and dark dress socks	+ Short afternoon or cocktail dress or + A little black dress + Long dressy skirt and top + Dressy separates
Festive Attire (usually for holidays)	+ Seasonal sport coat or blazer in color of choice and slacks + Open-collar shirt or dress shirt + Tie—festive or with a holiday theme	+ Cocktail dress or + Long dressy skirt and top + Dressy pants outfit or separates + A little black dress + Feature holiday colors and accessories

OCCASION	MEN	WOMEN
Business Formal*	+ Dark business suit + Matching vest (optional) + Dress shirt + Conservative tie + Dressy leather shoes and dark dress socks	+ Suit + Business-style dress + Dress with a jacket + Stockings (optional in summer) + Heels, low or high
Business Casual*	+ Seasonal sport coat or blazer with slacks or khakis + Dress shirt, casual button-down shirt, or open-collar or polo shirt + Optional tie + Loafers or loafer-style shoes and socks	+ Skirt, khakis, or pants + Open-collar shirt, knit shirt, or sweater (no spaghetti straps or décolleté) + Dress
Dressy Casual	+ Seasonal sport coat or blazer and slacks + Dress shirt, casual button-down shirt, or open-collar or polo shirt + Optional tie	+ Dress + Skirt and dressy top + Dressy pants outfit + Nice jeans and dressy top
Casual	+ Khakis or good jeans (clean, no holes) + Cargo or Bermuda shorts— depending on occasion and climate + Plain T-shirt (no slogans), polo shirt, or turtleneck + Casual button-down shirt + Sweater + Loafers, sneakers (with or without socks), or sandals	+ Sundress + Long or short skirt + Khakis or nice jeans + Shorts (depending on occasion and climate) + Plain T-shirt (no slogans), polo shirt, or turtleneck + Casual button-down blouse

*Always check and abide by your company's dress code.

should I bring a hostess gift?

✦ ✦ ✦

A gift for your host or hostess is a lovely way to thank them for their hospitality and is always appreciated. It doesn't have to be elaborate or expensive; simply consider the nature of the occasion and local custom when making your choice. In some parts of the country, a hostess gift is considered obligatory, while in other places a gift is brought only on special occasions. If it's the first time you're visiting someone's home, then it's a very nice gesture to bring a small gift. If you have a few extra minutes to wrap it, even if you only use tissue or a decorative bag, it adds to the gesture.

Wine, flowers, specialty food items, and small items for the house all make good hostess gifts. Flowers are terrific too, but if you want to go beyond Etiquette 101, bring them in a simple vase (a glass canning jar is fine). You could also offer to put them in water yourself when you arrive so your host doesn't have to arrange them. If you bring wine, don't expect your host to serve it that evening—the wines may have already been chosen for the meal. And don't bring food for the meal unless you've been asked to. Otherwise you risk putting your host on the spot and

upsetting the menu. Here are a few tips on what to bring when:

Casual dinner party. Dinner party guests usually bring a hostess gift unless they are close friends who dine together frequently. Gift possibilities include wine, Champagne, flowers (preferably in a vase), a potted plant, chocolates, specialty food items such as jams and jellies or other condiments, fancy nuts, olives, olive oil or vinegars, or items for the house, such as cocktail napkins, guest soaps and lotions, a picture frame, or a scented candle. A CD or book is also appropriate if you know your host's taste.

Formal dinner party. Gifts aren't usually taken to large, formal dinners.

When there's a guest of honor. If it's a birthday, anniversary, graduation, or shower, bring a gift for the honoree.

When you're the guest of honor. Bring a gift for your host or hostess, or send flowers before the party. After the party, send a thank-you note.

Housewarming. It's customary to bring a gift to a housewarming. It doesn't have to be expensive, but it should be something lasting for the house. Possible gifts include guest towels, a houseplant, a patio or garden plant, glasses, dish towels, a picture frame, specialty foods like a great olive oil or preserves, or a cheeseboard and/or cheese knives. Update an old-fashioned house-warming tradition of giving salt, and bring fancy sea salt and/or a saltbox or saltcellar. If the housewarming is for a neighbor new to your town, consider putting together a welcome kit containing area maps, the town paper, restaurant menus, bookmarks from your favorite bookstore, transportation schedules, and information on local parks and recreation facilities—anything that will make it easier for her to feel welcome and at home in her new community.

Weekend visit. Either bring or send a gift. Your gift choice will depend on the length of your stay and how elaborately you're entertained. While you don't have to break the bank, your gift should be sincere, thoughtful, and personal. (For gift ideas, see Chapter 15, Hosting House-guests, page 223.)

party manners 101

❖ ❖ ❖

As a guest, it's your job to display all your positive qualities: enthusiasm, congeniality, consideration, and thoughtfulness. You won't go wrong as long as you practice the following party manners basics:

Arrive on time. Anywhere between five and fifteen minutes after the designated start time is okay—but *never* show up early. If you're going to be more than fifteen minutes late, call your hosts with an ETA so they can decide if they should start without you. (And no, texting doesn't count! You don't know that they'll see it.)

Turn off your cell phone. While you're at a party, consider yourself unavailable. If you're expecting a call or must be reachable, put your phone on vibrate and excuse yourself to another room to take the call. Never use or answer a host's phone without permission. If you are asked to answer the phone, say, "Scherr residence."

Be a willing participant. Take part in—or at least try—whatever your host offers, whether it's charades, mushroom soufflé, or the opportunity to chat with new people. At a seated dinner, be an active—but not dominant—participant in the conversation, and be sure to spend time chatting with the people on both your left and your right.

Practice moderation. Try not to overindulge, whether in the shrimp cocktail or the Pinot Noir. You don't want to imply that the food or drinks are more important to you than the people present.

Unless invited in, keep clear of the kitchen. Some people love to cook with an audience; others really can't concentrate. If your host says no, go enjoy yourself at the party.

Offer to help when you can. Obviously this depends on the circumstances of the party, but where assistance is welcome there are lots of things guests can do to help out: pass hors d'oeuvres, light candles, help serve dessert. If your offer is turned down, don't insist—just enjoy yourself, knowing you did your best to pitch in.

Don't switch place cards. Your host has gone to the trouble to come up with a seating plan. Your spot was chosen especially for you, so enjoy it!

Be considerate. Wipe your feet before entering. Don't put your feet on furniture. Use a coaster for drinks. Leave the bathroom neat for the next person. If you're a smoker and there are no ashtrays, go outside to smoke. If you have a cold or other spreadable illness, call with your regrets and stay home.

Be complimentary. About the food, the decor, the garden, the company. You don't have to gush—just be gracious and sincere.

Respect your host's trust. Don't snoop in medicine cabinets, closets, or desks. Take care with your host's belongings. If you break something, let your host know immediately—and offer to pay for the repair.

Leave with the pack. Don't settle in as others are saying farewell, unless you've been invited to stay. In general, dinner guests are expected to stay for about an hour after dinner. If you need to leave early, let your host know before the party or when you arrive so they aren't surprised (or worse, insulted) by your early departure.

Thank your hosts on the way out. As you're leaving, make sure to say good-bye and thank you to each of your hosts. If they're not by the door, seek them out and thank them personally before you go.

thoughtful afterthoughts

✦ ✦ ✦

The really thoughtful guest thanks her host twice: once as she's leaving the party and again the next day. The written thank-you note is always, always appreciated, but is only *expected* after a formal dinner party or an overnight visit. If you don't send a note, do call or send an e-mail expressing your thanks within a day or two of the party. If someone hosted a party in your honor, or you were a houseguest, or you had an especially enjoyable time, now's the time to send flowers or a thank-you gift (if you didn't arrive with a gift in hand).

tag, you're it

✦ ✦ ✦

Some invitations—to weddings, balls, official functions, and events you pay to attend—don't carry any reciprocal obligation. But invitations to social events in someone's home or a private party hosted at a restaurant or club do call for some sort of reciprocation. This isn't a quid pro quo. The goal is not to replicate the event you were invited to, but simply to return the hospitality you've enjoyed and spend some social time with your hosts. So, a dinner invitation may be returned with an invitation to lunch or a brunch with a barbecue. If your hosts put on a lavish gourmet feast and you're not an accomplished cook, treat them to an evening out at a favorite restaurant or an afternoon sail and picnic on your boat. An invitation to a private club or beach or to a cultural or sporting event is also a good alternative.

Whatever you decide on, try to arrange to get together within a few months of the original party. If your hosts can't accept your first invitation, give it at least one, and preferably two, more tries. If you're still not successful, put the return engagement on hold for a later date.

If you attended a large gathering, include your hosts the next time you entertain in a similar way. However, we don't recommend throwing one big "payback party" for everyone who's recently hosted you. This may seem the perfect way to even the social score, but too often your intent will come across as obvious, with your guests recognizing it for what it is. If you're a popular guest, it's better to host several smaller parties throughout the year for those who've hosted you.

Lastly, if you decline an invitation to a party or dinner, are you still obligated to return the favor? In this case your obligation isn't as strong—but since the intent was to include you, you should still try to send a return invitation in the not-too-distant future.

Your Little Black Book

It's a good idea to keep some sort of social diary, either as a part of your calendar or in a separate notebook. You'll want to keep track of invitations you've accepted, the name(s) of your host(s), the date, and what type of event it was. When you've returned the favor, you can check off those names.

frequently asked questions

Questions for Anna and Lizzie

My friend called and accepted our dinner invitation and then called a few days later and asked if she could bring her kids. What do I say to her?

For some reason, many of today's parents think their kids are automatically included in invitations to adult parties. You'll need to practice being graciously firm: "We planned on dinner just for the grown-ups and aren't including the kids. We hope you can still make it."

One of my guests brought a date who turned out to be a vegan. Most of my menu was off-limits. I felt bad—what could I have done?

Truly, the fault isn't yours. It's important for guests to alert their host ahead of time that they have a food allergy or a specialized diet, or offer to bring a dish prepared according to their restrictions. It spoils the idea of a communal meal when one guest can't eat the food. That said, if you're caught off guard, see if there's any way you can amend your menu: Reserve a portion of salad and dress it with oil, vinegar, and salt, leaving out any cheese, meats, or fish; microwave a sweet or white potato; dress a portion of vegetables with olive oil; serve a beautifully sliced piece of fruit. Remember that while this may be an awkward situation for you, the vegan will be used to having to make choices or abstain when others prepare a meal.

What do I do when a guest arrives at my party and has obviously already had too much to drink?

Here's a situation where safety trumps etiquette—and any breach of etiquette isn't yours. You've been put on the spot, and there's no gracious way out of this situation. It's best to be direct. If your newly arrived guest is in the happy or tipsy phase, collect his hat, coat, and car keys. Don't serve him any more alcohol during the party, and spread the word among the other guests not to give him a drink either. Even if he seems to have sobered up during the party, give him a ride home or call him a cab.

It's a week before my party, and I still haven't heard from several people. Is it rude to call and ask for an answer?

No, it's not rude; it's a *must* if you don't want to be surprised at party time. In fact, it's rude not to respond to an invitation right away. "Hi, Jim, it's Tina. I hadn't heard from you and was wondering if you'll be able to make it for dinner on Saturday?" Perfectly pleasant, perfectly reasonable request, no finger-pointing. If Jim is still unsure, set a deadline for an answer. "Could you please let me know by Wednesday? Thanks!" And yes, it's also possible that the invite might have gone astray—and Jim would never have known about the party if you hadn't called. Giving someone the benefit of the doubt is always the kind and considerate thing to do.

I'm not sure if an acquaintance has a significant other or not, and I'd like to send her an invitation to a cocktail party. What should I do?

It's a must to invite spouses, people who live together, or those in a serious relationship as a couple. You can do a little sleuthing and ask someone who knows her better, or take the direct, sure-to-get-the-right-answer approach and call her. "Gloria, I'm sending you an invitation for a cocktail party and wanted to let you know that I'd be delighted if you want to bring a date." This gives Gloria the chance to say, "Thanks, Julie, I'm seeing [living with] this really great guy right now." "Terrific—what's his name? I'd like to include him in your invitation."

If a friend calls and asks for a "plus one," are you really going to say no?

Even though your friend is putting you in an awkward situation, you're right, you probably aren't going to say no. Do everything you possibly can to fit the extra person in. If it's just not possible, tell him exactly that.

As the bartender was setting up at my house, I noticed he had put out a tip jar. I asked him to remove it. Was I right?

Yes, you were. At a private party, tipping is entirely the host's responsibility, whether the party is at the host's home or another location. When you hire them, let your help know that you will be responsible for all tips and they shouldn't accept any money from guests. Your guests shouldn't have to carry anything more than cab fare in their pockets—everything else is on you.

I had a party and I wasn't happy with the caterer I hired. How do I discuss this with him, and can I expect a reduction in the bill?

While some people may choose to overlook it and just pay the bill, we think that whenever you are dissatisfied with a service that you are paying for, you should speak up. The key is to have a conversation that's forthright and respectful. First, take a look at the contract to review what was agreed to. Next, stick to the facts. Make a list of the areas where the service fell short. "The food was lousy" or "Your staff did a really bad job" is too vague. Be specific: The staff was a half hour late; the hot hors d'oeuvres were cold; the food wasn't fresh; the kitchen wasn't tidied. Now make your call. Start with what went well, then discuss your concerns over the phone or agree to a meeting. Present your case calmly—no drama!—and be prepared to listen, too. A reputable caterer will most likely offer some kind of accommodation. Your future business and your recommendations are important to him.

How long should I hold dinner for a late guest?

Be flexible, but don't let a late guest disrupt your party schedule and make your other guests suffer the consequences. Fifteen minutes past the time you were planning to serve dinner is the standard "hold time" for a latecomer. After that, go right ahead and serve dinner as planned. When Mr. Late does arrive, serve him whatever course is in progress. If that happens to be dessert, have a little pity and serve him the main course first.

What should I do if I'm going to be late for a dinner party?

Get on that cell phone, pronto! Call your host, apologize, and provide an ETA. This lets your host know (a) when to expect you and (b) that it's okay to start without you. When you arrive, offer your apologies again and join the party. *(P.S. Texting isn't sufficient—speak to your host in person!)*

What should I do if my host is serving something I don't like?

Take a small portion and do the best you can, without making remarks. But don't feel obligated to finish something you truly hate or that's making you feel ill!

My husband and I attend many holiday parties hosted by his company and his clients. Should I write a thank-you note to the hosts?

Absolutely! Adding a personal touch is so appreciated by the people who organize or host business parties. If it's a company party, your husband should send a thank-you note to his boss or department head. If a client is hosting, he should write to the person he works with at that company. Taking the time to write a personal, handwritten note is sure to be noticed by your husband's boss or client. Not only is it the gracious thing to do, but it also makes good business sense. And in general, the best answer to "Should I write a thank-you note?" is always yes.

We've been invited to several holiday parties this year, some on the same day or evening. Is it okay to "double book"?

This is one of those times when it's fine to double book and go from one party to another. The casual, drop-in nature of most holiday parties makes this perfectly okay. Just be sure you do each event justice—a lightning-quick drop-by simply doesn't cut it. And don't double book when you've been invited to a dinner party or a small gathering with a set time to arrive and a limited number of guests.

I'm planning my son's second birthday party. Is it okay to put his clothing size and the activities he likes on the bottom of the invitation to help guests with gift ideas?

No. Other than "No gifts, please," don't include any gift suggestions on an invitation. Mentioning gifts on the invitation puts the focus on the gift, not the guest. It's his presence that is important, not the present. Those who want gift suggestions or sizes should ask when they RSVP.

My kids are invited to so many birthday parties that it's impossible to go to all of them. What's the gift-giving protocol when you don't attend a party?

You don't have to give a present if you miss the party. It's not expected, and doing so could put a big dent in your wallet. However, if the party is for a cousin or a close friend, your child could still give a gift either before the party or at their next get-together.

My child has been invited to a joint birthday party for siblings. He only knows one of the children. Should he bring a gift for each?

No; it's really not expected. He should bring a gift for his friend. It's nice to bring a card for the other birthday child to acknowledge her day, too. However, some people feel uncomfortable about not bringing a gift for the second child. In that case, an inexpensive gift or a gift certificate toward books, movies, or ice cream will do the trick.

My husband and I recently moved to a resort town. It seems like everyone we've ever met has asked to come for a visit. I'm already tired of scheduling visitors and changing sheets. How can I make it stop?

Just say no. It's better for your friendships if you're straightforward, rather than being a reluctant host. Say: "We're so busy with our jobs right now, we're not having guests until things let up." Or "I can't commit to anything right now, but I can give you the name of a nice inn down the road. We'd love to get together with you for dinner." Or "I'm sorry, but we have family visiting then." Just be truthful in whatever explanation you offer. You don't have to give a specific reason, but saying that you're "unable to commit to having visitors" can soften the blow. Be careful, too, when talking about your new town, not to sound as though you're extending an invitation unless you mean to. And when you do take on houseguests, set parameters—even for family and A-list friends. A two- or three-night limit usually works best.

When I'm visiting someone for the weekend, how can I gracefully excuse myself for a while to give us both some space?

As long as you don't do it in the middle of dinner preparations or a planned activity, you'll probably make your hostess's day if you disappear for a couple of hours so she can regroup, take a nap, or simply not feel obligated to entertain you for a while. Just say, "Jenna, all this sea air has wiped me out—would it be all right with you if I took a nap?," or "If you don't need me for an hour or two, I think I'll drag out my laptop and check my e-mail," or "That hammock looks so inviting—if nobody else has claimed it for the next hour or so, I'd love to try it out with the book I've brought along."

Is the host responsible for providing all of the meals for houseguests?

Normally that's the standard, but you also need to take the length of stay into consideration. With an overnight or weekend guest, the host pays for the groceries. If a houseguest is staying longer than that, he should offer to contribute to or split the grocery bill and come to an arrangement with his host. It's fine for a guest to treat the host to a restaurant meal as a thank-you for the visit. Otherwise, decide how to handle any restaurant bills ahead of time. The host should make it clear that he's treating, if that's what he'd like to do, or it should be clear that the bill will be split. If a restaurant is proposed that seems to be out of a guest's budget, he should let his host know: "I'm sorry, it looks great, but I think Chez Antoine is a little out of my reach. Is there someplace else we could go?"

My mother-in-law never lets me help in the kitchen when we visit. I hate not pitching in. What can I do to contribute?

Don't take it personally: Some people prefer to work solo in the kitchen. And remember, the kitchen's not the only place where you can help out. Offer to run errands, set the table, walk the dog, or just keep her company while she preps the meal.

My host has slippers by the front door and asks everyone to remove their street shoes. Is that rude? What should I do?

In some cultures and some parts of the United States, especially where the weather's snowy or wet, it's considered polite to remove your street shoes or boots when entering someone else's house so that mud and dirt aren't tracked in, and most guests bring "indoor shoes." Other reasons to remove shoes are to protect hardwood floors or to keep a cleaner environment when there are young children who crawl or play on the floor. Considerate hosts, especially if they insist on shoe removal, will keep a basket of clean socks or slippers by the door in case a guest forgets to bring them. Whatever the motive, though, we recommend that you go with the flow and let your feet enjoy a little coziness.

I was at a party recently and knocked over my wineglass. Not only did I spill red wine all over the tablecloth, I broke the glass as well. What should I have done?

In this situation, an immediate "I'm so sorry" and damage control are the first things you should do. Assist with the mop-up—use paper towels and sponges (or whatever your host prefers to use) rather than your napkin. After dinner, find a moment to talk to your host privately. Offer to work out a way to make it right that's within your means: Pay the cleaning bill for the tablecloth, purchase a replacement wineglass if it's feasible to do so, or help with a repair. If your host refuses to let you, leave it at that and include an apology in your thank-you note.

PICTURE CREDITS

INVITATIONS

Sabrina and Eunice Moyle, Hello Lucky: http://www.hellolucky.com

Amanda Love, LoveLeaf Press: http://www.loveleafpress.com

Calligraphy on all envelopes and invites: Michele Papineau, Papineau Calligraphy

http://www.papineaucalligraphy.com/

PLACE CARDS

Calligraphy on all place card settings and name tags: Michele Papineau, Papineau Calligraphy

http://www.papineaucalligraphy.com/

Macaroons: http://www.paulettemacarons.com/

PLACE SETTINGS

Gumps

CUPCAKES

Gabrielle Feuersinger, Cake Coquette: www.CakeCoquette.com

index

Note: Index entries with asterisk* have photographs in color inserts.

handling accidents and mishaps, 20–22, 250

insurance and liability issues, 58

making small talk with guests, 19

Hot tray, 8

Houseguests, 223–32

  arrival and departure times, 224

  gift ideas for host, 230–32, 241

  guest rooms for, 227–28

  handling, when host has party invitation, 234–35

  meals for, 225–26

  offers to help from, 250

  planning activities for, 224–25

  previsit information exchange, 226

  proper manners and behavior, 228–30, 249–50

  saying no to, 249

  welcoming into home, 226

Housewarming parties, 186, 240–41

I

Iced tea, 112

Insurance, liability, 58

Introductions, 18

Invitations, 35–48

  addressing, 45–48

  for children's parties, 210–11, 216

  for cocktail parties, 117

  details and information on, 36

  determining guest list, 36

  for dinner parties, 139

  by e-mail, 37, 235

  by e-vite, 37–38, 235

  extras to include on, 42

  formal style, 39

  handwritten, 38

for holiday office parties, 200–201

for housewarming parties, 186

inviting spouses and significant others, 246

by mail, 38, 235

matching with party style*, 38

"No Gifts, Please" on, 45

for open house parties, 186, 194

by phone, 37, 235

for potlucks, BYOB, and BYOF, 43–44

responding to, 41, 234–35, 246

for showers, 85

specifying dress code on, 43, 195, 237–39

what not to put on, 44

when to send, 40–41

J

Juicers, 8

Juices, serving, 112

K

Kitchen, tidying up, 70

Kitchen equipment, 7–8

Knives, 8

Kwanzaa, 193

L

Lanterns, 67

Lemonade, 112

Lighting, 65–67, 158, 192

Lists

  guest lists, 36, 118, 210–11

  party checklists, 32–33, 140, 194

  shopping lists, 32–33

Living room, tidying up, 70

Luncheons, 89, 182

M

Magicians, 212

Mailed invitations, 38, 235

Maps and directions, 42

Mardi Gras, 204

Margarita glass, 108

Martini glass, 107–8

Menus, 77–94. *See also* Food; Recipes

  Anna's birthday lunch, 182

  for barbecue, 159

  basic guidelines, 77–78, 89–91

  for catered meal, 56–57

  for cocktail party buffet, 123

  estimating food quantities, 87–88

  for holiday open house, 195, 196

  for outdoor party, 153, 159, 165

  for picnics, 165

  seasonal and local foods for, 9

  seasonal fall menus, 79–80

  for spring dinner party for eight, 144

  for Sunday dinner, 176

  for wine-tasting party, 135–36

Microplane, 8

Mixers, for cocktails, 106

Mixers and food processors, 7–8

Music, 67–68, 163, 193

N

Napkins*, 7, 71, 72, 75

Neighbors, 159

New Year's Eve, 203–4

Notebooks, party, 34, 244

O

Open house parties, 186, 194–96

Outdoor parties, 151–72

  backyard barbecue, 154–56